Aging Bodies

Images and Everyday Experience

Edited by
Christopher A. Faircloth

ALTAMIRA PRESS

A Division of Rowman & Littlefield Publishers, Inc.
Walnut Creek • Lanham • New York • Oxford

ALTAMIRA PRESS
A Division of Rowman & Littlefield Publishers, Inc.
1630 North Main Street, #367
Walnut Creek, California 94596
www.altamirapress.com

Rowman & Littlefield Publishers, Inc.
A Member of the Rowman & Littlefield Publishing Group
4501 Forbes Boulevard, Suite 200
Lanham, Maryland 20706

PO Box 317
Oxford
OX2 9RU, UK

British Library Cataloguing in Publication Information Available

Library of Congress Cataloging-in-Publication Data

Aging bodies : images and everyday experience / edited by Christopher A.
Faircloth.
    p. cm.
Includes bibliographical references and index.
  ISBN 0-7591-0235-X (hc : acid-free)—ISBN 0-7591-0236-8 (pb :
acid free)
  1. Aged. 2. Aged—Social conditions. 3. Aging. I. Faircloth,
Christopher A., 1966–

HQ1061 .A4547 2003
305.26—dc21

2002154536

Printed in the United States of America

♾™ The paper used in this publication meets the minimum requirements of American
National Standard for Information Sciences—Permanence of Paper for Printed Library
Materials, ANSI/NISO Z39.48-1992.

CONTENTS

CONTENTS

DIFFERENT BODIES AND THE PARADOX OF AGING: LOCATING AGING BODIES IN IMAGES AND EVERYDAY EXPERIENCE

W hen I began to write the introduction to this collection, I mentioned it to my mother and father, who had rarely expressed interest in my work. However, they certainly expressed great interest here, because, as my father put it, "Our bodies sure aren't getting any younger." Given this response to my stated concerns with the aging body, I mentioned it to others that I considered "aged." They seemed to all be fascinated by the topic and all had comments and opinions on it—usually in relation to their own bodily experiences in aging. In fact, when I mentioned it to younger people, they also expressed significant interest in their own aging body, the decline they were feeling, and often a concern with the inevitable, as they saw it, future failure of their body.

Certainly, if this were such an important topic to people in their everyday lives, their mundane practices, if you will, then it would be a topic of great interest to social gerontologists and sociologists. But, strangely enough, for the most part, this has not proven to be the case. This is not to suggest that the aging body is "absent" in gerontology (Öberg 1996), but it certainly seems as if we are lagging behind the people that really count in any academic discipline that enhances the "social"—individuals and their lived place in society. Why is this? And why has this occurred when the body is being theorized so much in many other substantive areas? It is certainly an interesting question and one that bears answering. After all, is it not the physical body that readily marks us as aging?

Research into the body, as a social construct, has, if you pardon the expression, gained much steam as of late, like a train running faster and faster down the track. Indeed, one might consider it one of the "sexiest" topics in the social sciences today. The literature on the body has exploded. Scholars such as Bryan Turner, Chris Schilling, Judith Butler, and Margaret Lock have emerged at the forefront of this new theoretical "assault" on the body in the social sciences.

The body in sociology, as Hughes (2000, 13) notes, is "highly contested. . . . Sociology can deal with all sorts of bodies, largely because it relates to them primarily as either the source or the outcome of meaning." As Williams and Bendelow (1998, 1) note that "recent years have witnessed a veritable explosion of interest in the body within social theory . . . from the reflexive body of late modernity to post-structuralist celebration of the body." We have bantered about such concerns as the body as a passive, docile object (Foucault 1977), its own government (Turner 1996), its role as a civilizing presence (Elias 1978), and its own lived experience (Nettleton and Watson 1998). These are certainly only a few of the seemingly endless examples of "body theorizing" in the social sciences. The body, whether in theory or in practice, is, as Chris Shilling (1993) notes, an unfinished entity. And a popular one at that.

Social scientists have focused much substantive concern on arenas of the body such as its medicalization, sexuality, gender, work and capitalism, emotion, disability, and sport, among others. Obviously given the nature and limitations of an introduction, I am unable to discuss each in turn or in perhaps the needed depth. Given this, I will concentrate on three of these substantive concerns—medicalization, gender/sexuality, and the body as consumer.

As one might expect, the literature is quite thick, perhaps even voluminous in respect to each area, and much more than I can cover in the space provided for in this chapter. Due to this, I will briefly introduce each area of study and then provide a limited discussion of major works in that specific arena. As previously mentioned, the explosion in body theorizing has already occurred, and the sound of it still seems to be reverberating throughout the social sciences. I investigate each of these areas in turn and then switch analytic attention to the missing piece of the body in social theory—the aging one.

This collection is organized around two major themes of the aging body—its everyday experience and the social and personal impact of its imagery. Nettleton and Watson's (1998) collection *The Body in Everyday Life* points us to the importance of the mundanity of the "lived body"

(Williams and Bendelow 1998) and the reflexive meaning-making process that surrounds it. As the editors, Nettleson and Watson, point out, "[Their] concern is to examine how people experience their bodies and in particular how they articulate their experiences" (p. 9). Their phenomenological perspective focuses analytic attention on how individuals experience what they term the "lived body" and how they then articulate these experiences. While their arguments are grounded in the theoretical foundations of phenomenology, other approaches, such as symbolic interactionism and ethnomethodology, add much to this same concern—how do *we* experience the body as a social entity?

A concern with body and imagery takes us down a bit of a different path. From film, to comic strips, to magazine advertisements, and to self-image, bodily imagery plays an important role in meaning making and individual conceptions of one's own body. The visual representations of aging in our culture make for a constant self-monitoring of bodily transformation. After all, "the visual signs of age, like the weather, are a universal topic of everyday conversation among adults" (Bytheway and Johnson 1998, 243). We see it in various media imagery, from comic books to photographic collections. Perhaps the most significant point here is that this imagery has an important impact on self-conceptualization both in the present and in the future.

Locating the Biomedical Body

The prevailing conceptualization of the body in modernity has been that of the medicalized body (Hughes 2000). The body in the twentieth century was discursively constructed in the language of biomedicine. It has dominated our perceptions of the body and its functions during this period of time, no matter its faults:

> [It] is reductionist in form, seeking explanations of dysfunctions in invariant biological structures and processes: it privileges such explanations at the expense of social, cultural, and biographical explanations. In its clinical mode, this dominant model of medical reasoning implies that diseases exist as distinct entities; that these entities are revealed through the inspection of "signs" and "symptoms," that the individual patient is more or less a passive site of disease manifestation; that diseases are to be understood as categorical departures from normality. (Atkinson 1988, 180; as cited in Hughes 2000, 14)

3

The development and application of the biomedical model stems from the positivistic philosophy of Descartes, the first philosopher to establish a large and insurmountable gap between mind and body. Modern medicine has followed this, attending specifically to the body's mechanics and its failures. By focusing on the actual mechanization of the body, biomedicine sees illness/disease as having specific causal relationships to the body. Of course, by identifying causes, one can then treat specific pathologies as they exist independent of the social, static world, but rather in the frozen, stable presence of the biological body (Hughes 2000).

As social scientists of various ilk, as well as doctors (Sacks 1981, 1986), have noted, this approach does have specific problems. The first is that many disorders have no link to any causal relationship. An example of this would be the growing number of behavioral disorders such as chronic fatigue syndrome (CFS) and anorexia nervosa. These conditions are not only due to physiological malfunctioning but must also be related to the social world in which the body exists. In addition, the biomedical model can simply not treat many disorders adequately. This argument attends most closely to chronic illness. In addition, cross-cultural variations in illness inform us of major problems inherent in the biomedical model (Turner 1995).

Developing from these initial criticisms is Bryan Turner's (1995) seminal text on the biomedical body *Medical Power and Social Knowledge* (see also Leder 1992 and Lupton 1994, 1995 for further discussions of the relationship between medicine and the body). Arguing that the sociology of the body is the very foundation on which medical sociology must exist, Turner proposes a general theory of medical sociology that rests on our conceptualizations of the body. Pulling from various theorists from Erving Goffman to Talcott Parsons, the author returns, again and again, to the work of Michel Foucault as the broader base on which his argument rests.

Foucault, as Turner (1995, 10) notes, "was concerned to examine the relationship between certain medical discourses and the exercise of power in society, that is the development of alliances between discourse, practice, and professional groups." Foucault's thoughts on biomedicalization and the body were organized around a central theme of what he terms the "surveillance society," embedding us in a "regime of total health" (Armstrong 1983); that is, medical discourses emerged in relation to a growing concern with the overall disciplining of large groups of people, or populations. Specifically, Foucault found himself concerned with adopting Jeremy Bentham's term "panopticism," as it is embedded in social institutions from the prison to our major concern here, the clinic. This, Turner suggests, provides "a powerful framework for the development of theoretical medical sociology addressed to the central issues of meaning, structure, social order, and power" (p. 11).

The introduction and development of a biomedical model and the resulting growth in scientific medicine led directly to the extreme medicalization of society. If you recall, the biomedical model is the most prevalent and powerful discourse of the body. The model pinpoints disease as a deviant entity, a phenomenon that both Parsons (1937, 1939) and Conrad and Schneider (1980) have further alerted us to. The construction of disease as deviant rests in the power of those in charge, if you will, of the biomedical model—physicians. The scientific body of knowledge embedded in this model provided doctors with the ability to achieve considerable social power, not simply scientific power.

Turner (1995, 12) points this out when he notes that "[t]he clinical gaze (as Foucault called medical power in *The Birth of the Clinic* [1973]) enabled medical men to assume considerable social power in defining reality and hence in defining deviance and social disorder." Foucault continues by making the argument that indeed it is doctors, not the police, and so on, who exert the most social control on modern, and in turn postmodern, society. Foucault's concern with the body and medicine went as far as to lead him to see that sociology is inherently a sociology of medicine. If we take sociology to inherently be about the ongoing maintenance of order, then this is certainly no leap. Medicine is part of a totalizing regime whose purpose is to "manage" bodies through normalization. Medicine, and in turn the biomedical model, is the primary messenger of governmentality, or the mechanisms through which bodies are regulated and controlled in Western society (Burchell, Gordon, and Miller 1991; Turner 1995).

Note that Turner suggests the everyday "phenomenological body" as a way to approach the study of illness. Phenomenology's contribution is that it places the experience of illness with the social parameters of what Schutz (1967) referred to as the "life world"—the experiential labyrinth in which we reside. According to Turner (1995, 237), "We need to understand the body in the processes of action and interaction at the level of everyday reciprocities and exchange." While a phenomenological approach certainly does not answer all questions in regard to the placement of illness with structure, it does point us toward an understanding of how people experience the body as a mundane entity and the processes by which they give meaning to it. Other scholars, such as Atkinson (1988) and Williams and Bendelow (1998), though coming from slightly different perspectives (Atkinson as an ethnomethodologist), have expanded on this and developed a further understanding of everyday bodily production and conception.

Locating the Sexual and Gendered Body

The body is often represented in terms of a patriarchic definition that constructs the body in terms of gender, sex, and sexuality (Tuner 1995). Social theory has explored this in great detail, especially from the stance of queer and feminist theory. Underpinning much of this concern is a philosophical and theoretical concern with woman as "other." That is, in a world shaped by dualisms such as body/mind, nature/culture, and emotion/reason, women are relegated to secondary status. This is especially evident when one considers the transferal to these dualisms to women—reproduction/production, family/state, and individual/social (Williams and Bendelow 1998). In the Western social world, women are consistently compared against men, establishing the male gender as the norm, and female as "other." The male body is the yardstick against which the female body must be measured (Martin 1987).

This is notably evident in the portrayal of women in present day medical textbooks. As Williams and Bendelow (2000, 115) observe:

> Even to the present day, contemporary medical textbooks continue to portray the male body as the standard against which the female body is judged, and comparative references to female anatomy continue to employ terms such as "smaller," "feebler," "weaker," "less well developed," to demonstrate how women differ from men. (Scully and Bart 1978; Lawrence and Bendixen 1992)

These arguments have led to an increased medicalization of the female body. However, this argument places oneself in a bit of a theoretical quandary—how much does one attend to social difference at the expense of the consideration of biological difference? In the everyday body, women are defined and define themselves in relation to their body and female biology (Birke 1995). The intersection between nature and culture, as discussed in the preceding, is an integral part of an understanding of the female body and its construction in a patriarchic culture.

Following these theoretical concerns, Judith Butler is one of the leading theorists of the body as it intersects with gender and sexuality. In her 1993 book *Bodies That Matter*, Butler attends to the hegemonic relationship between heterosexuality and Western culture. Butler sees the body as a discursive construct, much as Foucault did. Like Foucault, her explicit concern is on discourse as power and the ways in which it constructs the body within a hierarchy of relations—a hierarchy that works to control and constrain bodily performance and presentation based on the cultural hegemony of heterosexuality. Butler's analysis takes us toward a concern with the identification of the subject solely by sexual means and the ways in which heterosexuality determines these means. Identity itself is constructed around a complex interplay of sexuality and gender and embodies performance. From this emerges her concern with sexual difference.

However, from our perspective, Butler's argument has a problem—it is not grounded in any concept of "real performance," but instead in that philosophical never-never land of the body, a fault of so much work on the sexual and gendered body. So how do we get it back down to earth in the images and everyday practices that work to construct our reality? How do we get sex and gender back down on the ground? Where can we locate it?

One way of exploring this is by investigating something that has important implications in real time for women in modern Western society—the size and shape of their own bodies (Tunaley, Walsh, and Nicolson 1999). If the majority of women are dissatisfied with their bodies (Cash and Henry 1995; Cash, Winstead, and Janda 1986), then its importance in real, everyday time, cannot be understated. This concern with bodily perfection has important implications for everyday practice and our pursuit of the "perfect body." The authors (Tunaley, Walsh, and Nicolson) note that

> Not only are women's bodies supposed to conform to the sylph-like silhouette of an adolescent or even pre-adolescent girl, they are also expected to have the soft, hairless and unwrinkled characteristics of youth and sexual immaturity. (P. 744)

The study focuses analytic attention on how women themselves account for the meaning of body size through social scripts of beauty ideals. Intersecting image and everyday practice, the authors argue that "women may reflect on the images of women they see around them or on the social discourses which surround these images" (Tunaley, Walsh, and Nicolson 1999, p. 745). The women in the study displayed, as one might expect given basic theoretical arguments, a great sense of dissatisfaction with their bodies. This played itself out in food consumption and exercise. The older women that were studied focused on the "thin body" as the perfect body and defined their own sexual attractiveness in terms of slimness. Pressure was placed on the women by those around them to lose weight, to eat right, to exercise, and to "take care of themselves."

However, with the incorporation of age into the study, the results emerged as much more complex than in other studies of body size among women. Age provided a kind of "freedom discourse" where the women had more leeway in their bodily presentation. In essence, age provided a discursive resource for defining their bodies in more of a laissez-faire manner. Unlike younger generations of women, older women used the very constructions that society imposed on them due to their age as a way of invoking a kind of freedom in bodily construction and presentation.

In their article, "Cybersex: Outercourse and the Enselfment of the Body," Waskul, Douglass, and Edgley (2000) take us in a different direction in their consideration of the intersection directly between sexuality, gender, and the body—the direction of the "virtual body" and the hyperreal (Baudrillard 1983). Beginning with the argument that sexual intercourse provides us with the ultimate in embodiment, or as they note, "a corporeal experience in which physical bodies interact" (Waskul, Douglass, and Edgley 2000, p. 375), the authors lead us to consider the sexual body through a much different frame. Using data on cybersex gathered from Internet Relay Chats (IRCs), bulletin board systems, and the World Wide Web (WWW), the authors discovered new sexual uses of the body where the physical body is completely removed from the actual encounter. This disappearance of the body allows for the enactment, as they state, "of new forms of selfhood and provide insights into new relationships among bodies, selves, and social interaction" (p. 380). In other words, their concern emerges along the lines of the "enselfment of the body," not the "embodiment of the self," as social theorists so often argue.

8

In this world of sexual performativity, one might assume that any body can be presented. However, the authors make a much different argument. Drawing from Geertz's (1973) concept of "local culture," they suggest that bodies, and in turn, selves, are "more likely to adhere to cultural and social prescriptions appropriate to the situation" (Waskul, Douglass, and Edgley 2000, p. 390). Participants present a virtual body in these sexual encounters that is prescribed by dominant cultural and social prescriptions of sexuality and gender. Small breasts, small penises, bad vision, and being "overweight," all disappear from the scene. Indeed, participants can present a body that is beyond normal physical constraints—"the fluidity of both body and self-presentation does not free participants from the shackles of the beauty myth but only allows them to redefine themselves in accordance with that myth" (p. 390).

So instead of destabilizing the "beauty myth" (Wolf 1990), participants engaged in virtual sexual encounters present a body that further enhances the myth and is defined by it. Indeed, virtual sex strengthens the beauty myth and provides it with further cultural and social legitimacy. Everyone online is gorgeous. Everyone online is sexually attractive. Sociocultural discourses of body and beauty determine the very ways in which one must define him- or herself in a "virtual land," where many have assumed this to be free.

Their argument is especially intriguing because it documents an intersection of everyday activity and wider social and cultural images. The participants find bestowed on them scripts of beauty. The images these scripts write, document for us what exactly beauty is in postmodern Western culture. Participants then put these images into play, as it were, in the cultural confines of virtual reality. The body here is no less "real" than it would be in actual physical encounters, but is instead a perfect, sexual body playing itself out in real-time, practical encounters depending on a culturally defined imagery of the perfect body.

Locating the Consumer Body

As we have entered the new millennium, we find ourselves embedded in what we might term a "consumer culture." The development of this new culture is associated with various changes in Western society. According to Jagger (2000, 45), these changes include "the rise of the media and advertising . . . the decline of heavy manufacturing industries and the growth in service sector industries." Turner (1991b) furthers this alluding to such changes as the shortening of the workweek and mandated retirement and the ways in which these have led to "an emphasis on consumption, hedonism, and play" (Jagger 2000, 45).

The question, of course, is exactly, How does this intersect with the body? While various theorists have dealt with this topic in varied degrees (see Bourdieu 1984; Baudrillard 1988; Giddens 1991), I turn to the arguments presented by Mike Featherstone (1991) in "The Body in Consumer Culture." Featherstone's arguments are closely tied with images of the body and consumer wants and needs. Featherstone leads off this work by discussing the ways that the capitalistic economic system in late modernity (or postmodernity) provides us with images that we hunger to adopt. For example, drawing from Turner's (1991b) work on diet and the body, Featherstone speaks to the very task of consumer culture, its production of "stylized images," and its relationship to mundane practice and consumption:

> Consumer culture latches onto the prevalent self-preservationist conception of the body, which encourages the individual to adopt instrumental strategies to combat deterioration and decay . . . and combines it with the notion that the body is a vehicle of pleasure and self-expression. Images of the body beautiful, openly sexual and associated with hedonism, leisure, and display, emphasize the importance of appearance and the "look." (P. 170)

What Featherstone suggests is that the body is itself an integral part of consumer culture. We act on or work to maintain the body because of the images of the perfect body presented to us by the media, advertising, and so forth, and these industries must, in turn, have the body to actively work on. To borrow a phrase from the ethnomethodologists, the body is both part and parcel of consumer culture.

Featherstone focuses analytic attention on the maintenance of the body and takes us down a path awash in imagery of the perfect body. He uses this quote by Kern (1975, ix) to introduce his concerns:

> Ours is an age obsessed with youth, health, and physical beauty. Television and motion pictures, the dominant visual media, churn out persistent reminders that the lithe and graceful body, the dimpled smile set in an attractive face, are the keys to happiness, perhaps even its essence. (P. 177)

The body is what we find the greatest pleasure in as individuals. It is the vehicle, consumer culture tells us, through which we can pursue this. We long after great health, beauty, and fitness. We long after the perfect body accentuating its form in clothing. Consumer culture allows us to flaunt our bodies, or at least attempt to achieve the body "worthy" of flaunting. And this body we can achieve through "bodywork." We can achieve the perfect body if we simply work hard enough. We can get that look we have always hoped for and longed for: the image of the body embedded in our television, our advertisements, our movies, and in turn, our dreams. These images lead directly to everyday self-work on the body, pushing us from image to practice.

One cannot overstate the importance of imagery in our consumer culture. The way we perceive our own bodies is dominated by the plethora of ever-expanding images of the body provided to us for our own consumption: "[I]ndeed the inner logic of consumer culture depends upon the cultivation of an insatiable appetite to consume images" (Featherstone 1991, 178). Again, these images link with everyday practice. We have a day-to-day knowledge of what we look like, what we feel like, and how we must appear to others as they come upon us in our daily lives. These images make us acutely aware of our "external appearance" as we fall under the watchful gaze of a world awash in perfect bodies.

Featherstone (1991) links this closely with the emergence of Hollywood cinema and its ties to the development of a consumer culture. It is the cinema, after all, that gave us "the look." As he notes, "Hollywood publicized the new consumer culture values and projected images of the glamorous celebrity lifestyle to a worldwide audience" (p. 179). These images, not words, drew great attention to the body and its "rightful" appearance. It oriented the consumer to the clothes to wear, the drinks to consume, the way to act, and even the correct way of smoking a cigarette. The body as a posed and easily manipulated entity was introduced to us through the "silver screen" (see Markson, chapter 3 in this volume).

While we are provided images of the body to long for, we must work to attain these images, which I have previously referred to as bodywork. Featherstone also terms this "body maintenance." What is intriguing about this terminology is its association with the mechanization of the body that "like cars and other consumer goods, bodies require servicing, regular care, and attention to preserve maximum efficiency" (1991, 182).

And we must work harder and harder, longer and longer, to maintain our body. This is a fascinating leap. Because now "free time" must be transposed into "body time." We work out, we eat differently, we shop for the "right" clothes, and so forth. We maintain an ongoing orientation to the body even in our own free time. In turn, this ongoing and seemingly endless body maintenance takes away what we once thought of as free time and has simply replaced it with another form of work.

Through time, media images and the health industry have become intertwined. Listen to what Featherstone says on this subject:

> Preventative medicine offers a similar message and through its offshoot, health education, demands constant vigilance on the part of the individual who has to be persuaded to assume responsibility for his (sic) health, introducing the category "self inflicted illness," which results from body abuse . . . health educationalists assert that individuals who conserve their bodies through dietary care and exercise will enjoy greater health and live longer. (P. 183)

Health education pushes for a culture where the individual must assume more and more self-responsibility for their own body and the effort needed to maintain this body. From what we eat, to how we dress, to the exercises we do, to the way we even stand or sit is placed on the individual's shoulders—it is *your* responsibility. From this, a whole industry has proliferated to help us self-maintain.

This leaves us in a place where this volume takes us as well—the intersection of practice and image. As the images of the perfect body emerge around us in every way, we are forced to practice ways to reach these perhaps unattainable, at least for the vast majority of us, body images. On this, consumer culture rides. The performative body finds itself dependent on knowledge of the perfect body embedded in images and the way in which we might present these images for others through daily habits, routines, and activities.

Locating the Gerontological Body in Imagery and Everyday Experience: Organizing the Text

At the initiation of the introduction, I articulated that the body has not been entirely absent in gerontological theorizing. It was Peter Öberg

(1996) who first discussed this important topic. What exactly did he mean by this? It is an important and necessary way to begin our discussion of the aging body. His article was a major impetus for the recent growth, as minimal as it may be outside of Britain, of gerontological interest in the body.

Öberg suggests that in Western thought the body is separated into a mind–body dualism. Of course, this springs from the philosophical reflections of Descartes and Plato. Descartes' arguments center around the "fact" that the body and mind exist completely separate from each other. In a hierarchical system, the body is subjugated to the mind. It is a subordinate entity.

This dualism has sprung into gerontological thought as well, being that "many dominating concepts within gerontology are based on and perpetuate this dualism" (Öberg 1996, 703). We apply what he terms as a "mechanical trilogy" in aging research, separating the body into the physical, psychological, and social dimension of aging. The study of the body is divided into two separate branches of study—as an area of study, the body resides in geriatrics, while gerontology focuses on other aspects of the aging experience.

Therefore, due to its placement in geriatrics, the body is an invisible structure in social gerontology. Öberg provides a wonderful example of this in his discussion of the absence of body talk in gerontological textbooks:

> If one looks up the word "body," "body image," "appearance," and "physical appearance" in gerontological manuals one finds nothing (Birren and Schaie 1977; Palmore 1980; Binstock and Shanas 1985; Binstock and George 1990; Birren and Bengston 1988; Cole et al. 1992). In *Emergent Theories of Aging* (Birren and Bengston 1988) under the catchword "self," we find a reference to "body and self" where it is briefly stated that we both are and have a body. (P. 703)

On the other hand, as just noted, the body has been a central feature of geriatrics. However, its conceptualization of the body is vastly different from what we experience in social theory. The aging body in geriatrics has been conceived as a *"thing, product,* and *diagnosis."* What this means is that the body is seen as an entity that is stable, that can be made pure, and that can be treated. Social gerontology, on the other hand, has ignored the body as a construction, whether as a symbol or as culturally or socially defined.

I have mentioned that the body has begun to make a small presence in gerontology. How has this occurred and in what ways have we begun to think of this "thing"? Following Öberg, Emmanuelle Tulle-Winton (2000) suggests that we have indeed made attempts in gerontology, again, primarily European, to account for the aging body. However, these either have been the body as a biological entity or have, to some degree, removed it from the aging experience, instead placing it in a cultural framework. In other words, we have dismissed its everyday practice. The corporality of mundane practice has been ignored.

This ignorance of the aging body might be best exemplified in the sociology of aging, which has failed miserably in discussing the aging body. Instead, sociology has centered its analysis around

> Popular stereotypes about old people, usually centered around the inevitability of old age and its manifestation as physical decrepitude from which cultural irrelevance could be inferred. Old age was therefore outside the social because it was an essentially biological process. (Tulle-Winton 2000, 67)

Given what sociology has and has not done, it has been a major contributor to the omnipotent discourse of old age that prevails in Western social thought. It produces and reproduces this discourse, thus neglecting the actual "practices, structures of thought and habits that we came to know as old age" (Tulle-Winton 2000, 68). This is not to say that sociology, and in turn, social gerontology, has not made recent strides in its consideration of the aging body. Nevertheless, for the most part, it has been an ignored entity. Indeed, it has been, to some degree, absent.

Drawing explicitly on the thoughts of Foucault, Stephen Katz (1996) takes us in a much different direction in his book *Disciplining Old Age: The Formation of Gerontological Knowledge*. Following Foucault's use of genealogy, Katz searches to unveil the historical movements and ruptures of gerontology as a controlling discipline. Katz's argument rests on the fact, as he states, that gerontology "discovered" the aging body as it is embedded in "institutional, discursive, technical, and political relations of power" (p. 29).

Katz proposes an interesting point in his separation of geriatrics and gerontology and the ways that each dealt with the body of the aged, especially the increased attention paid to the body by geriatrics as a stable, static, physical entity. The development of these two areas of study can be followed back to France in the eighteenth and nineteenth centuries as medical research developed a discourse of senescence, "a new organization of associated ideas that captured the aged body through three commanding perceptions" (p. 40). The three perceptions include the aged body as signifier, the aged body as a separate entity, and the aged body as a dying entity. Let us turn to the aged body as a signifying presence first.

Here, biomedicine first enters the picture. The advent of modern biomedicine led to the body as no longer being seen as an entity embedded in social relations with others, but rather as only a surface that points toward what is "layered in the body." As Katz notes, "the body in this sense became a signification system running from the surface to its microscopic interior, a generalized site where meanings could be localized" (1996, 40–41).

In a sense, the body has become its own local culture (Geertz 1973) that only needs to be unearthed by the gaze of the physician. The job of the physician was to go beneath the signifiers existing on the surface of the body. Her or his job was to probe, unearth, and uncover what exists beneath the surface—to see what is *really* happening. This shift in how biomedicine constructs and focuses attention toward the body is perhaps most aptly stated in Foucault's (1973) seminal text, *The Birth of the Clinic*, and his concept of the "medical gaze." The transcendence of Western medicine meshed closely with the Enlightenment's project of investigation, "probing, dissecting, fathoming, magnifying, codifying, and classifying" (p. 41). In short, the birth of the body as having an interior quality is embedded in the explosion of the Enlightenment.

In the conception of the aged body as a separate entity from the social world, medicine plays the role of the agent that reconstructs the body as a pathological entity easily identified by symptoms and the need of specialized therapeutic practices. Age now becomes a vital concern of medicine. Indeed, it is needed for medicine to function and for its knowledge to expand. Where age had previously been ignored, modern medicine and its treatments would grow to depend on it; "the problem was less the health, vitality, or prolongevity of an elder than the progressively degenerative diseases that defined their state of aging" (p. 41). Age, in other words, demanded the medical gaze as the body was now seen as a deteriorating entity, located in its decrepit surface presence. After all, as I remarked at the beginning of the introduction, the body visibly marks us as aging. Here, Katz takes us on a journey into the emergence of the word *senility*. While it is not necessary to discuss this here, the term indicates a "pathological state" and in its initiation, *senile*-conveyed weakness.

In the aged body as a dying presence, the concept of the aged body as a degenerative presence is continued. The body is now seen as an entity in the constant practice of *dying*. The concern is no longer with preservation of the body's life, but rather death as simply a part of life:

> The aged body became reduced to a state of degeneration where the meanings of old age and the body's deterioration seemed condemned to signify each other in perpetuity. By recreating death as a phenomenon in life, rather than of life, medical research on aging became separate from the earlier treatises that focused on the promise of longevity. (Foucault 1973, 41)

Death is no longer the destruction of the body, but simply another stage in its presence on earth. It is a unique and important shift that determined geriatric medical practice through time.

These three new concepts of the aged body inclusive of geriatrics and gerontology provided the opportunity of a discourse of senescence to change the very bodily meaning of the aged from premodern times. The body surface no longer points to the poor alignment of the cosmos, but rather pathological behavior of the interior body as a mechanized machine. Indeed, the discourse of the normal and pathological legitimized the new conceptualization of the body in Western medicine.

Importantly, and needed for its longevity, a discourse of senescence was embedded, and remains so, in institutions such as the hospital. Its presence in institutional relations of power further legitimates the exercise of medicine as a means of bodily creation and management. Its incorporation in sites such as the hospital allows the new discourse of the aged body to spread into what Foucault terms the "human sciences." By this, Foucault alerts us to the development of criminology, demography, and public health. Now, whole *bodies* of people can be managed. Part of the population most closely monitored were the aged population—their bodies, in decline, threatened the well-being of the rest of the population—the healthy population.

While the preceding represents a theoretical treatise on aging, Featherstone and Hepworth (1991) provide us with a seminal work that alerts us to the importance of images of aging and their primacy in everyday practice. In their piece, "The Mask of Ageing and the Post-modern Life Course," the authors work to explain the place of the aging body in postmodern culture. Explicitly, they examine the life course and its place in postmodern theorizing, drawing on such well used terms as deconstruction to explain the emergent views of postmodernism as a critique of cultural representations and to point out that the "new" postmodernism has direct links to gerontology.

Embedded in postmodernist approaches to aging is the contemporary dilemma of aging in which we find ourselves searching for and ever extending the time span of middle age. The linear life course has been disrupted phenomenologically, and these views are immersed in the images of aging we are presented with in our daily lives. As Kastenbaum (1981) points out, aging individuals do not consider their age in chronological terms, but rather in terms of life experiences, past, present, and an expected future.

One manner of denying old age is the concealment of "inner feelings, motives, attitudes or beliefs" (Featherstone and Hepworth 1991, 378). This is the "mask of aging." That is, age is seen as a mask that hides the true feelings of the person "underneath." Kaufman (1986) makes a similar argument in *The Ageless Self*. Listen as the authors (Featherstone and Hepworth 1991) tell us of the increasing presence of this mask, "the view of the aging process as a mask of disguise concealing the essentially youthful self beneath is one which appears to be increasingly popular" (p. 379).

The aging mask alerts us to three primary issues related to the aging experience. First, there is a gap between the physical presentation of aging on the external body and the subjective experience of aging that lies beneath. As we age, this subjective sense predominates in our own thoughts on the aging experience, whether negative or positive. Second, the vocabulary of aging, or its discourse, provides the aged with limited potential for the expression of their subjective, personal feelings, separate from prevailing stereotypes of the elderly. In our society, we fix the aged in a single place; ignoring the various places of life they might actually place themselves. They are not just old; they are many things.

Third, we find generational change. While the "image of the mask seems to remain the most appropriate as far as the present generation is concerned" (Featherstone and Hepworth 1991, 383), this seems to be changing. As increasing members enter middle age (or middle life), images are changing. A new discourse is emerging around age and aging. This new language is much more expressive and allows the aging person to speak of themselves in a much more positive manner. This is an important shift and presents new, positive ways of seeing the aged.

Featherstone and Hepworth's (1991) argument on images/masks of aging provides a segue into a discussion of the chapters and their organization. Since this volume is centered on two aspects of the aging body—its imagery and everyday practice—let us turn to these two arenas for a final discussion. Images of the aged body abound in our society. Visual representations of the elderly provide us with concert images of what it is like to be old, both in the way we look and the way we act. Increasing amounts of study have focused our attention on aging bodies as they are represented through visual representations (see Blaikie 1999; Blaikie and Hepworth 1997; Bytheway 1993; Bytheway and Johnson 1998; Woodward 1991). These images, as Tulle-Winton (2000) notes, are the way that we actually assess whether we are old or not, "they provide us with models of appropriate expectations and conduct, and they also illustrate deep-seated collective and personal fears about the 'reality' thus represented" (p. 69).

The study of photographs are vital to this area of interest. An example is the studies of "trendy retirement magazines" of the 1970s by Featherstone and Wernick (1995) and Hepworth (1995). What they find is that images of aging carry a "normative, moralizing content." They suggest what the correct way of aging is. For example, in the study of these magazines, the various authors found that the images presented in the magazines show us "good," successful aging people. They show us the well-preserved elderly. This is a group that has maintained an identity embedded in midlife, never departing to the darkness of late life. The models are "perfect" and represent the ideal aging body. Of course, great effort is extended to create the "perfect, aging body":

> The photographic conventions used in these magazines are designed to smooth out the aesthetic deficiencies of old bodies—by choosing attractive models who are usually young-looking, and presenting them in soft

focus, or, in more recent publications, engaged in sporting activity. (Tulle-Winton 2000, 69)

By using images such as these, individuals are taught that they have a responsibility to attain this perfection—to preserve middle life by increasing financial independence. From these forms of presenting images of the elderly that are fully clothed, the aging body is presented in its ideal state, creating a contrast between ideal perfection and failures on the individual. The photographs present images that tell us that we can end up like this, too, if we just make the right decisions and work hard enough—two arguments that fit clearly in the concept of the consumer body, as discussed earlier.

Everyday practice takes us down a road that, though in many ways is closely connected with imagery, pushes us toward the mundane practice of the "living" or the "real" body. It is a body embedded in individual perceptions and social interaction. It attends to the everyday methods of persons as they deal with their body as an aging, or aged, entity. The aging body is embedded in language games (Wittgenstein 1958), local cultures, and organizational constructs that provide the individual with delineated methods of interpretation. It is an artful entity, yet still subjected to discursive constraints. A fascinating construct, the body has no central meaning as a physiological "thing," but finds itself constructed through wider discourses of the body and sites of micropolitical interaction. The body, as embedded in everyday practice, is much more than an image, but a meaning-making and meaning-constructed entity that acts and is acted on. Every day of our lives is an embodied day (Nettleton and Watson 1998).

Drawing on these two approaches, the "separation" of this edited volume into sections on images and everyday experience occurred quite naturally. Papers were solicited from contributors without any request that their papers fit into a prescribed organization. The importance of everyday practice and interaction and the significance of images of aging flowed as time went on. Perhaps, more than anything else, this alerts us to the importance of these two things in the way that the aging body is conceptualized and experienced in Western thought.

The first four chapters of the volume focus attention on images and the aging body. Bill Bytheway, drawing on the work of Jean Baudrillard, attends to the role that photographs, and the textual construction that surrounds them, play in giving meaning to the aging body. Drawing on collections of photographs and advertisements in British retirement magazines, Bytheway searches out the role of images of later life, especially those organized in collections and carefully constructed magazine advertisement, and how they play in constructing reality and in offering us a vision of exactly how old life *should* be.

Betina Freidin drives us down a different road into an area most often left out of social thought about the aging body—that of death. Though a growing area of concern in social gerontology, it has really received little notice as an act connected with the imagery of a future body embedded in religious discourse and articulated through images and meaning-making practices of organ transplantation. Using data gathered in Buenos Aires, Freidin takes us to a place where symbolic images of bodily parts—the mechanized body—play out in concerns with death and the body as an organic whole. The body, as Shilling (1993) tells us, is unfinished and constantly plays itself out. Indeed, it continues to play itself out in the symbolic imagery of bodily organs and death.

Film has played an enormously important role in depicting images of the body. Drawing on this important foundation, Elizabeth W. Markson, in chapter 3, uses a representation depicted in *Sunset Boulevard* to focus on the theme of the aging female body through the examination of how the aged female body and mind have been presented to us in feature films. In particular, Markson focuses on three representations: the dressed body; the sexual body; and the ill or dying body. The chapter presented here by Markson is part of a larger study grounded in the portraits of older women in feature films. She has an outstanding knowledge of this subject matter, and it is readily evident in her work in this volume.

Last, Peter Öberg leads us into the section on everyday practice by pointing out an important analytic distinction between images of the aged body and the actual experience of it. This is an intriguing piece since Öberg argues that the two do not coincide in all cases, thus negating, or at least arguing against, the implications of imagery on aging. As he notes, gerontology has approached the body as a problematic entity layered with imagery and hopelessness. His study participants, however, do not always feel this way, providing a critical perspective on an ongoing stance in the cross discipline of social gerontology. In short, he introduces us to a series of "contradictory" images of the aging body and their intersection with subjective concerns of the aged themselves.

Turning to everyday practice, Julia Twigg leads off with a chapter on the interaction between community care employees and elders in terms of the personal care they receive at home. Drawing from her previous work on the same subject (Twigg 2000), she points out that the basic tasks of bathing and washing of elders exemplify the day-to-day, mundane activities of the aged. Due to this, they have received little attention by gerontologists. In short, it is seen as a rather boring and unimportant subject. But if so much of our time is taken up with body care, from washing one's hair to shaving, then it is most certainly a vitally important area of research on the body. Twigg takes this to heart, touching on the various discourses in which community bodily care are encoded.

Dana Rosenfeld continues her impressive efforts on the experience of older gays and lesbians by extending her discussion into the construct of the body and this group. The aging body, as Rosenfeld and her respondents see it, is immersed in its distinctive historical location. The time and social place of being queer, and the resulting discourse of the sexual body provided by these locations, has important implications for the techniques in which the sexual body sees itself.

Next, American sociologists Jaber F. Gubrium and James A. Holstein continue their long-standing focus on mundane practice and reality construction. Drawing on Shilling and his stance that the body is an "unfinished entity," the authors criticize, to some degree, a commonly held stance in considerations of the aging body. The body, Gubrium and Holstein argue, is not omnipresent. In fact, in everyday interaction it is sometimes "invisible." That is, it is an object of experience whose visibility is determined by meaning-making action. The visibility of the aging body in everyday practice is dependent on the complex intersection of the "objective body" and the social circumstances in which the body is directly encountered.

In the fourth chapter of this section, Emmanuelle Tulle pulls from the theoretical considerations of scholars such as Pierre Bourdieu and Michel Foucault to look at what we must consider the *aging* body, not the aged one. Her work focuses on long-distance, master runners and the manners and techniques in which the aging body plays out in their running practices. Tulle locates the ways in which they deal with a declining body within various theoretical perspectives.

Last, the chapter by Steven P. Wainwright and Bryan S. Turner concludes this volume. The authors look at the place of, once again, the aging body, within professional dancers. Drawing on substantive data, they, like Gubrium and Holstein, take a critical perspective toward much bodily theorizing. Concerned with the overarching dependency on Foucault in studies of the body, the authors argue against this "radical social constructionism," instead arguing that we need to focus more on reality and the body as a lived presence, not its theoretical construction. That is, the aging body as it matters.

References

Armstrong, D.
> 1983 *Political Anatomy of the Body: Medical Knowledge in Britain in the 20th Century*. Cambridge: Cambridge University Press.

Atkinson, P.
> 1988 Description and Diagnosis: Reproducing Normal Medicine. In *Biomedicine Examined*. Edited by M. Lock and D. Gordon. London: Kluwer.

Baudrillard, J.
> 1983 *Simulations*. New York: Semiotext(e).
> 1988 *Selected Writings*. Cambridge, U.K.: Polity Press.

Binstock, R., and L. George, eds.
> 1990 *Handbook of Aging and the Social Sciences*. 3rd ed. San Diego, Calif.: Academic Press.

Binstock, R., and E. Shanas, eds.
> 1985 *Handbook of Aging and the Social Sciences*, 2nd ed. New York: Van Nostrand Reinhold.

Birke, L.
> 1995 *Our Bodies, Ourselves? Feminism, Biology, and the Body*. Centre for the Study of Women and Gender, University of Warwick.

Birren, J., and V. Bengston, eds.
> 1988 *Emergent Theories of Aging*. New York: Springer.

Birren, J., and K. Schaie, eds.
> 1977 *Handbook of the Psychology of Aging*. New York: Van Nostrand Reinhold.

Blaikie, A.
> 1999 *Images of Ageing*. Cambridge: Cambridge University Press.

Blaikie, A., and M. Hepworth
    1997 Representation of Old Age in Painting and Photography. In *Critical Approaches to Ageing and Later Life*. Edited by A. Jamieson, S. Harper, and C. R. Victor. Buckingham, U.K.: Open University Press.

Bourdieu, P.
    1984 *Distinction: A Social Critique of the Judgment of Taste*. Cambridge: Harvard University Press.

Butler, J.
    1993 *Bodies That Matter*. London: Routledge.

Bytheway, B.
    1993 Ageing and Biography: The Letters of Bernard and Mary Berenson. *Sociology* 27: 153–65.

Bytheway, B., and J. Johnson
    1998 The Sight of Age. In *The Body and Everyday Life*. Edited by S. Nettleton and J. Watson, 243–57. London: Routledge.

Burchell, G., C. Gordon, and P. Miller
    1991 *The Foucault Effect: Studies in Governmentality*. London: Harvester.

Cash, T., and P. E. Henry
    1995 Women's Body Images: The Results of a National Survey in the United States. *Sex Roles* 33: 19–28.

Cash, T., B. A. Winstead, and L. Janda
    1986 Body Image Survey Report: The Great American Shape-Up. *Psychology Today* April: 30–37.

Cole, T., D. Van Tassel, and R. Kastenbaum, eds.
    1992 *Handbook of the Humanities and Aging*. New York: Springer.

Conrad, P., and J. Schneider
    1980 *Deviance and Medicalization: From Badness to Sickness*. St. Louis, Mo.: C. V. Mosby.

Elias, N.
    1978 *The History of Manners: The Civilizing Process*. Vol. 1. Oxford, U.K.: Blackwell.

Featherstone, M.
    1991 The Body in Consumer Culture. In *The Body: Social Process and Cultural Theory*. Edited by M. Featherstone, M. Hepworth, and B. Turner, 170–96. London: Sage.

Featherstone, M., and M. Hepworth
1991 The Mask of Ageing and the Post-modern Life Course. In *The Body: Social Process and Cultural Theory.* Edited by M. Featherstone, M. Hepworth, and B. Turner. London: Sage.

Featherstone, M., and A. Wernick, eds.
1995 *Images of Aging: Cultural Representations of Later Life.* London: Routledge.

Foucault, M.
1973 *The Birth of the Clinic.* London: Tavistock.
1977 *Discipline and Punish: The Birth of the Prison.* London: Tavistock.

Geertz, C.
1973 *The Interpretation of Cultures.* New York: Basic.

Giddens, A.
1991 *Modernity and Self-Identity: Self and Society in the Late Modern Age.* Cambridge, U.K.: Polity Press.

Hepworth, M.
1995 Positive Ageing: What is the Message? In *The Sociology of Health Promotion: Critical Analysis of Consumption, Lifestyle, and Risk.* Edited by R. Bunton, S. Nettleton, and R. Burrows. London: Routledge.

Hughes, B.
2000 Medicalized Bodies. In *The Body, Culture and Society.* Edited by P. Hancock et al., 12–18. Buckingham, U.K.: Open University Press.

Jagger, E.
2000 Consumer Bodies. In *The Body, Culture and Society.* Edited by P. Hancock et al., 45–63. Buckingham, U.K.: Open University Press.

Kastenbaum, R.
1981 Habituation as a Model of Human Aging. *Journal of Aging and Human Development* 12: 159–70.

Katz, S.
1996 *Disciplining Old Age: The Formation of Gerontological Knowledge.* Charlottesville: University of Virginia Press.

Kaufman, S.
1986 *The Ageless Self.* Madison: University of Wisconsin Press.

Kern, S.
1975 *Anatomy and Destiny: A Cultural History of the Human Body.* New York: Bobbs-Merrill.

Lawrence, S. C., and K. Bendixen

1992 His and Hers: Male and Female Anatomy in Anatomy Text for U.S. Medical Students. *Social Science and Medicine* 35: 925–34.

Leder, D.

1992 *The Body in Medical Thought and Practice.* Chicago: University of Chicago Press.

Lupton, D.

1994 *Medicine as Culture: Illness, Disease, and the Body.* London: Sage.

1995 *The Imperative of Health: Public Health and the Regulated Body.* London: Sage.

Martin, E.

1987 *The Woman in the Body.* (Milton Keynes, U.K.) Boston: Beacon Press.

Nettleton, S., and J. Watson, eds.

1998 *The Body and Everyday Life.* London: Routledge.

Öberg, P.

1996 The Absent Body: A Gerontological Paradox. *Ageing and Society* 16: 701–19.

Palmore, E., ed.

1980 *The International Handbook on Aging.* Hampshire, U.K.: Macmillan Press.

Parsons, T.

1937 *The Structure of Social Action.* New York: Free Press.

1939 The Professions and the Social Structure. *Social Forces* 17: 457–67.

Sacks, O.

1981 *Migraine: Evolution of a Common Disorder.* London: Pan Books.

1986 *A Leg to Stand On.* London: Pan Books.

Schutz, A.

1967 *The Phenomenology of the Social World.* Evanston, Ill.: Northwestern University Press.

Scully, D., and P. Bart

1978 A Funny Thing Happened on the Way to the Orifice: Women in Gynecological Textbooks. In *The Cultural Crisis of Modern Medicine.* Edited by J. Ehrenreich. New York: Monthly Review Publications.

Shilling, C.

1993 *The Body in Social Theory.* London: Sage.

Tulle-Winton, E.
2000 Old Bodies. In *The Body, Culture and Society.* Edited by P. Hancock et al., 64–83. Buckingham, U.K.: Open University Press.

Tunaley, J., S. Walsh, and P. Nicolson
1999 I'm Not Bad for My Age: The Meaning of Body Size and Eating in the Lives of Older Women. *Ageing and Society* 19: 741–59.

Turner, B.
1991a Recent Development in the Theory of the Body. In *The Body: Social Process and Cultural Theory.* Edited by M. Featherston, M. Hepworth, and B. Turner, 1–35. London: Sage.
1991b The Discourse of Diet. In *The Body: Social Process and Cultural Theory.* Edited by M. Featherstone, M. Hepworth, and B. Turner, 170–96. London: Sage.
1995 *Medical Power and Social Knowledge.* 2nd ed. London: Sage.
1996 *The Body and Society: Explorations in Social Theory.* London: Sage.

Twigg, J.
2000 *Bathing: The Body and Consumer Care.* London: Routledge.

Waskul, D., M. Douglass, and C. Edgley
2000 Cybersex: Outercourse and the Enselfment of the Body. *Symbolic Interaction* 23: 375–97.

Williams, S., and G. Bendelow
1998 *The Lived Body: Sociological Themes, Embodied Issues.* London: Routledge.

Wittengstein, L.
1958 *Philosophical Investigations.* Oxford, U.K.: Blackwell.

Wolf, N.
1990 *The Beauty Myth: How Images of Beauty Are Used Against Women.* New York: William Morrow.

Woodward, K.
1991 *Aging and Its Discontents: Freud and Other Fictions.* Bloomington: University of Indiana Press.

Part One
IMAGES

CHAPTER ONE

VISUAL REPRESENTATIONS OF LATE LIFE
Bill Bytheway

With the rise of early and phased retirement and anxieties about ageist stereotypes, later life is now conceptualized in a confusing variety of ways. Traditional certainties about "old age" and "the aged" have been overtaken by the ambiguous and relativist connotations of "later life" and "elderly," "aging" or "older" people. In this chapter, I use the terms "later life" and "older people" in the open sense of "later rather than earlier life" and "older rather than younger people." In exploring various ways in which images of the aging body are used to convey age identities, I compare two very different examples of collections of photographs. These are part of a continuing series of the analyses of images of later life.

In Johnson and Bytheway (1997), we focused on a magazine specializing in community care. This revealed four dominant images of care: the "teacher" shot in which the caregiver is portrayed in a supervisory role in relation to a number of older people; the "portrait" in which caregiver and older person are presented as if they were members of a loving family; the "cared for" shot, which shows the caregiver engaged in cleaning work, delivering meals, or dressing the older person; and the most significant in the context of cultural changes in later life, the "caring about" shot: care being typified by the prize-winning photograph of a younger caregiver touching the older person being cared for. We were particularly struck by the consistency of these standard images and by how they were used to reinforce certain basic messages regarding "good care practice."

Following this, in Bytheway and Johnson (1998), we discuss how age might be seen and recognized. We analyzed a number of readily available images of older people and considered the question, how might the older person interpret these images and compare them with the image seen in the mirror? In Bytheway (2000), I undertook a content analysis of one particular advertisement for an antiaging product. Although the advertisement itself appears to be of little apparent significance, it became clear that the text used presented the image of an allegedly older woman in a particularly subtle way. Initially she is a salesperson addressing the consumer in friendly if teasing terms. Gradually, however, the text turns the image into that of the prospective mirror: "This could be you!"

French social theorist Jean Baudrillard (1983) alerts us to how in contemporary society we live in a world awash with images. He argues that the "hyperreal" world we live in is embedded in these very images, images that coordinate, evaluate, order, and construct our daily lives. It is, he argues, the *only* reality: "In hyperreality, class, gender and race are no more real than Mickey Mouse or Donald Duck, except as their images might be conveyed as such" (Holstein and Gubrium 2000, 66). Aging can certainly be added to the mix.

In most forms of mass media at the start of the twenty-first century, later life is now represented predominantly by photographic images of older people. Magazine features, newspaper articles, advertisements, encyclopedias, and the Internet are all media that have "old age" as a recurrent topic. And in an increasingly visual world, there before you is a photograph, and often a series of photographs of older people, accompanied by text that confirms that, by association, *this* is old age. This chapter is intended to examine this phenomenon and address the question, what might gerontologists deduce from these kinds of visual representations about dominant cultural understandings of the life course?

Identifying with the Image

Susan Sontag (1979, 7) argues that photography became a central element in the mass media following the 1840s and 1850s: "photography's glorious first two decades." In her essay *Photographic Evangels,* she challenges its long association with realism:

> most of the contradictory declarations of photographers converge on pious avowals of respect for things-as-they-are. For a medium so often

considered to be merely realistic, one would think photographers would not have to go on as they do, exhorting each other to stick to realism. But the exhortations continue. (P. 119)

Discussing Walt Whitman's vision of the "Great American Cultural Revolution," in which there is "concord in discord, oneness in diversity," Sontag (1979) argues that realism dominated American photography from Steiglitz's work of 1903 to 1917 through to Edward Steichen's 1955 ambitious exhibition, *The Family of Man*. This she describes as the last attempt to prove that humanity is "one":

> Steichen set up the show to make it possible for each viewer to identify with a great many of the people depicted and, potentially, with the subject of every photograph: citizens of World Photography all. (P. 32)

This mirror-like identification with the subjects of photographs raises a number of important issues for gerontology. As we slowly grow older, how do we interpret the image in the mirror, and how do we relate and compare it with photographs that purport to portray "the elderly"? Is this, I wonder, how people become recognizable—both to themselves and to others—as being one of "them": those who are now "elderly" (Bytheway 1995, 118)?

It is important to begin with a simple distinction. Some photographs are portraits of particular people who happen to be taken at the end of long lives; others are taken to *represent* old people *in general*. So, for example, in her retrospective collection, Jane Bown's 1984 photographic portraits of Dora Russell and Naomi Mitchison are simply named and dated with no reference to age or biography (Bown 1986, 94–95). It is only in the introduction to this retrospective collection (written by Suzanne Lowry) that we read:

> Some of the older women, the survivors, she [Bown] loves for their toughness and for the sheer photogenic qualities of an ageing face; writer Naomi Mitchison and Dora Russell are in marked but unvarnished contrast with the artifice of Helena Rubinstein.

Viewers may, of course, note and comment on Mitchison's much-lined face, looking critically at the camera as if it were a mirror. They may know of her work and her biography, and some may know her to be of their own generation, and so they may use the image to help them interpret what they see in the mirror. But her image is not published to "represent" old age or "the elderly." It is no more and no less than that of Naomi Mitchison in 1984.

In contrast, other photographers have set out to specifically create images that represent later life. The personal identity of the subjects is secondary. They appear in the book, exhibition, or collection only as visual representations of later life. Even though the collected photographs may be of many different people, they are included solely in order to portray the one social phenomenon. In this chapter, I compare the content of two contrasting examples of this second category of images.

A Published Collection of Photographs

As noted in Bytheway and Johnson (1998), it is expensive to acquire "systematic representative samples" of specific kinds of media portrayals. For some purposes, it is sufficient to include what is readily available; images at hand that allow the researcher to focus on the "mundane" and readily available. Drawing on this method, over the last ten years I have acquired a small collection of books and magazines, purchased primarily on impulse rather than obtained systematically through bibliographic searches. Each presents multiple images of later life. For the purposes of this chapter, I picked—rather arbitrarily—*After Ninety*, a collection of eighty-two black and white photographs, taken by the celebrated American photographer, Imogen Cunningham (1977). Using her skills in photography, she provides us with a wonderful collection of detailed representations of older people.

At the beginning of the book there is a foreword from the publishers. This registers the fact that Cunningham died in 1976 at the age of ninety-three. The previous year, she had

> decided that it was time to create a new body of work. This book is the result of that decision, and with only a few exceptions contains photographs made by Imogen since her last publication [in 1974].

The foreword indicates that she was "exacting but not obstructive, interested in every phase of the physical design of the book, the evolution of the textual content and, of course, the quality of reproduction of the photographs." Unfortunately, there is no introductory commentary by Cunningham herself. Rather it was Margaretta Mitchell who wrote a twelve-page introductory essay. This begins with a quote by Simone de Beauvoir (1972) from her book, *Old Age*:

> Let us recognize ourselves in this old man or in that old woman. It must be done if we are to take upon ourselves the entirety of our human state. (P. 12)

Mitchell's purpose, like de Beauvoir's, is to remind us that our future includes the prospect of being as old as these people. As we view images of this old man or that old woman, we are urged to see ourselves in them and, thereby, to gain insight into the whole of our lives. De Beauvoir's exhortation is very similar to Sontag's comment on Steichen's objective in 1955: both refer to the act of viewing and interpreting photographs.

Echoing the publisher's foreword, Mitchell (1977) introduces Cunningham and her photographs in this way:

> No words can describe old age as well as the photographs reproduced in *After Ninety*, which is a direct result of Imogen's own confrontation with life after ninety. (P. 7)

This sentence contains two bold claims: photographs are better descriptors than words, and photographs result from personal experience. The viewer is being offered an insider's description of what life is truly like after ninety. In a wonderful and telling statement applauding Cunningham's courage, Mitchell also argues that taking these photographs had enhanced that experience:

> to look through the lens and see herself mirrored in others, always looking with a childlike curiosity, learning from another's reality ways to be strong, active, interesting, and useful. (P. 18)

Mitchell (1977) visited two of Cunningham's subjects and obtained the following eloquent commentary. It sheds light on Cunningham's strategy in engaging her subjects and sharing a sense of age:

> She was a model of what I would like to be at ninety-three. [He was only ninety-one] . . . She relaxed us with great skill. In fact, we seemed to feel

like intimate friends in a very short time. She was encouraging, got us to talk, gave us self-reliance. The next thing we knew we were talking as if she were an old friend. Usually photographers try to get you to look cheerful, happy, gay. They say "Smile, please for the birdie." She made no such effort. I think the picture is the only serious picture I ever had made of me. I like it very much, but my children loathe it. They want papa laughing, smiling, you know, happy. (P. 18)

The Photographs

Turning the pages, the viewer is repeatedly faced with photographic portraits accompanied by cryptic captions based on Cunningham's (1977) own taped comments. The first, for example, reads: "John Roeder worked in an oil refinery, but was really an artist." Many captions describe the taking of the photograph: "He's a chemist, and I asked him to put something on the blackboard for the photograph." In such ways Cunningham endeavored to consolidate a constant and distinctive identity for each subject. So a man in dungarees and displaying a potato is captioned: "He's proudest of his potatoes and he gave me this big one," and another, reflecting the way the subject is dressed in the portrait: "This lady likes Indian jewelry." A few relate to past achievements: "She was a famous pianist." Some are autobiographical; the last, for example (taken in 1937), is "My father after ninety." Only three of the subjects are quoted. One woman for example, illustrating a certain wit, said: "When we were young we were all puritans and all we talked about was whether it was right or it was wrong. And then I married a man from Sardinia."

Most are upper-body portraits with the head near the center of the image (Cunningham 1977). About one in three display symbols of their continuing interests (such as the potato and the Indian jewelry), and a similar proportion are taken out of doors. It seems likely that, in some instances, Cunningham or her subjects or both gave attention to dress. One photograph, for example, is of two sisters and the caption reads: "I had to pick out the clothes for one of them for the sitting. So I picked the most ornate things she had." About half are wearing spectacles, and six have a walking stick. At least half are seated. Half the subjects are looking directly at the camera and only seven are actively engaged in some activity other than posing for the camera. Only one of these involves vigorous bodily movement.

In *After Ninety* (Cunningham 1977), old age, broadly speaking, is portrayed as a time of contentment, fulfillment, and continuing engagement in former activities. There is a pervasive sense of calm and dignity. There are only ten captions that unambiguously celebrate achievements, two for example use the significant word "still": "He's still teaching the history of American films at three universities every year," and two refer to a length of time: "She was a high school teacher for more than fifty years." Most of the remainder are much more oblique, with statements such as "This man was in the city engineer's department," for example.

There were four male subjects (Cunningham 1977) where the captions suggest that there had been some conflict between photographer and subject. Cunningham teased one (who she describes as "over ninety") who came to her house to be photographed. She told him that "he should have no trouble climbing my steps since I managed it with my groceries every day." Rather more challengingly she commented on another: "I couldn't understand how such a creative filmmaker could be right wing"; another was described simply as "the hardest man to photograph."

The fourth man was sitting in the sun: "He didn't want me to take his picture but I did." Below this are four images of him resisting the attempt, and, on the opposite page, there is a smiling, but somewhat defeated, image headed: "This was the result." Also there is a woman who is portrayed displaying her heavily tattooed chest and arms: "This woman had been in the carnival all her life, but I found her in a hospital. It looks like lace, doesn't it?" The woman does not appear to be wholly happy about sitting up in her hospital bed, exposing her body in this way. One wonders what she felt about being asked to pose in this way. Another woman is pictured with the exceptionally long caption: "She is a distinguished radiobiologist who asked me to photograph her. I wasn't taking on commissions any more, but I did it because she didn't care if she looked old, and she didn't hate her face."

Again, despite the negative implication of not caring how she looks, this caption suggests that often there was negotiation between Cunningham and her subjects to convey a certain reality regarding how people look at ninety.

There are only four photographs that convey an image of struggle or defeat. One is of a woman with a forlorn look on her face: "She lived down my street, and I saw her sitting in the window and asked her how she spent her days. She said, 'I just try to get through them.' She is nearly a hundred." On the following page, there is a handsome man in a broad-brimmed hat, but the caption reads: "He was one of the earliest industrial designers, and feisty. The last time I saw him all the fight had gone out of him. I couldn't get him to argue about anything." Then there is a photograph of a somber man in a dressing gown under the caption: "These were taken in a Berkeley 'convalescent home.'" On the facing page, there is a black woman whose little cap and dress seem to confirm that she too was in the home. The caption reads: "She said to me, 'When you come here nobody knows where you are.'" Her facial expression reflects this: a frown and a wistful gaze toward the window.

Recruiting the Subjects

Mitchell (1977) acknowledges the contribution of certain academic colleagues from the social sciences in the planning of the book. They had participated in discussions about aging and so it is appropriate to consider how it might relate to gerontology:

> These photographs are a kind of visual research, straightforward studies of the way people are at the end of life, revealed in a face, an expression, a gesture, a posture. (P. 11)

Mitchell (1977) also acknowledges "the fine folk whose presence here makes a worthy portrait of old age" and, with only a few exceptions, Cunningham's subjects are each given the same amount of space in the book. So just as much gerontology is based on representative samples of older people who are systematically given the same amount of attention, can the eighty subjects of Cunningham's "research" (1977) be considered a representative sample? If so, of whom and for what purpose? A key question is, How did she recruit her subjects?:

> When she went to see homes for the aged, she did not like what she saw, and she became progressively aware of the true situation confronting many elderly persons in our culture. So often they had become dependent, as a result of circumstances over which they had lost control, but Imogen sought out individuals whose independent spirits had managed to transcend their problems. (Mitchell 1977, 11)

Thus, Cunningham decided not to portray the negative side of old age, despite this being the "true situation" of many. Rather, she wanted to illustrate positive aging. A place where problems had been overcome. That said, as the preceding analysis has shown, a few examples of people who had been defeated were included.

As a sample, the eighty are biased toward men: thirty-three single men compared with twenty-nine women, along with six married couples, and three other photographs each including two subjects. None of these nine multiple images could be interpreted as representing "care relationships" resulting from "dependency." The possible exception is that of a father and daughter: "He is a hundred this year, and I was invited to his birthday party on Fidalgo Island, but I couldn't make it." The daughter looks proudly at her father and lightly holds his arm, but apart from a discreetly held walking stick, he shows no sign of dependence. However, for the caption, they could easily be mistaken as a married couple.

Clearly from the captions and dates, forty-four of the eighty were photographed specifically for the book, and they were approached through Cunningham's social networks in California: neighbors, friends of friends, and so on. Quite probably, accomplished and professional people are overrepresented. Mitchell (1977) notes that "Imogen set out to photograph only people over the age of ninety, but she found that too many elderly people were interesting and just had to be included even if they were somewhat younger" (p. 11). Later she notes that "usually the people she found were younger than she, if only by a few years" (p. 18). Ages are given in only nine of the captions (all except one—"late eighties"—aged ninety or over).

These contemporary photographs were interspersed with others from the 1950s and 1960s (including some taken in Europe) and five from the 1930s, including those of her parents. Most of these subjects are not named, and it seems unlikely that Cunningham inquired about their ages. For example, one taken in the 1950s is of a woman sitting on a bench. The caption, "This was at a bus stop in the fifties," suggests that there might have been only the briefest of exchanges between the two. So, by implication, what we have is a collection of photographs of "interesting elderly people," most around the age of ninety. Essentially, these were older people who had "transcended" their problems.

Cunningham clearly did not set out to represent life after ninety as experienced by a representative sample of people who had attained that age. She chose not to provide evidence of dependence, depression, or failure. Nevertheless, she clearly intended that her subjects should "represent" a wide variety of people of great age and that the photographs should generate a general and positive image of old age. In the interplay between herself and her subjects, the mirroring of experience and appearance, and in the selection of photographs for inclusion in the book, she intended that a *particular* understanding of old age should emerge, an image of how late old age *can* be a positive phase in life.

Nevertheless, there is also a tension in this introduction between "our society" and Cunningham's subjects. For example, Mitchell (1977) comments: "These are the helpless victims of the stereotyped view that sees . . . their ability to contribute to our fast-paced consumer society [to be] a thing of the past" (p. 9). In addition to mirroring Cunningham's own experience of life after ninety, the collection portrays "them" as helpless victims of "our" society. The question of who are "we" and who are "they" is central to current debates over ageism (see *Ageing and Society* 2001). Despite her intention to challenge the stereotyped view, Mitchell's use of pronouns, along with the emotive term "helpless victims," serves to consolidate the sense of distance that has already been created through Cunningham's focus on the age of ninety. There appears to be strong, underlying assumptions that we the viewers of these photographs are (1) "contributing" to "our fast-paced consumer society" in our various ways and (2) have failed to recognize that among us there are people of great age who, far from being helpless, non-contributory victims, are actively contributing too. There is no acknowledgment of the possibility that we who view the photographs might be of great age ourselves.

For the cultural gerontologist, this book, like many other collections of photographic portraits, provides fascinating insights into the construction and interpretation of images of old age. Often these collections reflect the view, well expressed by Mitchell, that old age is most clearly illustrated ("better than any words") by portraits of older people; better, for example, than images of residential homes, or of older people participating in social activities, or of people in need or receiving care services. Rather it is the aging body (gestures, postures, and, in particular, the expressions of the aging face) that is the classic representation.

Market Images

I now turn to the second example. This series of photographic representations of later life builds on an interest in how age is represented in advertisements that emerged out of work undertaken in Bytheway and
Johnson (1998) and Bytheway (2000). In undertaking an analysis of how
the aging body is represented in ads, I decided to focus on a source that is
associated with later life and in which the viewer is faced with multiple
images of older people. Recognizing that Cunningham's portrait of old
age is based in a privileged, university-related Californian world, I was cu-
rious to note the similarities and differences between her collection and
the very different work of advertising photographers, charged with the
task of marketing goods for older people in the U.K.

Focusing on the emerging third-age consumer market, Blaikie (1999)
argues that advertising practices in regard to older people changed "quite
markedly" following the publication of Sontag's *Saturday Review* article
on the double jeopardy of aging (1972), coinciding as it nearly did with
the publication in the *New York Review of Books* of the first of her influ-
ential essays on photography (Sontag 1979).

While older people have always been active customers in a variety of
traditional marketplaces, they have been increasingly targeted as a group
who, through their participation in new markets, are being persuaded that
there are alternative lifestyles that they too might enjoy (Sawchuk 1991).
Typically, as with most marketing, satisfaction is associated with positive
attributes such as happiness, utility, and personal fulfillment. This trend has
attracted the interest of cultural gerontologists. In the U.K., the most well-
known example of empirical work in this area is the analysis of the changing face of *Retirement Choice* magazine (Featherstone and Hepworth 1984,
1995; Blaikie 1999). The interest here is how the target group for the magazine shifted over the twenty years that followed the first issue in 1972, and
how this is reflected in editorials, features, and, in particular, the content of
its cover. However, although Featherstone and Hepworth (1995) note the
use of celebrities on the cover of the magazine (p. 38) and of younger models to demonstrate changing fashions in age-appropriate clothing (p. 34),
they do not attempt to analyze the content of visual representations.

The purpose of this analysis is to explore in detail the *visual* representation of later life in a similar magazine and to see what messages are

associated with these images. I wanted to compare the images and apparent messages of Cunningham with those being produced by a very different publication in a different cultural context. I decided on purely pragmatic grounds to focus on one particular edition of one magazine. Based on this decision, I purchased the January 2002 edition of what I knew to be the market leader in magazines directed at older people in the U.K. Alongside magazines directed at women, sports fans, motorists, and so on, virtually every news agency in Britain displays the latest edition of *YOURS* magazine. In 1995, Featherstone and Hepworth identified it as one of the four leading magazines in the "expanding commercially-produced retirement literature in Britain" (1995, 33). In the edition I purchased, the monthly sales over the first six months of 2001 as "measured by independent auditors" are reported to be 350,363. This confirms that it is indeed highly successful and, arguably, in 2002, the market leader in its subject area.

The Target

Like many other readers (indeed I suspect like most people familiar with the U.K. magazine market), I know that *YOURS* is aimed at older people. Significantly, however, there is no clear indication of this on its cover. The name *YOURS* is particularly enigmatic. The most obvious connotation is that of possession: "This magazine could be yours" or "This magazine is about things that are yours—dreams, dogs, old friends, chunky jackets, etc." But there is also an echo of the word "years," which for some might more directly associate it with age.

Beneath its name, the claim is made on the cover that it is "Britain's most-read magazine." The cover is made up of two photographic images and the following lines (reading roughly from the top to the bottom):

1. WIN £500 of ORGANIC FOODS
2. Make *your* dreams come true in 2002
3. 20 inspirational life changes
4. Dogs are my heroes says EastEnders Pam
5. Nana looks to the future
6. Meet UK's most CARING WARDEN
7. "End NHS age bias" say campaigners

8. Find old friends—we show you how
9. Plus knit our chunky jacket—3 pages of travel ideas

There is only one explicit reference here to age (number 7) and, arguably, only two other allusions to later life (numbers 6 and 8). The possibility that the magazine is directed at older people is supported by the photographic images (which are linked to numbers 4 and 5). Both are of celebrities (Pam St. Clement, a star of the TV soap opera EastEnders, and Nana Mouskouri, the Greek singer). Prospective purchasers of the magazine might be excused for thinking that it falls into the category of a celebrity magazine, but some of the accompanying lines would contradict this.

Not only does "NHS age bias" refer explicitly to age, but "caring warden," referring to people employed to "keep a neighborly eye" on residents of sheltered housing or assisted-living schemes, is a direct reference to organized care. Many would recognize Pam St. Clement and know that in EastEnders she represents a certain kind of older woman. Similarly, they might appreciate that only older people would recognize the photograph of Nana Mouskouri, having been taken when she became famous in the late 1950s. So in looking at the cover, it is only through a series of "hints" that a new customer might recognize the magazine to be aimed at older people.

Inside, the contents page is similarly full of hints without any explicit guidance. Nevertheless, a browse through the pages will provide plenty of evidence that older people are prominently featured. One section in particular is unambiguous regarding the readership. A feature titled *Friends of YOURS* offers help in finding a friend. The box headed "How to use our FREE Find a Friend service" ends with instructions in small print that "we must restrict appeals to those who are 50 or over only." Participants are asked to cut out the printed coupon, write up to twenty-five words, and send in a photograph.

A total of 218 appeals are published and the twenty-five words are quite revealing. Many closely resemble the ads that appear in dating magazines (the acronym TLC—tender, loving care—is popular), but there are other kinds of requests. There are special sections for those wanting a penfriend who lives overseas and for those wanting to share a holiday with someone. Overall, 190 (87 percent) come from women (the majority identifying themselves as widows), and all but 23 (i.e., 89 percent) include information about age. This ranges from fifty to eight-four years, with nearly half (103) of the people in their sixties (see table 1.1). A total of nine women describe themselves as "young-at-heart" and five others use the word "young" in describing themselves (as in "young 60s" and "young-minded"). None of the men uses such age terms. Ten appeals are accompanied by photographs—eight women and two men. Although not representative of readers as a whole, these statistics suggest that the large proportion of readers are women in the fifty-five to seventy year age group. As such, they are a generation younger than those portrayed by Cunningham.

Table 1.1.   Age and Sex of Those Seeking a Friend

Age	Women	Men
50s	15.3	10.7
60s	46.8	50.0
70s	27.4	25.0
80s	0.0	3.6
Not stated	10.5	10.7
Total (= 100%)	190	28

Toward the end of the magazine there is a section titled *Caring & Keeping Mobile*. It includes two feature items: "Rewarding the unsung carers" (acknowledging "a special breed of people who care for others") and "*YOURS* wardens roll of honour" (listing the names of about 330 honored wardens). This section is designed to attract the interest of caregivers as well as older people. Apart from passing references to "pensioners" and "senior citizens," there is little explicit reference in these two items to age, until the final paragraph where the editor comments that

> The YOURS Warden of the Year contest has confirmed something we at the magazine already knew—that older people much prefer to have contact with a warden rather than an intercom system.

In this subtle way, the editor is building an alliance with caregivers, both in supporting older people and in promoting its live shows and the sales of the magazine. Caregivers, such as wardens, will warm to the vote of confidence that the contest represents and, as a result, will more readily participate in the magazine's activities.

The Content

The editors place a heavy emphasis on reader participation. On pages 18–19, for example, there is a report on *YOURS Live*, the magazine's "first national show." This included a series of celebrity events, displays, fashion shows, and awards (for example, the "Good Neighbour of the Year"). There are invitations to contact the magazine on 50 of the 148 pages. For example, "the hottest topic" at *YOURS Live* is the cost of transportation "for pensioners," and readers are invited to comment; pages 4 to 7 are taken up with *Meeting Place* ("Britain's brightest and best letters page"); *Talkback* on page 7 invites readers to comment on recently published letters; on page 36 there is a survey questionnaire on the Royal Family; and on page 49 an invitation to win £500 is offered for a competition designed to promote handwritten letters.

The magazine also provides help and advice to the reader. On pages 14 to 16, three women on the editorial team are *Happy to Help*: "We aim to help solve your problems," including the advice of the magazine's "agony aunt." On page 22, there is *Ask the Experts*: four men advising on money, benefits, legal matters, and pet care; and on page 24, *Help Desk* provides contact details to seventeen advice agencies. These relate to various money matters, accommodations, care, disability aids, and travel. Pages 28 to 33 are given over to "the *YOURS* doctor," and under the column *Illness Support*, readers are invited to "offer help, support and first-hand experience to one another."

Regarding visual representations of later life, there are a variety of small photographs of readers, experts, and celebrities in the magazine's features. Many of these are portraits with the subject smiling at the camera. In contrast, relatively few offer a broader image of age. A photograph of a grandmother and granddaughter sharing a book, a man sorting out his tax returns, and a couple perusing a photograph album illustrate advice-giving articles. A feature on life for older people in Stoke-on-Trent, includes photographs of a volunteer-run shop in a retirement village and of a woman with a walking stick being helped out of a minibus to attend a day center. On the following page, there is a feature on a campaign against age discrimination in the health service that includes a photograph of a party from the Portsmouth Pensioners' Association and their large banner. The feature *Make Your Dreams Come True in 2002* includes photographs of skydiving, holidaying, obtaining a degree, and a visit to a war memorial in Belgium. These sustain familiar images of later life: reflection and fulfillment, travel and activity, and advice and support.

Advertisements

The magazine is made up of 148 pages (including front and back covers) and five inserts. Although the contents page gives no indication of this, there are a number of clearly defined sections (some indicated by color-coded margins), and these help to classify and segregate the advertisements (see table 1.2). The most prominent ads are those in the main section. These tend to feature the positive side of life: holidays, finance, and fashion. Advertisements relating to mobility problems tend to appear in the later pages, close to and within the section *Caring & Keeping Mobile.*

Table 1.2. Advertisements by Sections

Section	No. of Pages	Advertising Space (%)	No. of Full-Page Ads
Front cover and contents page	3	33	1
The main section (including the lead features)	95	37	29
Find a Friend	17	44	4
Caring & Keeping Mobile	12	83	1
Competitions	5	30	0
Fiction	4	25	2
Armchair shopping (including "holiday selection")	7	100	0
YOURS services, office, next edition, and "Leaving you smiling"	3	0	0
Back cover	2	100	2
Inserts	34	100	18

In total, 44.8 percent of the pages are taken up by advertising. There is 1 two-page ad, and 38 one-page and 58 half- or quarter-page ads. There are also 117 smaller ads, making a total of 214 ads. Together with the five inserts (including a mini-catalog with 79 ads), the reader faces nearly 300 advertisements in just this one edition of the magazine. The magazine is a marketplace in itself where many of the distinctive "needs" of later life are being met.

The advertisements include the largest visual representations of later life that appear in the magazine. The analysis that follows focuses on two separate issues: (1) what products are being advertised, and (2) how these ads are portraying later life. Table 1.3 indicates how the 64 ads in the magazine that take up at least a quarter of a page can be classified.

There are five ads where the product is either a coat, suit, or dressing gown, and the image includes the whole of the model. All five are female, and what is significant here (see also Featherstone and Hepworth 1995) is that all the models are clearly well under fifty years. There is no attempt to reflect the age of the magazine's targeted readers. The same can be said about the models demonstrating chairs, baths, and beds.

In contrast, the model demonstrating a vacuum cleaner has gray hair, lines on her face, and veins showing on her arms. Moreover, adjacent to the image there is a named testimonial: " You'll be amazed at what this super lightweight Vac will pick up! Miss L. Baraclough—London." Regardless of whether the model is Miss Baraclough, the reader is being encouraged to identify with both. The model herself appears to be providing verbal testimony: the words "It's so light and at the touch of a button it converts to a hand Vac" are quoted alongside an insert photograph of her using it on a staircase. In this way, despite the signs of age that the model displays, the advertisers emphasize convenience rather than need; there is no attempt to portray her as *needing* a super lightweight Vac as a result of age or disability. Indeed, she is dressed as elegantly, and poses in a similar way, as the younger models displaying clothes.

Table 1.3. Classification of Larger Advertisements

Clothing	9
Travel/holidays/cameras	8
Equity	7
Medicines/food supplements/cosmetics	6
CDs/videos/fiction	6
Footwear/foot therapy	5
Chairs	4
Beds/bedding	5
Information (books, etc.)	3
Furniture covers	2
Baths/showers	2
Mobility aids	3
Funeral plans	2
Garden	2
Housing	1

There is only one other advertisement, for the "Senior Railcard," that attempts to produce a positive image of people approaching pensionable age. A man, dressed in a wetsuit, looks back over his right shoulder as he carries a large surfboard into the sea. The text reads: "60 isn't what it used to be. There are sights to see, friends to visit, and waves to catch. Instead of taking the car, take the train." The model has been selected to represent the contemporary, active, adventure-seeking sixty-year-old male. His hair may be gray and thin and his face lined, but he looks strong, healthy, and adventurous.

Older Models

There are eight ads in the main section of the magazine that use models who appear to be older than these two. Likely, all the models are over sixty years of age and several are in their seventies. One is an advertisement for a range of health supplements (such as vitamin tablets) and another for retirement housing. The other six are all advertising equity release offers. This is significant in that it represents later life as a time when personal assets may need to be reviewed and rationalized. With the fall in income that accompanies retirement from paid employment, a major anxiety for many older people is the cost of maintaining their homes in good repair. Equity release schemes are intended to generate income to cover this by "releasing" capital that is otherwise tied up in the house itself. These financial schemes have become big business in the U.K., and they reflect the rapid policy shift that has taken place over the last two decades on housing for older people: from the provision of specialized rented housing to schemes designed to promote and sustain owner-occupation (Oldman and Quilgars 1999).

All except one of these six advertisements feature a seemingly happy couple. The target of such schemes is the older couple who own a house. Potentially such people present an image of successful aging: married and home owning. The various schemes being advertised purport to sustain this. So exactly what kind of visual image do they construct? Consider each of the couples in turn.

On page 20, all we see are their heads and just enough of their upper bodies to note that, as his right arm hangs over her shoulder, she holds his right hand with both hands. They are smiling as they look into each other's eyes and the sun is shining. The details indicate that the scheme is available to couples who are both over seventy. The text of the ad reads:

Do your homework.
You've worked all your life to pay for your home, now sit back and let your home pay for you with an equity release plan.
When you retire you want to enjoy your time—and your home—without financial worries. You may have repairs or bills but don't want to use savings to pay them. Or maybe you just want to continue the lifestyle you enjoyed when working.
We bring good things to life.

On page 27, there is a couple who are not quite so white haired; again just their heads and shoulders are displayed, but this time they are smiling at the camera. Although sitting on a garden bench, there is no evidence of sunshine. The text twice uses the phrase "the retirement you deserve." The coupon to be returned indicates that you should be aged sixty or over.

There are three smaller, quarter-page ads for equity schemes. The first, on page 111, has two miniscule images of the model couple. In the first, they appear to be enjoying the garden sunshine, drinking tea. The second shows them astride a motorbike by the new bridge over the River Tyne. Arguably, these are intended as alternatives. Like the Senior Railcard surfer, the latter represents the adventures that could result from implementation of the New Year's resolution suggested in the slogan: "New year—new desires?" No age limits are indicated.

On page 113, the couple is standing in a well-lit, perhaps sunny room, with arms around each other. "A wonderful difference" is the caption, reflecting the consequence of joining the scheme. The text reveals the way the advertisers encourage the reader to "imagine" an alternative future:

Pension not enough?
Imagine—a cash lump sum—without any borrowing . . .
Imagine relaxing, having paid off your mortgage, loans or other debts . . .
Imagine enjoying the benefits of a significantly improved lifestyle. Perhaps home improvements . . . new car . . . holidays . . . etc.
Imagine a cash lump sum, immediately solving all your money problems . . .

Are you 60 or over (both) and own your own home?
Do you deserve a happy and worry-free future?

Similarly, the text of the advertisement on page 115 evokes a dreamlike other world. The couple is smiling at the camera, and the man appears to have his arm around the woman. He is in an open-necked shirt and she is in a summer dress with a pearl necklace:

Homeowners aged 60 plus
Within weeks your money worries could be just a distant memory.
Now you can enjoy a wealthier, more comfortable retirement, safe in the knowledge that your home remains yours for the rest of your life.
Use the cash in any way you want . . . home improvements . . . extra income . . . holidays . . . repay your mortgage and other debts. Don't delay—get rid of your money worries for good by calling.
YES, please help me improve my retirement lifestyle by sending your FREE brochure.

Before we consider the sixth equity release advertisement, it is interesting to note the similarity of the preceding five to the vitamins and retirement housing ads. In the former (the only two-page ad), the benefits of vitamins are represented by a couple with their arms around each other and a small girl sitting (rather awkwardly) on the man's shoulders. She is covering his eyes, and all three are laughing: an unambiguous image of active, fun-loving grandparenthood. The benefits of retirement housing are represented by a couple, both admiring a lily he appears to have taken from a large bouquet that she is holding. Again the sun shines and both smile. The slogan, echoed in the choice of the lily perhaps, is "Retirement flats—tailor made for you." No age limits are specified. It is not difficult to imagine these same couples serving as models for equity release schemes.

All seven images represent life over sixty (or seventy) as happy, vigorous, home-owning coupledom, a time when the sun always shines. It is particularly interesting then to compare them with the remaining equity release ad. Here there is just one model, a man, and the image is much larger than those of the other ads: his face takes up almost a quarter of the page. The top of his head is cut off but there is white hair above his ears and white flecks in his eyebrows. He rests his chin on his hands, and there are many lines visible below his eyes. The skin on his fingers appears thin and his hands are heavily veined. He looks relaxed and smiles directly at the camera. His eyes are bright and his teeth are even. He wears a tweed jacket over what appears to be a collar and tie. The background is dark and unspecific, and there is no evidence of a wife or any other person. The slogan above the brief text reads: "Release some of the money locked in your home to do the things you want."

The advertisers for this particular scheme appear to have decided to target the individual rather than the couple. Regardless of whether he represents the married man or the widower, he looks the reader in the eye, and surrounded by the slogan "Homeowner over 70? Boost your retirement income," he presents the image of someone (of that age) who has taken advantage of the scheme. He challenges the reader to follow suit. Although still substantially younger than Cunningham's subjects, this portrait has a marked similarity. Like them, he appears to exhibit the kind of confidence of someone who knows his own mind, who has exercised choice, and who is challenging the viewer to follow suit.

Aids to Daily Living

Many of the ads in *YOURS* would certainly not be out of place in magazines directed at groups other than older people. The fact that most of the clothing advertisements use younger models, for example, suggests that these are indeed "all-purpose" advertisements that are published in other magazines. Nevertheless, they construct an image of what are perceived to be the distinctive needs and wants of older people. For example, reflecting the perceived values of older people, many of the clothes are advertised as "comfortable" or "classic."

In contrast, a number of advertisements list age-related illnesses and impairments. An advertisement for a "foot cradle," to be worn inside shoes, offers "instant relief" for those who suffer from any of ten listed complaints. Similarly, a reclining chair is endorsed by a "Harley St. orthopaedic consultant" and offers "therapy and comfort" to sufferers with five specified complaints "and many other mobility and painful ailments." A range of beds brings "blissful positional relief and night-long rest" to sufferers of eight listed conditions. A range of baths and showers includes such aids as "LegLift," side entrances, belt lifts, and power-assisted seats.

The section *Caring & Keeping Mobile* has a total of twenty-seven advertisements, including nine for baths and bathing products, eight for scooters and other mobility aids, and six for stair lifts. Of the ads for baths, seven include models, typically middle aged and in various poses and states of dress. An eighth is demonstrated by Dora Bryan (a well-known actress in her seventies: "It's so simple and easy—it's amazing"). The ninth is quite interesting in that it shows a woman literally having a bath with the aid of a "saddleband." Although her hair is fashionably cut, it is gray, and her face, arms, and shoulders suggest she might be a typical reader. Printed over the bath bubbles is the following testimony: "I've found it easy and comfortable to use, and it enables me to have a bath with no problems. Mrs N. Lee on Solent."

Of the scooters, one is demonstrated by a man posting a letter. He has gray, thin hair and so perhaps is intended to represent an older user. In contrast, a PowerTrike (giving you "the power to enjoy a whole new world of possibilities") is demonstrated by a Paralympian Gold Medalist.

Climbing stairs has long been recognized to be a problem for some disabled and older people (Haslam et al. 2001) and the stair lift is offered as a solution. Like the wheelchair, it is a powerful visual symbol of disability. It is difficult to look dignified while using one. Of the six advertisements, three choose not to demonstrate its use. Rather they display a photograph of the unoccupied lift and detail its qualities. One of these includes a small inset of a couple smiling at the camera (much the same picture as the equity release images). Of the three demonstrators, one is clearly middle aged; the other two, much older. The image of one, smiling at the camera as she waits for the lift to take her upstairs, is adjacent to a quote that indicates that she trusts the firm "to give you best advice, best price & the largest choice." The second features Dame Thora Hird, born in 1912 and one of Britain's most popular actresses. Her recommendation is that it is "the only stairlift company I trust and I recommend them to you."

The advertisements in this section are, for the most part, addressed to the older user. Together they confirm that some older people have problems in bathing, getting upstairs, and getting out and about. Their products offer solutions. What is significant for this analysis is the message that despite the implicit difficulties that you might face in undertaking these routine domestic activities, there are actions you can take. Act and your life might be transformed.

Conclusion

The editorial team at *YOURS* magazine has succeeded in keeping the magazine in publication for a number of years. This is most likely because it has identified, defined, and developed an area in the wider marketplace to which both customers and manufacturers are attracted. Products have been promoted, advertised, and purchased by readers who in general, it would appear, have been satisfied and who have remained active participants in the market.

The area is defined primarily, but not explicitly, by age. Anyone is free to purchase the magazine, and a wide range of interests is covered. But the content is oriented to later life and the issues and activities that interest older people. The heavy investment in reader participation, coupled with the extensive use by advertisers of personal testimonies, reinforces the belief that readers have many shared interests and that they, as much as the editorial team, are involved in "setting the agenda." Many of the smaller photographic images are of older people smiling at the camera. Implicitly readers are encouraged to see themselves in these images.

The survival of the magazine, of course, depends largely on the willingness and ability of its readers to purchase the products that are advertised. Reading is largely an individual and private act, and so the magazine in its many complex ways is encouraging the reader to think positively about alternatives: new holidays, new adventures, and new lifestyles. While the clothing advertisements may appeal to enduring tastes and therefore compete in terms of cost, many of the others, particularly the travel and equity release schemes, promise to transform the reader's way of life. All that is required is financial reorganization and a whole new, bright, active, future opens up.

So in a completely different cultural context, the series of images of later life that is published in this edition of *YOURS* magazine (and, it is reasonable to assume, other editions) is constructing a portrait of "the aged" that has many similarities to those of Imogen Cunningham (1977). She was keen to promote the idea that a better old age can be achieved if steps are taken to transcend its "problems." In particular, by confronting age and learning from others, by being "feisty" and, where necessary, fighting the challenges of age, a sense of fulfillment can be achieved. *YOURS* is providing clear guidance as to some of the steps that can be taken.

Whereas her view was as much retrospective as prospective, drawing attention to what her subjects had already achieved, *YOURS* is almost entirely prospective. The combined message reads something like this:

> OK, you're in your fifties, sixties or seventies. Life's not over yet. You may live many more years. How's it going to be when you hit ninety? Take stock. Get your act together. Think positive. Spend what you've earned to get what you want. Then when you're ninety, guess what! You too could be doing something like publishing the photographs of your contemporaries.

Thus, these two very different collections of images share a constructed reality. This reality offers the viewer a glimpse, not of how old age is, but how it might be. For the aging person, the collections provide not a mirror of the present, but one of possibilities. Implicit in both collections is a judgment: act to achieve the possible and to avoid the otherwise inevitable. The distinction says much about the experienced realities of aging in contemporary society.

References

Ageing and Society. 2000. Forum. 20: 773–95.

Baudrillard, J.
1983 *Simulations.* New York: Semiotext(e).

Blaikie, A.
1997 Beside the Sea: Visual Imagery, Ageing and Heritage. *Ageing and Society* 17: 629–39.
1999 *Ageing and Popular Culture.* Cambridge: Cambridge University Press.

Bown, J.
1986 *Portraits.* London: Chatto and Windus.

Bytheway, B.
1995 *Ageism.* Buckingham, U.K.: Open University Press.
2000 Images of Age. *Ageing and Health* 7: 4–6.

Bytheway, B., and J. Johnson
1998 The Sight of Age. In *The Body in Everyday Life.* Edited by S. Nettleton and J. Watson, 243–57. London: Routledge.

Cunningham, I.
1977 *After Ninety*. Seattle: University of Washington Press.
de Beauvoir, S. 1972. *Old Age*. Harmondsworth, U.K.: Penguin.

Featherstone, M., and M. Hepworth
1984 Changing Images of Retirement. In *Gerontology: Social and Behavioural Perspectives*. Edited by D. B. B. Bromley, 219–24. London: Croom Helm.
1995 Images of Positive Ageing: A Case Study of *Retirement Choice* Magazine. In *Images of Ageing: Cultural Representations of Later Life*. Edited by M. Featherstone and A. Wernick, 29–47. London: Routledge.

Haslam, R. et al.
2001 What Do Older People Know about Factors Affecting Their Safety on Stairs? *Ageing and Society* 21: 759–76.

Holstein, J., and J. Gubrium
2000 *The Self We Live By: Narrative Identity in a Post-modern World*. New York: Oxford University Press.

Johnson, J., and B. Bytheway
1997 Illustrating Care: Images of Care Relationships with Older People. In *Critical Approaches to Ageing and Later Life*. Edited by A. Jamieson, 132–42. Buckingham, U.K.: Open University Press.

Mitchell, M.
1977 Introduction to *After Ninety* by I. Cunningham. Seattle: University of Washington Press.

Oldman, C., and D. Quilgars
1999 The Last Resort? Revisiting Ideas about Older People's Living Arrangements. *Ageing and Society* 19: 363–84.

Sawchuk, K. A.
1991 From the Gloom to Boom: Age, Identity and Target Marketing. In *Images of Ageing: Cultural Representations of Later Life*. Edited by M. Featherstone and A. Wernick, 173–87. London: Routledge.

Sontag, S.
1972 The Double Standard of Ageing. *Saturday Review*, September 23: 29–38.
1979 *On Photography*. Harmondsworth, U.K.: Penguin.

CHAPTER TWO

THE DEAD BODY AND ORGAN TRANSPLANTATION
Betina Freidin

In 1969, psychologist Elizabeth Kubler-Ross introduced both the academic and lay audience to the importance of death and the ways in which we, as individuals, cope with it. Interestingly enough, sociologists Barney Glaser and Anselm Strauss (1964, 1967) had introduced us to their own version of a "stage theory of dying," albeit from a sociological perspective centered around "birth work" in hospital emergency rooms. But a "sociology of death, dying, and bereavement," as an acknowledged area of sociological research fell to the wayside (Kearl 1989).

However, all of this has changed. Sociologists now find themselves concerned with the mundanity of death. From the intersections of death and work to death in the military to death and dying in popular culture, seemingly no stone has been left unturned, at least sociologically speaking. We find ourselves, as Kearl (1989, 63) puts it, "in the middle of a virtual renaissance of interesting endings." Death is central to our understanding of life and its embeddedness in the place of the individual in the social order.

The purpose of this chapter is to extend our interest in death by analyzing laypeople's symbolic representations of the human body in order to understand their willingness to donate their organs for transplants after death. In so doing, I deal with the relationship that people establish between the self and the body during life and their extension into death. In short, the intersection of body and self in life and death.

The world of human organ transplantation provides a particular opportunity for the social sciences to explore the social uses and the cultural definitions of the body. Since transplantation depends mainly on postmortem organ donation, it seems inevitable to ask how the dead body is symbolically constructed by laypeople.

The condition of the embodied self has been an important matter of interest for sociologists during the last years. However, sociological studies have generally been concerned with the living body and have rarely addressed the death of the embodied individual. If we have, it has certainly only been in recent years (Hallam, Hockey, and Howarth 1999; Lawton 1998; Seale 1998). Thus, academics, especially those who work in the field of medical sociology, have focused their work on subjects such as the experience of pain and illness of the embodied agent, the bodily changes that adult people experience throughout the process of aging, and the meanings that people attach to these changes and disorders related to the transformation of their social and self-identity. Therefore, little is known about how people describe the dead body. This is certainly true concerning the experience about their corporeal condition in the face of their own inevitable death.

Here, qualitative data on laypeople's symbolic constructions of the dead body are compiled in order to explore if such constructions do or do not harmonize with biomedicine's instrumental definition of the body. The biomedical model of organ transplantation and the technologies inherent to this is further investigated in order to see what underlies transplantation technologies and if they do or do not encourage organ donation among the citizenry.

The research findings show that a dominant lay dualism between the body and the self prevails when people discuss their own death in relation to organ donation. Even though this dualism is constructed on nonexpert ground, it is functional to the biomedical gaze of the body. An alternative, nondualistic view of the body and the self after death also appeared residually in the study, which I will turn to later.

I frame lay views of the body into two distinctive conceptual frameworks, termed "transcendental" and "nontranscendental." Within both perspectives, I distinguish those conceptions that encourage organ donation and those that discourage it. The term transcendental refers to supernatural notions that involve either religious or other spiritual beliefs. Nontranscendental alludes to more secularized views that either emphasize dualistic ideas of the body and the self or, on the contrary, highlight the intrinsic unity of the embodied individual, even postdeath.

I wish to move into the realm of the body as a nonlived entity. Here, at the very end of our social life, the intersection of self and body becomes quite complex. The self, as seen in relation to the body, can maintain an existence long after it has disappeared as a corporeal presence (Hallam, Hockey, and Howarth 1999).

However, if we look closer, it might actually not be that complex after all. At least not to "practical actors." Their ways of orienting might very well be much different than nonempirically driven theoretical propositions. Perhaps it is time we pay closer attention to them (Gubrium and Holstein, chapter 7 in this volume). How do people construct self in relation to the futuristic, dead body and the removal of its parts? If, as Bryan Turner (1998) argues, bodies and selves are synonymous, then the post-life body carries with it serious implications for individuals as they work to preserve a coherent, biographically intact, social identity.

The Human Body: Constructing an Elusive Object

The human body, like any other social and cultural object, is a symbolic construction; but one that represents a nonevident and ambiguous object (Le Breton 1995). Its peculiarity among other objects lies in its multiple conditions. As Shilling (1997) points out, the body should be seen as

> an unfinished biological and social phenomenon which is transformed, within certain limits, as a result of its entry into, and participation in, society. It is this biological and social quality that makes the body at once such an obvious, and yet such an elusive phenomenon.

Le Breton (1995) highlights that our representations and knowledge about the body depend on the broader social context and a general worldview and, concerning the latter, on an ultimate definition of the person. Therefore, as Foucault (1973, 1977) alludes, he emphasizes the culturally constructed nature of the human body.

The dominant vision of the body in contemporary Western societies is provided by biomedicine. Its influence cannot be overstated. Embracing this, Seale (1998, 75) suggests that

> Medicine can be understood as containing some of the most classificatory ideas of our culture, dividing the healthy from the dead . . . medical

care manages events, people, and body states . . . pushing aside the inevitable consequence of embodiment.

Modern medicine has conceptualized the body instrumentally by
making use of a machine-like model that conceives it as fragmented into
several parts, an object that can be studied and treated as an autonomous
entity detached from the self. These considerations are applicable to the
living body and the corpse. In the present era of transplantation (human
bodies conceptualized as sets of interchangeable *spare parts)*[1] and *cyborgs*
(individuals composed of both organic matter and machinery)[2], the machine analogy not only persists, deepening a dualistic view of the body and
the self, but also blurs the frontiers between nature and culture (see Lock
2000; Samson 1999; Featherstone and Turner 1995; Turner 1992).

Existing beyond the scientific world, religions and other spiritual or
transcendental meaning systems also provide cultural categories for common people to define and experience their body.[3] However, in contemporary secularized societies the reflexive relationship between the self and
the body has become an important and controversial component in the
construction of self-identities (Shilling 1997; Sharma 1996).

People belong to several life worlds that share discourses and symbolism. The images and beliefs that common people relate to the body are
grounded in their interpretations of scientific, religious, and spiritual discourses and nourished by commonsense knowledge and ritualized practices. This applies when talking about both the living and the dead body.
How do laypeople describe the dead body and the symbolic meanings that
they attach to it when accounting for their organ donation decisions? This
question and the ensuing analysis enables one to observe how social agents
apply "meaning systems," "cultural distinctions," "models," "schemes," or
"interpretation repertories" (Alasuutari 1995) in order to define the human body and its proper treatment.

The Dead Body: Organs as
Parts and Their Transplantation

As Mellor and Shilling (1993) stress, sociological studies of the body have
generally focused analytic attention on the living body and have only
rarely addressed the demise and death of the embodied individual (see also

Walter 1996). More interest in the topic has developed in the field of anthropology (Le Breton 1995; Joralemon 1995, 1996; Himmelman 1997; Lock 2000; Scheper-Hughes 2000) as well as social psychology and psychiatry (Belk 1990; Bermudez, Marcel, and Eilan 1998; Youngner 1992).

As a sociohistorically and culturally constructed object, the dead body constitutes a realm of agreements and disputes about its meaning. This is particularly evident in the field of organ transplantation. Joralemon (1996, 2) describes the issue quite accurately:

> To ask someone to consent to donate is to ask him or her to adopt a set of associated ideas about the human body, the self, and death that are familiar to the medical subculture, but still substantially alien to the society at large.

The author highlights the cultural resistance that biomedicine's assumptions may provoke among the public.[4] In the same analytical direction, Le Breton (1995) holds that the most recent technological advances of modern medicine have deepened the dualistic vision of the body in relation to the person and the instrumental definition and uses of the former. This tendency, Le Breton argues, may disturb laypeople's conceptions. A more extreme position on the matter is held by authors like Himmelman (1997) and Awaya (1994, as quoted by Scheper-Hughes 2000, 198) who employ the images of "cannibalism" and "neocannibalism," respectively, to describe the biomedical treatment of the donor's body in the field of transplant surgeries.

From the perspective of social psychology, Belk (1990) suggests that if we attempt to grasp the public responses toward organ donation, we should pay close attention to the cultural metaphors that are commonly used to define the human body during life and postlife. They express different emotional bonds between the self and the body, and therefore, while some symbolic representations dispose positively to offering organs, others may imply some troubles or barriers for soliciting organs for transplants.

Following Belk (1990), visions that favor the idea of organ transplantation represent the body as a symbolic garden or a machine. The "organic" view presents the human body as a natural object, or as a place where organs can be harvested and implanted. The mechanical image (dominant in modern medicine) is highly compatible with the idea of organ transplantation since the body is seen as a machine whose parts can be replaced and interchanged. In contrast, we find two other metaphors that are dissonant with the organ transplantation practice. The first describes the body as self, a central part of the individual identity, and body parts, at least some of them, are regarded as extensions of the self. Another metaphor constructs the body as a sacred vessel, in the religious sense, or even on secular bases, and highlights the reluctance to touch or spoil this sacred and mysterious object. In the next section, I observe how these metaphors are used by laypeople to describe the body, and how they are framed as available discursive sources of meaning.

Lay Descriptions of the Dead Body

Here, I summarize laypeople's descriptions of the body after death and during life as well as connect these images with their attitudes toward organ donation. The data come from a qualitative research on postmortem organ donation. All the participants shared the following characteristics: they were nonexperts (i.e., did not belong to the medical subculture by virtue of formal knowledge or training), and, additionally, they did not have direct life experience in organ donation and transplantation.[5] Participants' representations of the body have been "thickened" through systematic analysis of focus group interviews conducted among the middle and lower class in Argentina.[6]

The methodology was selected on the assumption that the feedback generated by the group discussion itself would enable participants to express their ideas and emotions more freely than in face-to-face interviews. The focus group strategy was considered particularly suitable to simulate the social process by which personal positions are formed and changed. During group discussions, agreement, disagreement, and complementation in verbal interaction facilitate the emergence of social representations and emotions. As Frey and Fontana (1993) point out, the stories produced in group context are more "polyphonic" since the range of opinions gathered is broader and the interviewer's influence on the interviewees, while not eliminated, is diffused by the very fact of being in a group rather than in a face-to-face interview situation.

The focus groups were conducted using a semistructured interview guide that included several topics connected with the willingness to become an organ donor, such as laypeople's trust in public agencies in charge of organ procurement and transplants and in the medical community, their images and ideas associated with brain death, the motivations that pre-dispose individuals to donate organs, and the symbolic representations of the body.[7] The following analysis focuses on the representations of the body, taking into account both cognitive and emotional components that nourish people's narratives.[8]

When participants talked of organ donation, they depicted and symbolized their bodies. A set of analytical dimensions was constructed to organize thematically the interviewees' spontaneous comments. These dimensions were (1) the images of organ ablation and the attitudes toward the transplantation procedure, (2) the representations of the dead body focusing on the relationship that people establish between the self and the body, (3) the importance of preserving the integrity of the corpse, and (4) the emotions that emerge around the idea of the biological decomposition of the body postmortem.

The following outline displays the connections between analytical dimensions. I began analyzing the images and emotions related to the organ ablation practice itself. Underlying these images, I found different symbolic representations that participants of the focus groups used to describe the body—"the disposable corpse" and the "untouchable body." Both representations were framed into two distinctive perspectives, transcendental and nontranscendental. Within them, I distinguished those conceptions that encourage organ donation and those that discourage it (figure 2.1).

The Disposable Corpse

During the group discussions, I observed that the dead body loses importance for most interviewees. For them, death means the end of the instrumental worth of the body and even its symbolic value, both for the dead person and for his or her relatives. The body is regarded as disposable for surgical interventions since it is described as a dehumanized cadaver, or sheer flesh. Therefore, the organ ablation practice for transplantation, defined by the participants as "body disassembling," does not provoke any emotional unease for them.

Such a detachment from the corpse is integrated into different interpretative frames—transcendental and nontranscendental ones. In the first case, participants referred to religious beliefs or other spiritual notions to

Figure 2.1. Organ Ablation Image

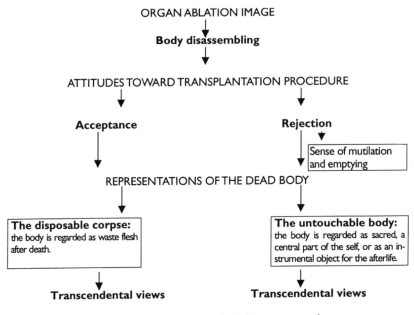

ORGAN ABLATION IMAGE
↓
Body disassembling
↓

ATTITUDES TOWARD TRANSPLANTATION PROCEDURE
↓

Acceptance   **Rejection**
↓   Sense of mutilation
and emptying

REPRESENTATIONS OF THE DEAD BODY
↓

The disposable corpse: **The untouchable body:**
the body is regarded as waste flesh   the body is regarded as sacred, a
after death.   central part of the self, or as an in-
                                      strumental object for the afterlife.
↓   ↓

Transcendental views   **Transcendental views**

Religious perspective   **Religious perspective**
Distinction between the immortal spirit or the   Critical view of modern medicine based on re
soul and the contingent body. Death deter-   ligious reasons. Importance of keeping the integ-
mines the inutility of the body for the afterlife. rity of the body after death: belief in the resurrec-
                                                 tion of the body or in the intrinsic unity of the
Nondefined religious perspective   person even after death. Defense of the dignity
Distinction between a universal vital energy and of the corpse.
the body. Death determines the uselessness of the
body and the survival of the spiritual force.

Nontranscendental views   **Nontranscendental views**
Distinction between self and body. Death de-   Critical view of the biomedical practices on
termines the temporal ending of the self and the   bodies based on the uncertainties to establish
instrumental worth of the body.   the temporal ending of the self. Intrinsic unity be-
                                               tween self and body.

IMPORTANCE OF CONSERVING THE INTEGRITY OF THE DEAD BODY
↓   ↓
NO, the body lacks in instrumental or   **YES,** the body bears symbolic or instrumental
symbolic value.   value.
↑

Rejection of the idea of the biological decomposition of the flesh

ATTITUDES TOWARD ORGAN DONATION
↓   ↓

Willingness to become a donor   **Unwillingness to become a
                                      donor**

highlight the distinction between the spirit, the soul, or the vital energy and physical body. In the second case, participants talked about death as the end of the existence of the self without integrating their narratives into transcendental perspectives. All of them—those who expressed transcendental notions and those who expressed nontranscendental views—shared a dualistic viewpoint of the body and the self that supported the idea of organ donation as it emphasized the utility that the body parts after death have for others who, at the same time, are still alive.

From a defined religious perspective, women who shared the Evangelical or Catholic credo explained that while the disembodied soul remains immortal, the body has an ephemeral value because of its contingent existence.[9] The body is important during life on earth because it has a sacred worth, but after death it loses not only instrumental but also symbolic value:

> I have read the Word and I understand it; what is important to me is my spirit not my body. During life the body is God's temple but when one dies the spirit separates from the body. We are a vessel of clay, and when we die the spirit goes to heaven and the body remains on earth. The body is not important to God."[10]

> God wants the soul, and once you die you will not feel anymore.[11]

The Catholic belief in resurrection of the soul, as a disembodied human state after death, was also mentioned as a reason that disposes positively to organ donation:

> I am Catholic and I believe in resurrection, therefore my spirit will wander here [not my body]; the resurrection is of the soul.[12]

Other interviewees, considered as having nondefined religious transcendental beliefs, also supported their accounts of the body on spiritual ideas that stress the dualism between the spirit and the flesh. However, they did not refer to any specific religious credo. They felt an emotional detachment from the dead body. These participants believed in reincarnation or in the existence of vital cycles. This means that a universal energy is liberated after the individual's physical death. The dead body is represented by them as a container that is abandoned by a disembodied consciousness or vital force, and even the self is experienced as disembodied while one is alive.

> I consider that after death one is not this [the body], this is simply a container. I believe in reincarnation, and so, I say that one is not this, I am not this [my body], this is just a transitory vessel that will disintegrate. I am not too attached to *this* body; so okay: if my eyes are useful, take them. If my legs are useful, take them too.[13]

> I believe that human life is energy that manifests itself in different bodies. . . . perhaps what I am saying sounds a little spiritual because coherently you can't see energy, but I think that when you die, energy is suddenly liberated, and this is a cycle like I see in nature.[14]

All the preceding descriptions share transcendental notions when referring to a dualistic view of the body and the self. On the other hand, other accounts of the corpse also imply a dualistic viewpoint, but they do not bear such spiritual components. The dead body is described as lacking in symbolic value because death represents the unambiguous ending of the self experienced in the secular Western notion of personhood. As long as the person is represented as a center of consciousness, sensitivity, and volition, the interviewees expressed that when one dies, he or she will not feel anymore. Therefore, what the physicians might do with the corpse is not important. The dead body is defined as dehumanized flesh that will start its own natural process of decomposition. In the prospect of this inevitable fate for the body, organ ablation is not seen as a biomedical practice that generates emotional troubles:

> When you are dead . . . I don't know, it's done, you don't lose anything [donating] because your body is nothing.[15]

> After death everything is over.[16]

> When I am dead they [physicians] can do whatever they want, because I won't feel anything anymore.[17]

> It doesn't matter if they draw and quarter me after death because I won't feel anything anymore, that does not affect me. . . . I would donate all my body parts because the body disappears when you die.[18]

The body in the prospect of death was also described using the analogy of cloth: when you are alive your body is a useful vessel (new cloth), but when you die it is useless for the owner (old cloth); so it becomes a thing that can be given away. Describing the body in such a way, separating away from its parts, would not cause emotional difficulties for the donor:

> Post-mortem organ donation is like donating old clothes that you don't need anymore. The body is not useful anymore for me so it doesn't matter to donate its parts.[19]

It was common that participants who did not express transcendental beliefs of surviving after their physical death mentioned their hope of the same kind of "symbolic immortality" (DeSpelder and Strickland 2002, 519), or the possibility of a "post-self" existence in the minds and hearts of loved ones (Shneidman 1995, 455). As they assume their impossibility to actually survive in some sense after death, they expect to be remembered by their loved ones:

> When a loved one dies what remains for the others is not his body, what is important is not material.[20]

> I will donate all of my body parts because what remains of you survives in your loved one's hearts.[21]

Even though for these participants the body loses importance both for the dead person and his or her relatives, some of them discussed a distinction among body parts. They differentiated the "outward" body from the "inward" body; the former visible and the latter hidden to loved ones. The distinction made among body parts leads not to finding obstacles to remove solid, internal organs, but to reject the idea of the ablation of body parts that could disfigure the corpse. Skin, bones, and corneas were mentioned as body features that participants would prefer not to be touched by physicians:[22]

> I would give all my organs but what is outside not [what is the *outside?*], the skin, the bones. . . . If they [physicians] are going to take my corneas I want that my eyes remain fine, . . . that *I* can look pretty.[23]

We can infer from these narratives that the body is regarded as a bearer of symbolic meaning for relatives, and that the expected "correct" treatment of the corpse is related to a more traditional idea of the presence of an embodied self. This certainly held true during the funeral, a ritualized practice of separation from the world of the living beings.

Among those participants who considered that conserving body integrity after death was irrelevant, the willingness to donate organs seemed to be reinforced by the negative image of the biological decomposition of the corpse and by the thought of imagining their bodies during this natural process.[24] Some see organ ablation as a way to avoid—or at least to reduce to its minimal expression—the biological degrading process. Moreover, some participants believe that the donor's corpse is wasted or cremated automatically (i.e., as part of the proceeding) after organ and tissue removal. Thus, organ ablation for transplantation seems to be a desired destination, or at least a preferred one, for the corpse.

During the focus group sessions, many interviewees spontaneously associated their positive disposition to donate organs with the preference for cremation, instead of burial as a method of body disposal.[25] The link between both practices—organ donation and cremation of the corpse— seems to be based on the rejection of the sense of inevitability that the image of human body decomposition provokes:

> Once I am dead I think that it is much better that I be disassembled by scalpel rather than eaten by worms. . . . I have a completely different concept of the putrefaction that the coffin signifies. . . . I think that it is much healthier to cremate the corpse than to wait for its natural disintegration.[26]

> The day I die I would like to be cremated to avoid the worms eating me, and I will offer my organs [for transplants]. Why would I leave them rot? It is better to give our organs to help other people.[27]

As discussed earlier, while some participants emphasized the negative images of human flesh degradation, others assumed the inevitability of this biological process. Their pragmatic attitude toward death was stressed when considering that organ and tissue removal was a good method to find a meaningful destination for body parts postdeath.

The Untouchable Body

Only a few participants in the research openly expressed their reluctance to become organ donors based on definitions of the dead body that differed from those described in the previous section. Like those who do not mention obstacles to donate organs for transplantation, these participants also describe the organ ablation practice as a disassembling procedure but, contrary to the former, they associate surgery with the negative senses of mutilation and emptying. I termed the underlying representations of the body that nourish this reluctance to organ transplantation under the category of the "untouchable body."

The self and body do not seem to be so easily separated from each other for these interviewees. They cannot precisely establish the temporal ending of the self. In their narratives, a dualistic viewpoint of the self and the body vanishes. Their accounts are grounded either in transcendental beliefs or in nonspiritual notions or intuitions.

Among the lower-class participants, the arguments against post-mortem organ donation were constructed around transcendental cultural values or religious ones. Even the Christian concern with the resurrection of the body was mentioned in opposition to biomedical practice. The body is defined as either sacred (as belonging to a suprahuman realm) or instrumentally (as a useful object that the person would need in the afterlife). Both reasons, sacredness and usefulness, support the preference of preserving the integrity of the corpse:

I don't want to donate [my organs]. I'm old fashioned, I want to die. . . . I want to be buried with my whole body. I don't like to be touched.[28]

It is horrible that [physicians] open your body after death. If you are born one way, you have to die in the same manner. It is better that we go as God made us. To remove organs is cruel.[29]

And what happens if you believe that you can live after death and you find that you don't have some part of your body? I believe that [the possibility of afterlife] is present in the life of Jesus, who was resurrected.[30]

As can be observed, during the group discussions references were made to the dual role that Christian interpretations assign to the body after death.[31] While participants included in the previous section accounted for the continuity of the immortal soul to support their willingness to donate their organs, those who held the notion of the untouchable body highlighted the possibility of bodily survival after death to argue against organ donation.

When the preference to keep the integrity of the dead body appeared among middle-class participants, it was connected with a much different set of cultural categories. Their reluctance to donate organs after death was framed into a nontranscendental critical view of modern medicine's practices on bodies and expressed a certain unease of accepting the death of the self. These accounts indicate cultural obstacles to the assumptions of the machine model that transplantation technology implies. Hence, the participants expressed their resistance to donate organs after death. The feeling that underlies their positions seems to be an inextricable connection between the self and the body. These narratives express what Giddens (1991; as quoted by Shilling 1997, 184) stresses as the absolute uncertainty of the death of our subjective selves. Listen to what the subjects had to say:

> [Organ ablation] sounds like a mutilation. To be quartered, to be cut up is worse when you are dead than when you are alive. It is irrational, isn't it? When I die I want to be buried naturally. . . . I do not like it [organ ablation] . . . in general, I reject intrusive medical acts.[32]

> The feeling of being disassembled is a little bit heavy. . . . Ultimately, you don't believe that you will vanish. . . . You are afraid of suffering [because] you think that you will continue living someway . . . [organ removal]. It is something that I consider aggressive to my dead body . . . the body is yourself. . . . My identity is very attached to my body.[33]

Although participants who opposed organ donation based on body considerations were a minority during the group discussions, their testimonies reflect that organ ablation is sometimes considered a disgusting practice. As Joralemon (1995, 1996) argues, these people would express a kind of cultural resistance to the medical rationality and the assumptions that orient transplantation practices within certain discursive boundaries.

The absence of certainties about the temporal ending of the self and the sense of unity between the person and its corporeal condition reflect a different image and symbolism of the dead body. If the self, in some way, remains alive and attached to the physical body, it is possible to imagine the persistence of "proprioceptive awareness" (Eilan, Marcel, and Bermudez 1998). This kind of consciousness consists in the perception of the body from an inner perspective that leads to the perception and experience of it as a unique "object." According to this possibility, organ removal is defined as a harmful intervention on bodies that still contain and maintain a human presence.

These descriptions represent the body as self, an integral part of self-identity, or as sacred (Belk 1990). Consequentially, the dead body still appears as a bearer of positive meaning, and therefore its parts are not regarded as insignificant "things" (Le Breton 1995) but as "lively or spiritualized parts of the self which people would still like to take with them when they die" (Scheper-Hughes 2000, 211).

Conclusion

In this chapter, I have analyzed body representations that emerged spontaneously from group interviews focusing on postmortem organ donation. Participants were positively disposed to donate their organs when they considered the dead body as a machine or material vessel separated from the self. Death is regarded as a temporal instance that determines the self/body or the soul/body detachment. In such descriptions, the body loses its usefulness and symbolic meaning both for the donor and for his or her relatives. These considerations are built on transcendental beliefs—according to religious ideas or secularized ones—or nontranscendental notions of the temporal vanishing of the self. Although these ideas are based on different cultural grounds, they converge on a dualistic, instrumental view of the dead body that is functional to organ transplantation practices. Keeping the integrity of the corpse is not important, and this consideration is reinforced by the negative emotion that the biological decomposition of the human body provokes among some participants.

The reluctance to donate organs grounded in cultural rejection was expressed either openly, or with certain ambiguity, by a few participants who opposed the idea of organ removal. They argued that it is linked to images of mutilation and emptying. Often, their accounts were based on religious beliefs or traditional cultural preferences for preserving the integrity of the body. Lower-class participants, who attributed some kind of sacredness and mystery to the human corpse generally supported these ideas. Within the transcendental perspective, the belief of bodily resurrection was also mentioned as a reason against organ donation.

Middle-class participants who were reluctant in their support of organ removal for transplantation, gave reasons that suggested that the body and its parts were considered as central for a secularized self-identity. These participants expressed difficulties in accepting the end of the embodiment of the self. Taking into account different perspectives—one is transcendental and the other is nontranscendental—these later descriptions of the human body tell us that for some individuals the dead body is not reduced to a mere residue lacking in symbolic meaning.

To conclude, I would like to remark on the complexity of studying empirically the meanings that people give to the dead body. The focus group is a potent method to stimulate an informal conversation among participants. It collects rich details on complex experiences and accesses their own interpretations of their actions, perceptions, and attitudes (Carey 1995). In this study, I suggest that dead body representations and the imagery of death that they imply may be the deepest layer that we have to explore in order to grasp the laypeople's attitudes toward organ donation.

Some individuals might find it more difficult to talk about certain sensitive topics than to discuss other less sensitive ones in "public" (see Blaxter 1997). For instance, in Argentina, people express openly a general distrust of public agencies and of the medical community when discussing the possibility of organ donation. This issue appeared recurrently during our focus group meetings, showing a strong centrality for data analysis (see Freidin 2000). I consider this matter the most external of the layers that underlie organ donation positions and make them accountable in Argentina.

On the other hand, arguments against organ donation based on a preference for conserving the integrity of the dead body appeared residually, often embedded in other reasons. Some people were more reluctant to speak about their bodies postdeath due to what they perceived as the irrationally of their narrative. It is possible that some participants of the focus groups were inhibited in the open expression of their positions if they perceived them not to be grounded in logical reasoning, but rather on intuitions, and diffuse and subtle feelings. These accounts are difficult to articulate in the presence of others with whom one has not built bonds of confidence and familiarity. I suggest that complementary in-depth face-to-face interviews with a selected sample of participants are necessary after group encounters if we wish to delve deeper in grasping phenomeno-logical representations of the dead body.

Notes

The research project on organ donation was supported by the University of Buenos Aires and the National Council for Science and Technology (1998–2000). I am deeply grateful to Professor Ruth Sautu, my mentor, for her support, insightful guidance, and encouragement throughout the research process, as well as for her invaluable comments on the earlier versions of this chapter. My thanks also to Nora Liberalotto, the research assistant of the study, and to Ignacia Perugoría, who helped me with the English translation. Finally, my gratitude to Chris Faircloth for his insightful suggestions to improve the manuscript. Of course, I am in debt to the participants of the focus groups for their collaboration with this study.

1. Fox and Swazey (1992) use the expression of "spare parts" to describe the pragmatic vision of the "replaceable body" or "re-built people" promoted by biomedicine.

2. The term "cyborg" was conceptualized by Haraway (1991 as quoted in Lock [2000, 260] and Samson [1999, 12]).

3. Following Wuthnow (1987), a meaning system refers to the dominant meanings in a culture associated with a particular symbol or set of symbols. The meanings evoked by the symbols occur at the emotional and the volitional level, as well as the cognitive level.

4. Joralemon raises issues including the topic of the brain death criterion and the difficulties that this relatively new medical definition of death may generate among the public (see also Fox and Swazey 1992; Lock 2000; Scheper-Hughes 2000). I deal with this topic in other works (see Freidin 2000, chapter 2) where I show that the condition for organ donation is unknown among the public. From this, I analyze the lay images of the postmortem donor. Here, I focus on how the dead body is symbolically constructed.

5. I follow the definition of laypeople provided by Williams and Calnan (1996).

6. Twelve focus groups were conducted in Metropolitan Buenos Aires during 1998 and 1999. People were recruited according to social class, gender, and age criteria. The universe of study was circumscribed to men and women aged between eighteen and thirty years, belonging to the lower class (additionally, they reside in two shanty towns) and the middle class (professionals, businessmen, clerical workers, all with university studies). A pretest was conducted to check the interview guide and the dynamic of the sessions.

7. Unidentified organ-donation campaign posters were used at the beginning of the sessions to trigger group discussion. The pictures and drawings contained in the posters facilitated participants' free association with the topic at hand. The posters belonged to an official campaign that was not launched publicly. The institutional identification of the campaign was made known only at the end of the sessions.

8. It is assumed here, following Turner (1992), that affects, emotions, and feelings are social components of purposeful actions, and key elements for a sociology of embodied agents.

9. The religious arguments in favor of or against transplants arose spontaneously during the focus group interviews. We did not intentionally select people belonging to different religions to participate. The topic was introduced as part of the interview guide. While some participants framed their viewpoints on organ donation into the faith they profess, others who also share religious beliefs, especially Catholics and Jews, did not connect transplants with their religion.

10. Lower-class younger female group.

11. Lower-class younger female group.

12. Lower-class older female group.

13. Lower-class older female group.

14. Middle-class younger female group.

15. Middle-class younger mixed group.

16. Middle-class younger male group.

17. Lower-class older female group.

18. Middle-class older female group.

19. Middle-class female younger group.

20. Middle-class female older group.

21. Middle-class female younger group.

22. The distinction among different body parts is also found in other studies (see Sque and Payne 1996; Bigio et al. 1998).

23. Lower-class younger female group.

24. Morin (1994) points out that the horror of decomposition of the corpse is a trait of humanity that is connected with the taboo of impurity and the terror that the loss of the individuality means to human beings.

25. This association was also discussed by Perez San Gregorio et al. (1992).

26. Middle-class younger female group.

27. Lower-class older female group.

28. Lower-class older male group.

29. Lower-class older female group.

30. Lower-class younger female group.

31. This point was developed by Dixon (1992) who pointed out the diversity of opinions, emphasis, and ideas of this credo in relation with bodily resurrection.

The same is discussed by DeSpelder and Strickland (2002). Greely and Hout (1999) empirically document that people's images of the afterlife differ in the importance given to the body.

32. Middle-class female group.

33. Middle-class younger female group.

References

Alasuutari, P.
1995 *Researching Culture: Qualitative Methods and Cultural Studies.* London: Sage.

Belk, R. W.
1990 Me and Thee Versus Mine and Thine: How Perceptions of the Body Influence Organ Donation and Transplantation. In *Organ Donation and Transplantation: Psychological and Behavioral Factors.* Edited by J. Shanteau and R. J. Jackson Harris, 139–49. Washington D.C.: American Psychological Association.

Bermudez, J. L., A. Marcel, and N. Eilan
1998 *The Body and the Self.* Cambridge: MIT Press.

Bigio, L.
1998 Los sí y los no a los requerimientos de donación de órganos para transplante. *V Jornada Argentina sobre Aspectos Psicosociales en Diálisis y Transplantes.* School of Psychology, University of Buenos Aires. Mimeographed.

Blaxter, M.
1997 Whose Fault Is It? People's Own Conceptions of the Reasons for Health Inequalities. *Social Science & Medicine* 44: 747–56.

Carey, M. A.
1995 *Issues and Applications of Focus Groups: Health Qualitative Research.* Thousand Oaks, Calif.: Sage.

DeSpelder, L. A., and A. L. Strickland
2002 *The Last Dance: Encountering Death and Dying.* Boston: McGraw-Hill.

Dixon, D.
1992 Religious and Spiritual Perspectives on Organ Transplantation. In *Psychiatric Aspects of Organ Transplantation.* Edited by J. Craven and G. Rodin, 131–41. Oxford: Oxford University Press.

Eilan, N., A. Marcel, and J. L. Bermudez
1998 Self-Consciousness and the Body: An Interdisciplinary Introduction. In *The Body and the Self.* Edited by J. L. Bermudez, A. Marcel, and N. Eilan, 1–28. Cambridge: MIT Press.

Featherstone, M., and B. Turner
1995 Body & Society: An Introduction. *Body & Society* 1: 1–12.

Foucault, M.
1973 *The Birth of the Clinic.* London: Tavistock.
1977 *Discipline and Punish: The Birth of the Prison.* London: Tavistock.

Fox, R. C., and J. P. Swazey
1992 *Spare Parts: Organ Replacement in American Society.* New York: Oxford University Press.

Freidin, B.
2000 *Los Límites de la Solidaridad. Condiciones Sociales y Culturales para la Donación de órganos.* Buenos Aires: Lumiere.

Frey, J. H. and A. Fontana
1993 The Group Interview in Social Research. In *Successful Focus Groups*, 20–34. Edited by D. Morgan. Newbury Park, Calif.: Sage.

Glaser, B., and A. Strauss
1964 The Social Loss of Dying Parents. *American Journal of Nursing* 64: 110–21.
1967 *The Grounded Theory.* Chicago: Aldine De Gruyther.

Greeley, A. M., and M. Hout
1999 Americans' Increasing Belief in Life After Death: Religious Competition and Acculturation. *American Sociological Review* 64: 813–35.

Hallam, E., J. Hockey, and G. Howarth
1999 *Beyond the Body: Death and Social Identity.* London: Routledge.

Himmelman, P. K.
1997 The Medicinal Body: An Analysis of Medicinal Cannibalism in Europe, 1300–1700. *Dialectical Anthropology* 22: 183–203.

Joralemon, D.
1995 Organ Wars: The Battle for Body Parts. *Medical Anthropology Quarterly* 9: 335–56.

1996 Request for Consent as Cultural Encounters. *UNOS Annual Meeting Towards the Year 2000: Concepts and Considerations in the Consent Process.* Washington, D.C. Mimeographed.

Kearl, M.
1998 Endings: A Sociology of Death and Dying. Oxford: Oxford University Press.

Lawton, J.
1998 Contemporary Hospice Care: The Sequestration of the Unfounded Body and "Dirty Dying." *Sociology of Health and Illness* 20: 121–43.

Le Breton, D.
1995 *Antropología del Cuerpo y Modernidad.* Buenos Aires: Nueva Vision.

Lock, M.
2000 On Dying Twice: Culture, Technology and the Determination of Death. In *Living and Working with the New Medical Technologies: Intersections of Inquiry.* Edited by M. Lock, A. Young, and A. Cambrosio, 233–62. Cambridge: Cambridge University Press.

Mellor, P., and C. Shilling
1993 Modernity, Self-Identity, and the Sequestration of Death. *Sociology* 27: 411–31.

Morin, E.
1994. *El hombre y la muerte.* Barcelona: Kairós.

Perez San Gregorio, M. A.
1992 The Attitude Towards Death Influences the Donation of Organs in Intensive Care Units. *Transplantation Proceedings* 24: 24.

Samson, C., ed.
1999 *Health Studies.* Oxford, U.K.: Blackwell.

Scheper-Hughes, N.
2000 The Global Traffic in Human Organs. *Current Anthropology* 41: 191–211.

Seale, C.
1998 *Constructing Death: The Sociology of Death, Dying, and Bereavement.* Cambridge: Cambridge University Press.

Sharma, U.
1996 Bringing the Body Back into the (Social) Action. Techniques of the Body and (Cultural) Imagination. *Social Anthropology* 4: 251–63.

Shilling, C.
1997 *The Body and Social Theory*. London: Sage.

Shneidman, E. S.
1995 The Postself. In *Death: Current Perspectives*. Edited by J. B. Williamson and E. S. Shneidman, 454–60. Mountain View, Calif.: Mayfield.

Sque, M., and S. Payne
1996 Dissonant Loss: The Experience of Donor Relatives. *Social Science and Medicine* 43: 1359–70.

Turner, B.
1992 *Regulating Bodies. Essays in Medical Sociology*. New York: Routledge.
1998 Plenary paper presentation at "After the Body" Conference. University of Manchester, U.K.

Walter, T.
1996 British Sociology and Death. In *The Sociology of Death*. Edited by D. Clark, 264–95. Oxford, U.K.: Blackwell.

Williams, S. J., and M. Calnan
1996 Modern Medicine and the Lay Populace: Theoretical Perspectives and Methodological Issues. In *Modern Medicine: Lay Perspectives and Experiences*. Edited by S. J. Williams and M. Calnan, 2–25. London: UCL Press.

Wuthnow, R.
1987 *Meaning and Moral Order. Explorations in Cultural Analysis*. Berkeley: University of California Press.

Youngner, S.
1992 Organ Donation and Procurement. In *Psychiatric Aspects of Organ Transplantation*. Edited by J. Craven and G. Rodin, 121–30. London: Oxford University Press.

CHAPTER THREE
THE FEMALE AGING BODY THROUGH FILM
Elizabeth W. Markson

When the movie *Sunset Boulevard* appeared in 1950, silent film star Norma Desmond represented the dark side of Hollywood stardom: the prototypical has-been, aging woman, clinging to dreams of youth, romance, and a cinematic comeback as Salome. That her vision of regaining lost beauty and fame was absurd, not only forms the basis of the plot but is metaphorically forecasted in the film's opening scene. Joe (William Holden), the male protagonist, is desperately trying to outdrive the "repo men" pursuing him to repossess his car when he spots a long driveway: "At the end of the drive was a lovely sight indeed—a great big empty garage just going to waste." Parking his car in the garage, he goes up to a big mansion that he assumes is deserted:

> It was a great big white elephant of a place—the kind crazy movie people built in the crazy 1920s. . . . A neglected house gets an unhappy look. This one had it in spades. It was like that old woman in *Great Expectations*— that Miss Haversham and her rotting wedding dress taking it out on the world because she'd been given the go-by.

Gloria Swanson, who created the role of Norma Desmond, was herself fifty at the time; Powell, portraying Joe, a young out-of-luck would-be screenwriter, was only fifteen years her junior. Yet the point—as an assistant to Cecil B. De Mille comments later in the film, "She must be a million years old!"—clearly draws the line: the aging Norma Desmond *is* a Miss Haversham, over the hill both as a sex object and a woman.

Completing the image of the postmenopausal female, Norma Desmond suffers from involutional melancholia, a deep depression. Her butler (and former husband) points out to Joe that

> There are no locks anywhere in this house, Sir . . . the Doctor suggested it . . . Madame's doctor. Madame has moments of melancholy. There have been some attempts at suicide. . . . We have to be very careful; no sleeping pills, no razor blades; we shut off the gas in Madame's bedroom.

Drawing on the representation depicted in *Sunset Boulevard*, this chapter focuses on the theme of the aging female body raised in *Sunset Boulevard* by examining how the older female body and mind have been portrayed in feature films. In particular, I concentrate on cinematic representations of the dressed body; the sexual body; and the ill or dying body. These three categories provide a useful heuristic device for analysis but are not mutually exclusive; for example, the body is depicted in various states of dress whether sexual or ill, and some of these bodies die.

Data for this analysis are drawn from a larger study of portrayals of older men and women in feature films, portions of which have been previously published (Markson and Taylor 1993; Markson and Taylor 2000). The larger study encompasses a 14 percent random sample of 3,091 feature films containing all genres during the 1929–1998 period in which performers, who were nominated at least once in their lifetimes for an Academy Award, appeared in one or more films when aged sixty or over.[1] In this chapter, only female nominees for a "best" or "supporting" role are included. Not every performer is American, as foreign actresses also have been Oscar nominees, but all films in which they appeared were in English. Because it is beyond the scope of this chapter to include the entire sample of these films, I focus on a selection spanning the years noted in the preceding.

Throughout the past one hundred years or so, film has played a powerful cinematic and ideological role. Although cinematic representations permit spectators to play active roles in constructing and interpreting their meanings, the very act of watching a film fosters new modes of behavior and consciousness. Because we are usually engaged in the film's action, we rarely speculate about the implicit and explicit messages conveyed by gazing on the bodies of the protagonists. Film nonetheless has wielded a powerful influence on how women of all ages are perceived, on how they perceive themselves, and about appropriate or inappropriate age and gender behavior. It is no accident that feminist film critics have noted that the bodies of women are portrayed through male eyes. Annette Kuhn (1982, 4) remarked more than twenty years ago that

> One of the major theoretical contributions of the women's movement has been its insistence on the significance of cultural factors, in particular in the form of socially dominant representations of women and the ideological character of such representation, both in constituting the category "woman" and in delimiting and defining what has been called the "sex-gender system."

In this chapter, I explore the management of the older woman's body in movies. How filmmakers compose older women's bodies both reflects and shapes our idealized and existing social values about females, aging, and the culture and society producing them. Whether true or false, these cinematic images also provide elementary, anticipatory socialization for our own beliefs about, and behavior in, later life. The portrayal of the female body in this medium provides a kind of everyday politics of emotion and feeling that contour spectators' real, lived, emotional experiences. Indeed, as Mander (1974, 68) points out, "If politics is the present tense of history, media is the present tense of politics."

The Aging Female Body

Like the story of *Sunset Boulevard*, the story of aging begins with the body. Aging and old age have been understood primarily in relationship to bodily changes that in turn provide visual images and predictions of what it is like to be old—a system of visible signs carrying social meaning. In contemporary Western society, the human body of every age is medicalized, the object of the medical gaze (Foucault 1975). Accompanying the medicalization of the body has been its disciplining, where its every aspect is likely to be subjected to control (Foucault 1975, 1979, 1980).

Although Foucault said little about aging in his voluminous writings, particularly germane to the old female body are those disciplinary practices that transform a domain of human existence—being older and female—into the unfamiliar, the uncertain, or the problematic to create the "other" (Foucault 1980). Charcot's nineteenth-century work at the Salpetriere Hospital in Paris where primarily poor old women were objects of his medical male gaze, heralded the saliency of the aging body as "the other" in a state of terminal decline (Katz 1996, 1999). The creation of elder as "other" in turn elicits responses and interventions, transforming both the everyday and unusual into conundrums requiring the attention and skills of experts (Foucault 1984).

Developments in science and scientific medicine in the nineteenth century gave additional opportunities for the bodies and minds of the elderly, especially older women, to be medicalized and disciplined. As early as 1865, "involutional melancholia" and "climacteric insanity" were terms developed by physicians to describe postmenopausal women (Banner 1992). The medicalization of the postmenopausal female soon proved to be profitable to the emerging fields of gynecology and psychiatry, and special diagnostic categories, including "old maid's insanity" (Ellis, [1905] 1942), were coined to describe the older woman. By 1896, psychiatrist Emile Kraepelin had denoted involutional melancholia as "a disorder that sets in principally or perhaps exclusively, at the beginning of old age in men and in women from the period of menopause onwards" (Kraepelin 1896, as cited in Greer 1991, 79).

A crucial aspect of aging aside from menopause that distinguishes men and women is the latter's social position in contemporary society as objects not only of the medical gaze but, as previously mentioned, objects of the male gaze—bodies to be looked at, admired, and desired for their youth, beauty, and fecundity. The postmenopausal body, having lost its reproductive (and by implication, sexual) charm, neither is the object of the appreciative male gaze nor does it fit into contemporary cultural discourses about "ideal" female beauty. Moreover, from a psychoanalytic perspective, the older woman is mentally suspect:

> It is a well-known fact, and one that has given much ground for complaint, that after women have lost their genital function [the ability to bear children] their character often undergoes a peculiar alteration. They become quarrelsome, vexatious and overbearing, petty and stingy; that is to say they exhibit typically sadistic and anal-erotic traits that they did not possess earlier, during their period of womanliness. Writers of com-

edy and satirists have in all ages directed their invectives against the "old dragon" into which the charming girl, the loving wife, and the tender mother have been transformed. (Freud 1958, 323–24)

Freud's model of the older woman echoes the views of earlier Judeo-Christian theologians: because of their anatomical differences, females, lacking a penis, are always defective beings, and once past menopause their primary reason for existence is lost. From a psychoanalytic perspective, the body is paramount, and the postmenopausal woman is not only old but her dysfunction is engraved on her wrinkled body for everyone to see (Woodward 1991).

Women have been of little interest to subsequent psychoanalysts except as symbols of decline and depression once their status as mother has ceased to be their major source of identity. In psychoanalytic terms, strengthening the association between aging as loss, older women have been described as likely to experience the trauma of the empty nest after their children leave home (Tallmer 1989). Given the belief that the aging woman is particularly prone to depression, it is not surprising that the majority of antidepressant users seen in the advertisements of major medical journals in several nations are predominantly women (Lovdahl, Riska, and Riska 1999). Against the medical and social backdrop of physical and psychic deformity assigned to them, older women have suffered from a conjunction of pernicious cultural attitudes about age and gender.

The relevance of these attitudes for cinematic portrayals of older women was highlighted by actor Charlie Chaplin when interviewed about the transition from silent to sound film:

> It's beauty that matters in pictures—nothing else. . . . Pictures! Lovely looking girls . . . What if the girls can't act? . . . Certainly I prefer to see, say, Dolores Costello [a 1920s silent movie star], in a thin tale than some aged actress of the stage doing dialogue with revolting close-ups. (Chaplin; as cited in Walker 1979, 132)

Thus do the bodily changes of aging blast the image of the fecund sex goddess. The following sections examine a selection of the ways that older women's bodies have been shown in more than six decades of feature films and the extent to which they convey or negate the narrative of aging as decline.

Gazing on the Aging Female Body in Feature Films

The Clothed Body

Just as the sound stage or on-location setting of a movie frames the scene for action, how its characters are clothed informs the spectator about their probable roles and attributes. Whether in the media or in everyday life, clothing provides a "look," a "semiotic battledress" (Evans and Thornton 1989, 14), fraught with age and gender messages that go far beyond covering our nudity or keeping us warm or cool. Imprinted with the consumption patterns of various social classes and categories of people, clothes are cultural goods used to delineate boundaries, establishing status and consciousness of kind between individuals and social groups (Bourdieu 1984). Garments are systems of signs, communicating messages about the social roles and status of the wearer that discipline and manage the body. With every change in costume, age and gender coding is displaced from the body to its attire, and the body is set to play a specific part (Evans and Thornton 1989).

In film, as in the real world, specific modes of female dress convey not only sexiness and sensuality but wealth (Lucille Watson in *Everybody Does It*, 1949; Billie Burke in *The Barclays of Broadway*, 1949; Edith Evans in *The Importance of Being Earnest*, 1952, remade with Dame Judy Dench, 2002; and Mildred Natwick in *Dangerous Liaisons*, 1988), poverty (Marie Dressler, *Min and Bill*, 1930), power (Marie Ouspenskaya, a maharanee described as "the last queen . . . still dresses the queen" in *The Rains Came*, 1939), occupation (Jane Darwell, a housemaid in *Experiment Perilous*, 1944; Gladys Cooper as Mother Superior, *Thunder on the Hill*, 1951; Hope Emerson as a starched, white-garbed child care expert in *Rock-a-Bye Baby*, 1958), rebellion against conventional norms (Ruth Gordon as "The Dealer," a.k.a. Old Chap, *Inside Daisy Clover*, 1965), and so forth.

Clothing also gives information about life events and their conative emotional meanings; mourning clothes (Joan Plowright, *Widow's Peak*, 1994) are but one example. Outmoded apparel, too, carries meanings; the visual image of people clinging to obsolete fashions informs the spectator that their wearers are not keeping up with the times and are likely to have opinions and beliefs as outdated as the clothing (Hepworth 1995).

The clothed body in movies is central to establish the character portrayed, her probable age, personality, social status, penchants, and passions. Personal props often are used as bodily extensions, ranging from a wheelchair to a dearly loved pet, staking additional identity claims. Through the considered use of clothing and accoutrements (props) as identity hallmarks, the performer transmits messages about the character being played and whether she is "with it" or antique and sometimes whether she is framed as a "good woman" or "bad woman." The following two sections describe the clothing and context in which the older female body is set to play a specific role.

Clothing the "Good" or Benevolent Aging Woman

The body of the older woman is often dressed to represent the "good" mother or grandmother. A common stereotype of the benevolent older woman is "mother" or "granny" who is likely to fit into one of the following clothing categories: she wears a house dress and is unconcerned with appearance; she is dressed in fashions of a bygone era; she wears a shawl to denote her advancing age and fragility; or she wears an apron to denote her housewifery. Accoutrements further establishing her identity are likely to include rocking chairs, knitting, sewing or crocheting, preparing food, cleaning, and perhaps owning a small pet. Granny (Cloris Leachman) in *The Beverley Hillbillies* (1993) is the campy prototype of a good, old-fashioned grandmother. With gray hair in a tight bun and garbed in long dresses of an uncertain era, she cooks, mixes home remedies, and sits in a rocking chair. In a break with the prototypical persona of the sweet grandmother, Granny sits in her rocker holding a shotgun, rides a motorcycle through the family's new Beverley Hill mansion, escapes from a mental hospital, and stops a wedding to save the family.

More conventional "motherly" or "grandmotherly" images abound in feature films over the decades. These range from Aunt Polly (May Robson in *The Adventures of Tom Sawyer*, 1938) to the magical Mrs. Cavour (Maureen Stapleton in *Trading Mom*, 1993). Mrs Cavour is a "good witch" whose garden produces an uncanny number of spectacular vegetables and flowers and who can summon up a "mommy market" for children to select a new mother when they are dissatisfied with their real mom.

Strong, powerful, or ineffectual, the representation of the older woman clad as a mother has been popular. In the mixed genre gangster/espionage/comedy, Jane Darwell (Ma Donahue in *All Through the Night*, 1942) portrays the archetype of the strong, powerful, elderly Irish mother.

Garbed in housedress, apron, and hair in a tidy knot on the top of her head throughout most of the action, she is the mother of gangster/gambler Gloves Donahue (Humphrey Bogart) and the unmistakable head of the family (and thus of Gloves' gang). Ma Donahue's simple dress emphasizes her as an unpretentious down-to-earth woman, who, despite Gloves' wealth, remains both loyal to her Lower East Side, New York City neighbors and oblivious to Gloves' illegal activities.

Always reliant on her intuitions, she gets a "feeling" that the mysterious absence of the local German American baker from his shop is sinister and orders Gloves and his gang to investigate. While probing the disappearance, Gloves and his gang inadvertently find themselves involved with a group of Nazi fifth columnists who are plotting to blow up an American battleship. Gloves and his gang foil the sabotage at the eleventh hour, and the evil Nazi leader is killed in the explosion. The film concludes with another of Ma's intuitions "I've got a feeling . . . and you know when I've got a feeling . . . " that suggests further adventures for Gloves and his associates to be instigated by Ma.

Another "good mother" role is portrayed in *None but the Lonely Heart* (1944), a moody film about "the story of Ernie Mott who searched for a free, beautiful, and noble life in the second quarter of the 20th century." Clad as a dowdy, working-class older woman with a dog as her companion, Ernie Mott's mother (Ethel Barrymore) habitually wears a hat whether inside or outside the house, a scarf or shawl around her neck and shoulders, and an apron over her housedress or coat. The addition of the hat suggests that she is not only a housewife/mother but works outside the home. (She is the owner of a junk and used furniture store in Cockney London.) Like so many film mothers, in her first appearance, she is preparing food for her son. She despairs about Ernie's drifting, his lack of direction in life, and his disinterest in making an honest living:

> I get no more from you than I did from your dad. . . . Stay or get out. Do a man's job . . . [you are] wanderin' around like a homeless wind.

Ernie accepts his mother's challenge and leaves home, only to return when his mother becomes ill—a topic discussed later in this chapter. As the plot unfolds, Ma Mott emerges as the quintessential, working-class, self-sacrificing, and hard-working mother that her clothing suggests.

A more glamorous "good mother"—well coifed and expensively dressed as befits her status as an upper-middle-class matron—is depicted by Peggy Ashcroft in *Sunday, Bloody Sunday* (1971). Although freed from the economic problems that besiege the Mott family, her role, like that of Ernie Mott's mother, is as a concerned, caring mother. The plot revolves around her daughter's marital problems: Her bisexual son-in-law is both in love with her daughter and a male friend. As she tries to help her daughter save the marriage, she assures her that one must resist the temptation to act hastily, instead taking the bitter of a relationship with the sweet: "There is no whole thing. . . . You have to make it work. I left your father once. . . . I was mad to think I'd not miss him."

Two older women in *The Summer House* (1993) wear sharply contrasting clothing that differentiates their roles. Mrs. Munro (Joan Plowright), the mother of a son engaged to be married, bears a startling resemblance to Grandma in "Little Red Riding Hood." Outfitted in shawl plus a nightcap to cover her gray hair, she lies in bed with her obese pug dog and gloomily contemplates her empty future after the marriage of her coddled twit of a son, Syl, to Margaret, the girl next door. In a subsequent scene, she slices sausage while talking to her dog: "You're too fat and I'm too old . . . but that girl [Margaret, her son's fiancée] is too quiet!" Her feelings of impending uselessness in old age after she is no longer needed as a mother are evident: "You know, dog, in other countries when the aged have no more use, they are placed on ice floes, but there are no ice floes in Croyden [the town where the action takes place]."

In vivid distinction, Jeanne Moreau, as the flamboyant, sexily dressed friend of the bride-to-be's mother, is a sophisticate. Her youthful clothing and sense of style set the scene for a complex sequence of events. She inveigles Plowright to get drunk ("boozing—or what you call a knees-up"), to dance, to laugh, to throw champagne at her brother-in-law-to-be, and, most important, to cease her laments. Moreau is the catalyst both for Plowright's rejuvenation and for the final resolutions of the plot, including a revelation about Margaret's sexual molestation by her father and her decision not to marry Syl, but to become a nun. In one of the rare cinematic depictions of an older woman as sexually attractive and active, Moreau also contributes to the end of Syl's innocence by seducing him in the summer house. No mutton dressed as lamb could have done better!

Elderly and never married women, too, often have "motherly" or "grandmotherly" clothing. In the sentimental drama *Grand Old Girl* (1935), a paean to schoolteachers and firm, traditional values of right and wrong, actress Laura Bayles (May Robson) is the principal of a high school where she is known as old gunpowder. Wearing clothes reminiscent of the Edwardian era—long, near-ankle-length skirt, blouse with a jabot, jet brooch, and watch pin—the one contemporary for the 1930s aspect of her dress is her marcelled hair. Her wardrobe establishes her as a proponent of the "old school," representing stable, tried and true moral values during the social ferment years of the Great Depression. A spinster with a cat (male!), her cat and her students are her children.

Their care forms the core of her character: "It is my duty to build up character. . . . I'd dare anything for my children." And as a builder of character and good conduct, she castigates the school janitor who has sworn at a student: "Swearing is a disgusting habit. . . . why don't you try and cultivate yourself the way you do your flowers." Thus, nurturing both males and females, challenging male authority, and breaking up the local gambling ring in the soda shop frequented by her students, she is eventually rewarded for her nurturance in a homily by the President of the United States, a former student of hers, to whom he owes his own clear sense of right and wrong.

Older women not only nurture their children, students (and the occasional U.S. President), but dogs. Dally (Dame May Whitty, *Lassie Come Home*, 1943), who appears in the film roughly one hour into the action, is one of the many minor characters who Lassie meets in her peregrinations to return to her young former owner. Dally, arrayed in grandmotherly pink shawl and lavender apron over a brown dress with a lace collar, is sitting in her rocking chair and knitting when she hears a noise outside. She and her husband, Dau, both of whom are apparently childless, lonely, and no longer have new experiences to share, find Lassie, tired and ill after numerous misadventures. The elderly couple take in Lassie who is, according to Dally "Such a bonnie dog. . . . Now she's ours, Dau. . . . we're her owners." Dally's clothing and accoutrements (rocking chair, knitting, preparing food, and caring for Lassie) ensure that she will be perceived by the viewer as a compassionate old woman, seeking an object that she can cherish and give meaning to in her otherwise humdrum life. As the scenes unfold, she is such a "good mother" to the dog that Lassie's needs take precedence both over her husband's and her own desires:

> She's [Lassie's] not happy here. . . . she's too polite. . . . You see, Dau, I know about this dog. She's going somewhere. . . . She wants to be on her way but she's too polite and understanding. She doesn't want to hurt us. . . . All right, then, dog. If you must go, away with you. Goodbye, Herself—good luck to you!

Both clothing and personal props also dress the body for another charitable nurturing older woman, Ma Belden (Jane Darwell in *Excuse My Dust*, 1951), Joe Belden's (Red Skelton) mother. Set in 1895 in Willow Falls, Indiana, the story centers on Joe's numerous attempts to invent a working "gasmobile," his eventual success, and his contest with a wealthier suitor to marry his sweetheart, Liz. Dressed in pink and peach costumes of the period, plump, and gray hair pinned back, Ma's first appearance is on the porch of their farmhouse where she offers cookies to her son: "I declare, this boy hasn't had a bite to eat all day. . . . [turning to Joe's girlfriend, Liz] Maybe you can get him to eat, I can't."

In her second appearance, she stirs cooking batter. But Ma nurtures her boy in more ways than cooking. When Joe inadvertently burns down the farm's barn in one of his attempts to build the gasmobile, her response is supportive and once again includes food as a prop. Extraneous to the action, Ma, as his proud, loyal supporter, is the aging backdrop against which her son's life is played.

A break in the image of the "good" old woman as a mother figure is provided by Margaret Rutherford in the mystery/comedy *Murder at the Gallop* (1963). An adaptation of one of Agatha Christie's Miss Marple mysteries, the cinematic Miss Marple is the diametric opposite of Christie's original heroine, a sweet-faced, slightly-built woman who solved crimes by relying on her knowledge of village human nature while knitting woollies for babies. In contrast, Rutherford's Miss Marple is heavyset, baggy-eyed, and physically active, usually wearing massively flowing cloaks and scarves, tweeds, and outmoded hats as she seeks to solve the mysterious death of the elderly, wealthy, misanthropic Mr. Enderby.

In other scenes, she, dressed in riding gear of an uncertain era, rides a horse sidesaddle and, wearing an unexpectedly becoming evening dress, feigns a heart attack. Giving her generally frumpy appearance and unexpected comedic flair, she is not only an occasional baker of scones (still another instance of cooking as a prop for the older woman) but an audacious, intrepid climber of ladders, eavesdropper, peeper into windows, and skilled horsewoman who outrides the male owner of the combined bed and breakfast and riding school where much of the action is set. Disparaged by the local law enforcement authorities as a meddlesome, overly imaginative, and aging figure of fun, she has the last laugh when she brings the murderer to justice.

Another surprising figure is the frumpy Miss Froy (Dame May Whitty in Hitchcock's suspense film, *The Lady Vanishes,* 1938) who initially appears as a retired, tweedy, vacuous, and motherly spinster music teacher vacationing at a European ski resort. Despite being kidnapped and nearly murdered by enemy agents until her rescue by a much younger, romantically involved couple, she successfully evades armed soldiers in a daring flight and emerges as a powerful British spy, more clever than either her would-be captors or the young couple who had rescued her. Her clothing provides her with the perfect cover for a spy!

Clothing the Malign or "Bad" Older Woman

The benevolent or "good" older woman is alternately dowdy or chic, depending on the role and social status of the character. The malign or "bad" older woman, too, may be shabby, unfashionable, or stylish. Malign mothers nonetheless are wolves in sheep's clothing, even when their clothes and propensity for cooking and housewifery resemble "good" mothers. Ma (Margaret Wycherly) is the evil guiding force for Cody (James Cagney), her psychopathic and mother-obsessed gangster son, in the extraordinarily violent film *White Heat* (1949). Like Ma in the *Oxbow Incident*, Cody's Ma has no scruples about murder. Like a good lower-class cinematic mother, she first appears shabbily dressed as she cooks for Cody's gang that has just robbed a mail train and killed four men. In a subsequent car getaway scene, the ubiquitous shawl appears as a lap robe to keep her warm. Also like good film mothers, she is solicitous about Cody who has "fits." After his first fit in the film, she expresses her concerns:

> Not good for you son, it's the cold air. . . . Don't let 'em see you [the gang members] like that. Might give some of 'em ideas. . . .Top of the world, son [as she gives him something to drink]. Now go on out.

In a subsequent scene, Ma goes to the supermarket to buy one of Cody's favorite foods—strawberries—but the police spot her car and a chase ensues. Ma eludes them, thus instigating the gang's flight to a motel, justifying the action:

After Cody decides to turn himself in and go to prison for a crime that he did not commit in order to avoid prosecution for the train robbery, Ma becomes head of the gang and once again expresses her love for her son by laying the ground rules to protect Cody's interests: "Anything we get, Cody gets his full share. Anything different say it now. Or would you rather wait 'til Cody gets out?"

Her solicitude for Cody continues when she pays a visit to her son in prison and warns him that his wife, Verna, is having an affair with Big Ed, another gang member, who is plotting to kill Cody: "You've been hurt. . . . It's Big Ed and Verna. It's my fault; I let you down. . . . And I'll help you, Cody. . . . [She states she will kill Big Ed.] Anytime I can't take care of his kind I know I'm gettin' old. . . . Nobody does what he's done to you and gets away with it."

Although Ma is ultimately not able to save Cody, Cody's last words in the final scene just before he is blown up on top of an oil refinery tank echo what Ma has repeatedly told him about his place in life: "Top of the world!"

The body of the bad older woman is, however, more likely to be shown as grotesque, even asexually "unfeminine," than her good counterpart would. Traditional signifiers of femininity are abandoned for the exotic absurd. The witch or possessor of magical or occult powers is a reminder that evil lurks beneath her monstrous appearance. For example, Countess Renevskaya (Dame Edith Evans in *The Queen of Spades*, 1948), a witch who possesses the secret of how always to win at cards, is wrinkled, alternately hobbling or walking with a cane, and hard of hearing. Her feeble body is clad in obsolete fashions of a long past era often complemented by a shawl, and an extraordinarily elaborate and outmoded wig covers her hair.

When young and the most beautiful woman in Russia, she took a lover who robbed her of her husband's funding for his military regiment. Rather than admit her adultery and the robbery to her husband, she sought help from the mysterious and demonic St. Germain who gave her the secret of three cards guaranteed to win at all times. Extracting a pledge from her that she would never divulge this information, St. Germain demanded her soul in return. Although the secret of the cards enabled the countess both to recoup her husband's stolen money and to be invincible at cards, she was indelibly marked. Now a ludicrous, vicious relic, the countess's only kind words are for her dog with whom she talks baby talk and kisses. Her dress, cane, physical disabilities, and lapdog set the scene for the tale of her amoral power in old age plus the broader dangers of ambition and deceit that she triggers in others.

Flora Robson (*Clash of the Titans*, 1981), as one of three Stygian witches who makes the three witches in *Macbeth* appear as benign as the Sugar Plum Fairy, is clearly another grotesque. She and her fellow witches are garbed to represent the epitome of malevolent old-age hags as they crouch, cackling menacingly over a cauldron, in a dark, dank, and frightening cave. Stringily haired and blind with only one large and unattached eye among the three, their raiments are filthy rags. Cosmetic artistry not only makes their faces hideous but conceals their eye sockets, transforming their eye areas into disconcertingly flat surfaces.

Perseus, the hero of the film, has sought them in hopes that they will give him the secret to break the curse of Andromeda's sacrifice. To force them to yield the secret, he steals their eye. Once successfully gaining information, he throws the eye back at the blind witches who grovel and scramble about to find it to protect themselves. The leitmotiv of the old woman arrayed as menacing and powerful yet as a profoundly disabled victim is explicit.

A more recent depiction of the older woman as a grotesque witch is Diahann Carroll as Elzora (*Eve's Bayou*, 1997), an elderly voodoo woman and fortune-teller. In painted whiteface with lank, white hair, she first appears in an open-air market where she is a sideshow attraction. In return for money stolen by ten-year-old Eve, she agrees to put a curse on Eve's philandering father, Louis:

> I'll see what I can do. I'll need some hair. . . . You come back Thursday night and we will see. . . . [Later to Eve] I did not make you no voodoo doll. I made a wax coffin and buried it in the graveyard. . . . You said you wanted him dead!

Although Louis is subsequently killed by the husband of a woman with whom he is having an affair, Eve continues to believe that her father's death was her own fault.

Not all malevolent women, of course, are witches, although they may approach the grotesque or be just simply ugly and "unfeminine." Ma (Jane Darwell) is a boardinghouse keeper in *The Oxbow Incident* (1943), a dark Western of mob terror, set in 1885 Nevada. With gray hair slicked back and dressed in men's clothing, she carries a shotgun as she arrives on horseback. The only woman among the members of the posse who hunts and captures three innocent men, Ma's clothing and personal props immediately inform the spectator that she is as tough or tougher than any of her male cronies and well equipped to spur on the lynch mob. Successfully overruling those few people who protest the impending lynching, Ma gleefully comments to the men about to be hanged: It ain't that you're so dangerous—it's just that most of the men ain't seen a real triple hangin'. . . . Keep your chin up. You can only die once.

Even female villains like Ma, however, still cook. In her one "feminine" gesture, Ma prepares food for the three men to be hanged but offsets this apparent kindness with delighted chuckles at the prospect of their death. She proves herself to be merciless, offering to lead the mob in whipping out the horses for the hanging. While not a witch with supernatural powers, Ma's garb, props, and demeanor typify Freud's negative view of the older woman as a postmenopausal, sadistic "old dragon," genderless, neither female nor male.

The Sexual Older Body

Given the still persistent view succinctly expressed by Charlie Chaplin that lovely looking girls are preferable to some aged actress with revolting close-ups, it is hardly a shock that few older actresses portray roles where they are sexy or regarded as sexually attractive. With older women relegated to asexual motherhood, unattractiveness, genderlessness, or the grotesque, the female cinematic sexual body remains young, pure, and fecund for the male voyeuristic gaze and as female role model.

The character of the aging, sleazy, unkempt, and alcoholic prostitute, Marthy Owen (Marie Dressler in *Anna Christie*, 1930), both frames the declining sexuality of the older woman and redefines her basically as a motherly woman who nurtures and protects a younger one. At the outset of the film, Marthy lives with a coal barge owner, the aging Chris Christopherson (George F. Marion), where she serves as his mistress. When his allegedly sheltered and virginal daughter, Anna Christie (Greta Garbo)—who, unbeknownst to him, is also a prostitute—arrives from Minnesota to live with him, he asks Marthy to leave. Marthy sums up the situation by stating that "he didn't want no old wharf rats around a nice young girl." Despite her protestation to the young Anna that "I can have any man I want. . . . Plenty of guys on plenty of boats waitin' for me . . . always was," Marthy is beyond sexual desirability to anyone but Christopherson. A sexual fossil, she is unable to attract a clientele after leaving the relative security of the coal barge; when last seen, she is reduced to panhandling to support her alcoholism.

Although countless films portray older men as romantically and sexually involved with younger women, suggesting an ageless male sexual body, it is rare for the love object to be an elderly woman. An exception is the film, *Harold and Maude* (1971), in which the young, wealthy, and suicidal Harold falls in love with the soon-to-be-eighty Maude (Ruth Gordon, who was in fact aged 75). Maude, an attractive, well-proportioned woman whose red hair encircles her head in braids, may be the only female character in American cinema to have a romantic sexual entanglement with a man approximately sixty years younger than she. Unhampered by age and gender norms, the ebullient Maude advises Harold not to cheat himself out of life:

> Reach out! Take a jump. . . . Play as well as you can. Go, Team! Give me an L, give me an I, give me a V, give me an E—LIVE!! Otherwise you've got nothing to talk about in the locker room.

When Harold decides he wants to marry Maude, however, opposition mounts on all fronts. His psychiatrist sums the romantic attachment:

> A very common neurosis, particularly in this society whereby the male child subconsciously wishes to sleep with his mother. What puzzles me, Harold, is that you want to sleep with your GRANDMOTHER.

And the priest's commentary, specifically directed to the old body, is even more pointed:

> I would be remiss in my duties if I did not tell you that the idea of intercourse and the fact of your firm, young, body commingling with the

WITHERED flesh, SAGGING breasts and buttocks makes me want to VOMIT.

Harold's marriage plans are thwarted by Maude's suicide on her eightieth birthday; as she says, "80 is old enough." That Maude commits suicide provides a tidy end that would satisfy psychiatrist, priest, and many cinemagoers alike. The image of an old woman's body commingling with that of a young man is put to rest.

A very different view—but nonetheless unflattering—of the sexuality of the aging woman is portrayed in *The Adventures of Baron Munchausen* (1989). In a dual role played by Valentina Cortese, the older woman is a sex object who does not, of course, "look her age." As Violet, Cortese is one of several actresses appearing in a stage production of the adventures of the Baron (Bill Paterson). When the real Baron appears and challenges the actors' interpretations, she unsuccessfully attempts to seduce him.

In Cortese's second role—a sequence of the "actual," as opposed to the theatrical, enactment of the Baron's adventures—she appears as Queen Adriana, wife of the King of the Moon. Because mind and body are separated on the moon, Adriana's head is able to flirt with the Baron while her body is having intercourse with her husband. This mind-body split emphasizes at least two points about female sexuality. First, the female physical body is an object where psychological involvement is totally extraneous to the act of sexual intercourse. Second, regardless of her age, a woman's head is not always where the heart (body) is in sexual relationships.

The Ill or Dying Body

The disciplining of the aging body as a grid of disorders, distinct from younger bodies, is apparent in the depiction of older women. Whether portraying the good, the bad, or the ugly, older women are at particular risk of madness, decrepitude, death, or murder: visual reminders of the loss of mobility, loss of mind, loss of functional capacity, and possibility of lingering or sudden death associated with aging. Emphasis on the fragility of older women's minds and bodies strengthens and justifies the relegation of older women to "the other."

The Madness of Old Women

Many people believe that dementia is an inherent part of old age and in-terpret even mild memory loss as a dreaded sign of impending madness. Although relatively few films portray demented or insane older women, in those movies featuring such women, it is their major identity claim. The mentally deranged Countess Pelagia of Poland (Maria Ouspenskaya), who appears briefly in a pseudo biography of Napoleon (*Conquest*, 1937), is a woman who reportedly remembers nothing of the past forty years and be-lieves that Louis XVI is still king of France. In her first scene, the Cos-sacks have just been driven from her brother's palace after destroying the drawing room. As she views the destruction, she complains: "Ah, so there was a party! Why am I never told anything?"

When the Emperor Napoleon arrives to be quartered at the palace, she is asleep but wakes to say to him:

> Who are you? . . . Don't be impertinent, young man. . . . Oh, you are an emperor, are you? And my good friend Louis XVI abdicated in your favor? . . . This house is getting to be a lunatic asylum. . . . What were you before you became an emperor? . . . Are you Jesus, too?

In a more recent treatment of mental illness, Barbara Harris as Mary Blank in the black comedy, *Grosse Pointe Blank* (1997), portrays the insane mother of Martin Q. Blank (John Cusack), an accomplished hired killer who has lost his taste for his chosen profession. Returning to the Detroit suburb of Grosse Pointe where he grew up, Martin finds that his child-hood home has been demolished and his mother has been institutional-ized. In her only scene—set in either a nursing home or a mental hospital—Mary Blank is unkempt, wheelchair-bound, and on lithium. Although she initially recognizes her son, she soon forgets who he is and asks him his name. As she is wheeled away by a nurse, she chants the ap-parent non sequitur, "the colonel's lady and Judy O'Grady are sisters un-der the skin."

Judith Hearne's Aunt Darcy (Wendy Hiller in *The Lonely Passion of Judith Hearne*, 1987), always a demanding woman, becomes demented in the course of the film. Once a "grande dame" who conducted "musicales" in which her niece, Judith, performed for wealthy guests, she suffers a stroke and becomes bedridden, demented, and even more irascible:

The chop's burned! [As she throws the chop at her niece]. . . . No, no, I want the beans, please, please, Judith, I want the beans!! [Throws food again] . . . I want the cake, the cake, the cake!! [While beating the cutlery and having a temper tantrum]

Aunt Darcy's behavior is so extreme that her physician advises Judith to place her in a private mental hospital. When Judith finally signs the commitment papers, Aunt Darcy is furious. As she crawls on the floor, she accuses Judith of ingratitude: "You're telling them I'm mad, and I sheltered you when no one wanted you!"

Judith then promises that she will not let her aunt be institutionalized. Certifiably insane until her death, the aunt keeps her niece as a quasi-slave, the major reason for the niece's subsequent lonely alcoholic existence as a spinster piano teacher.

Physical Disability and Death

The disintegrating ill or dying female body provides a model against which spectators can perform a self-assessment, reassuring themselves of their own wholeness by projecting their fears of aging and death outward. One's own mortality is kept at bay, perhaps one reason that the portrayal of the aging female body as a tomb or a candidate for entombment is a prevalent movie theme. Incapacities may be multiple, as in *Whales of August* (1987) where an ever-patient, self-sacrificing, and concerned Lillian Gish takes care of her blind, rich, and always choleric sister (Bette Davis) who is possibly demented and openly wishes to become deaf so that she will be totally insensible to the world around her. Older women also have hysterical seizures; in *The Trip to Bountiful* (1985), a helpless widow (Geraldine Page), living with her greedy, selfish daughter-in-law and wimpy son, collapses in a fit of despair after she runs away trying to make her way back to her old home in Bountiful, Texas, and is thwarted.

Lingering illnesses are no stranger in the cinematic representations of older women. When Ernie Mott learns that his mother (Ethel Barrymore, *None But the Lonely Heart*, 1944) is stricken with cancer, he returns home. Attempting to conceal her pain and illness from Ernie, she is delighted that he has apparently decided to cease his life as an aimless drifter: "Look at him out there. You'd never know it was the same boy. There's such a thing as prayers being answered. . . . Lots of love in you, Ernie. Unbeknownst to her, however, Ernie has become a thief rather than living up to his mother's expectations for him to earn an honest living. The police discover that Ma's shop contains stolen goods received from Ernie and his partners in crime, and she is imprisoned. As Ma lies in the prison hospital dying, she pleads, "Love me, son. I disgraced you." After her death, Ernie decides to join the war effort and fight for the good life.

Strokes, heart disease, and other ailments take their toll even among the most sympathetic film characters. Dolly (Piper Laurie in *The Grass Harp*, 1996), a warm, simple, otherworldly, and youthful-looking spinster whose "spirit is pink," spends much of her time in the woods where she collects herbs that she uses to concoct an herbal medicine for dropsy. Her herbal medicine sales are so successful that both her strong-willed sister, Verena, and unprincipled "Doctor" boyfriend, plan to patent the medicine and turn it into a profit-making business. Dolly objects and runs away to live in her secret tree house in the woods where her young cousin, Collin, and the family housekeeper, Catherine, join her. Verena reports them as runaways to the town sheriff who attempts to bring them back, but a retired judge intervenes.

The judge begins to pay frequent visits to the tree house, falls in love with Dolly, and proposes marriage to her. In subsequent scenes, Collin is accidentally shot by the sheriff, Dolly returns home, and the two sisters are reconciled. All seems well until Dolly unexpectedly collapses while dancing with Collin, is taken to bed, and dies of a stroke. Collin, now older, decides to go to New York to become a writer. He, Verena, Catherine, and the judge go to visit the tree house together one last time to listen to Dolly's "grass harp—the harp of voices . . . the wind is us."

Ramona Calvert (Gena Rowlands in *Hope Floats*, 1998), albeit an eccentric taxidermist, is a good mother and grandmother. Like Dolly, she is youthful in appearance and unexpectedly dies of a stroke toward the end of the film. Her daughter, former high school beauty queen, Birdee Pruitt (Sandra Bullock), has returned home to live with Ramona after the humiliating revelation on a television talk show that Birdee's husband and best friend are having an affair. Ramona repeatedly tries to comfort the deeply depressed Birdee:

Why don't you just tell me when it first started? Cryin' over it won't make it clear. Life just moves along and you've got to go with it. Your love life has always been a disaster. You think life just goes on and on.

Birdee angrily tells Ramona that her depression and unhappy life are due to her mother, for Birdee had to be pleasing as a teen beauty queen to overcome Ramona's reputation as the town joke who stuffs dead animals in the front yard and came to Birdee's school with a bag full of road kill.

Throughout the film, there are intimations of Ramona's mortality. In one scene, Ramona is in the attic where she is cleaning out things from the past (one may also speculate about any hidden meaning in Ramona's profession as a taxidermist!). In a second scene, she is once again cleaning in the attic when she begins to feel sick. Subsequently, while in bed drinking a cup of tea, Ramona suddenly drops the cup, which shatters, and she dies. After Ramona's death, Birdee undergoes a transformation, taking on her mother's wisdom, strength, and some of her mannerisms.

Albeit representing different cinematic eras, in all three dramas, *None but the Lonely Heart*, *The Grass Harp*, and *Hope Floats*, the death of the caring older woman frees a younger individual to develop more fully as an adult. Ernie Mott ceases his criminal activity to fight for his country; Collin goes on to pursue a career as a writer, and Birdee is able to overcome her depression and feelings of inadequacy. The legacy of the deceased is their wisdom passed on to the next generation. Not all older women die of natural causes or leave a happy legacy to their relatives. The hypochondriacal Mrs. Bramson (Dame May Whitty in *Night Must Fall*, 1937) is an imperious, self-centered, autocratic old woman in a wheelchair (who can push her own wheelchair when unobserved). Another "old dragon," she is nasty, sarcastic, manipulative, class conscious, miserly, and disparaging to her devoted niece who works for her (or as Mrs. Bramson says, "pretends to work" for her).

Mrs. Bramson meets her match, however, with young, mass murderer Danny (Robert Montgomery) who wins her trust by asking what her ailments are. As the combination of a gigolo and the son she never had, Danny ensures her confidence by giving her a shawl that he claims was his mother's but that he has just purchased. He further solidifies his position by infantalizing Mrs. Bramson with songs such as *Rock a Bye Baby* and games such as "this little piggy went to market" with her toes. While encouraging her hypochondria, dependency, and regression into childhood, Danny is plotting to rob and murder her. Collapsed in hysterics when Danny reappears after a brief absence during which he has stolen her money, she describes herself as, "Poor old woman crying for Danny. . . .You're the only one who understands me . . . unkind husband . . . You have such a kind face." Soon after, Danny smothers her to death with a pillow.

Death also comes to claim other older women. Countess Renevskaya (*The Queen of Spades*, 1948) dies of fright when the ambitious, corrupt, Captain Sovotin, demanding her secret to enable him to become rich by winning at cards, threatens her with a revolver. Cody's mother (*White Heat*, 1949) is murdered by his estranged wife, Verna. In *What Ever Happened to Aunt Alice* (1969), both Miss Edna Tinsley (Mildred Dunnock) and Alice Dimmock (Ruth Gordon), housekeepers for a younger, eccentric widow who maintains her wealth through murder, deserve far better than Mrs. Bramson, the countess, or Cody's mother but are nonetheless bludgeoned to death by their employer. The disintegration of the body through death is lurking in the background for both the just and unjust older woman.

Conclusion

This examination of how older women's bodies are portrayed in film shows that through six decades of social change in women's social roles, certain basic beliefs about older women have remained constant. Despite changes in life expectancy, health, fashions, and the physical body itself, the message delivered remains the same. With a few rare exceptions, women's old age is not hidden in feature films; rather, specific images of aging and old age predominate and are often exaggerated. The older woman as a motherly or grandmotherly figure, whether compassionate, cunning, or cruel, is one such image; the older woman as an exotic grotesque whose body is debased by clothing and makeup is another. Aging is primarily estimated in visual terms, where the surface of the body, its garments, and its accoutrements provide the hallmarks by which one's age is judged.

However garbed, seeing the scantily attired aging female body on screen remains taboo. It would seem incongruous for the older Ruth Gordon, Jessica Tandy, or Katharine Hepburn to have appeared in a film while wearing a swimsuit. Even in her romantic interludes with Harold, Maude's naked or nearly naked body remains hidden from the spectator. Yet when the seventy-eight-year-old Kirk Douglas (*Greedy*, 1994) appeared in swimming trunks and successfully defeated his much younger nephew in water games, it merely established his character as indomitable albeit allegedly crippled. Viewing an older woman's body nude or nearly nude and not morphed by cosmetic surgery offends the female's social positioning as an object to be gazed at with admiration. Keeping the older woman's body clothed supplies both a "look" and a barrier to being perceived as other than asexual, sometimes ill, pathetic, or disgusting. The bodies of older male stars, however, are likely to be extended "into a fantasy of ageless sexual potency" (Kozlowski 1993, 8).

The portrayal of the older female body in film is, by definition, a masquerade. Film stars put on "a look" designed to make known information about the social status and character's personality being played; this "look" may or may not resemble the real-life appearance of the individual performers. The garbed, cinematic older female body, whether or not augmented with the accoutrements of wheelchair, rocking chair, cane, cooking pots, cookie batter, small pets, and so on, is divorced from the reality of the older woman acting a role. Bodily images in film are changeable and flexible, subject to replacement with clothing, makeup, and personal props that carry symbolic meanings essential to a specific plot. Yet the performer, too, is old and subject to the same fears about her own body going to pieces as does the character she plays. Kaplan (1999), using the illustration of Marlene Dietrich, suggested that it is women's social position as objects of the admiring male gaze that makes age especially traumatic:

This dark knowledge of aging as trauma is born out [*sic*], I want to suggest, in two of the images we see of Dietrich in the documentary film *Shadow and Light*. . . . (p. 175). The first shot shows a surprised Dietrich, sitting up in bed, dressed all in white, with her hair pinned behind a bandana, revealing an ugly forehead and cheeks white with a facial (attesting to her continuing concern with her image despite now being a recluse). . . . Posterity has the image she so feared—of a gaunt, aged face, trying to hide behind the windows of her Paris flat. . . . The second image is perhaps even more terrifying to me in relation to the trauma of aging. It is another still photograph from inside the flat—this time of an empty wheelchair, positioned at the tall glass windows. Presumably Dietrich (who so feared a gaze that would catch her wrinkled face) sat here in the afternoons and gazed out at the life going by in the street below, a life she had excluded herself from because of her own trauma of aging. She would control the gaze now—not because of the changes in her body per se, as we saw, but for fear of anyone seeing the changes. (P. 178–79)

Whether in cinematic depictions or in real life in a visually oriented, consumer society such as ours, the bodily imprints of old age are seen as both literally and figuratively unbecoming: not only unattractive to see but an indication of vulnerability and mortality. The body and the person within are going to pieces. Despite the proliferation of cosmetic techniques employed to discipline the aging body, the message of *Sunset Boulevard* remains; age can indeed wither her and custom stale her infinite variety.

Notes

I would like to thank my colleague Carol A. Taylor for her tireless identification of actresses and films that made the construction of the database a reality, plus her suggestions at the outset of ideas for this chapter.

1. Academy Award nominees were selected because they offered a sample of "notable" performers and greater availability of birth date information for Oscar nominees. Both nominees for best and supporting actress are included. Neither the selection of Oscar nominees nor the selection of films is intended as a commentary on artistic merit of the performance or on the quality of the film. Random sampling allowed the viewing of a broad range of both good and bad films, many of which one might not otherwise choose to see.

References

Banner, L. W.
    1992 *In Full Flower: Aging Women, Power, and Sexuality*. New York: Knopf.

Bourdieu, P.
    1984 *Distinction: A Social Critique of the Judgement of Taste*. Cambridge: Harvard University Press.

Ellis, H.
    [1905] 1942 *Studies in the Psychology of Sex*. Vol. 1. New York: Random House.

Evans, C., and M. Thornton
1989 *Women and Fashion*. London: Quartet.

Foucault, M.
1975 *The Birth of the Clinic: An Archeology of Medical Perception*. New York: Vintage.
1979 *Discipline and Punish: The Birth of the Prison*. New York: Vintage.
1980 *The History of Sexuality*. Vol. 1. New York: Vintage.
1984 Politics and Ethics: An Interview. In *The Foucault Reader*. Edited by P. Rabinow, 32–50. New York: Pantheon Books.

Freud, S.
1958 The Disposition to Obsessional Neurosis. In *The Standard Edition of the Complete Psychological Works of Sigmund Freud*. Edited by J. Strachey. Vol. 12. London: Hogarth, 317–26.

Greer, G.
1991 *The Change: Women, Aging, and the Menopause*. New York: Knopf.

Hepworth, M.
1995 Images of Old Age. In *Handbook of Communication and Aging Research*. Edited by J. E. Nussbaum and J. Copeland, 5–37. Mahwah, N.J.: Lawrence Erlbaum Associates.

Kaplan, E. A.
1999 Trauma and Aging: Marlene Dietrich, Melanie Klein, and Marguerite Duras. In *Figuring Age: Women, Bodies, Generations*. Edited by K. Woodward, 171–94. Bloomington: University of Indiana Press.

Katz, S.
1996 *Disciplining Old Age: The Formation of Gerontological Knowledge*. Charlottesville: University of Virginia Press.
1999 Charcot's Older Women: Bodies of Knowledge at the Interface of Aging Studies and Women's Studies. In *Figuring Age: Women, Bodies, Generations*. Edited by K. Woodward, 112–27. Bloomington: University of Indiana Press.

Kozlowski, J.
1993 Women, Film, and the Midlife Sophie's Choice: Sink or Souzatzka? In *Menopause: A Midlife Passage*. Edited by J. C. Callahan, 3–22. Bloomington: University of Indiana Press.

Kuhn, A.
1982 *Women's Pictures: Feminism and Cinema*. London: Routledge & Kegan Paul.

Lovdahl, U., A. Riska, and E. Riska
1999 Gender Display in Scandinavian and American Advertising for Anti-depressants. *Scandinavian Journal of Public Health* 27(4): 306–10.

Mander, A. V.
1974 Her Story of History. In *Feminism as Therapy*. Edited by A. V. Mander and A. K. Rush, 63–88. New York: Random House.

Markson, E. W., and C. A. Taylor
1993 Real versus Reel World: Older Women and the Academy Awards. *Women and Therapy* 14(1/2): 157–72.
2000 The Mirror Has Two Faces. *Ageing and Society* 20: 137–60.

Tallmer, M.
1989 Empty-Nest Syndrome: Possibility or Despair. In *The Psychology of Today's Woman: New Psychoanalytic Visions*. Edited by T. Bernay and D. W. Cantor, 231–52. Cambridge: Harvard University Press.

Walker, A.
1979 *The Shattered Silents: How the Talkies Came to Stay*. New York: William Morrow.

Woodward, K.
1991 *Aging and Its Discontents: Freud and Other Fictions*. Bloomington: University of Indiana Press.

CHAPTER FOUR

IMAGES VERSUS EXPERIENCE
OF THE AGING BODY

Peter Öberg

On the one hand, sociological and gerontological discourse has homogenized aging bodies as "problem bodies," constructing these bodies as viewed through a particular lens. As a result, the "misery perspective" on aging has been perpetuated. On the other hand, we have witnessed new images for older people in popular culture where they—especially the young-old—are looking and dressing youthfully, having sex, dieting, actively traveling, and so forth. Becoming older seems to present, as Chris Gilleard and Paul Higgs (2000) have suggested, at least as many opportunities as problems, both for the individual and society. The intention of this chapter is to show how the aging body in late modernity is situated in this "gap" or "tension" between opportunities and problems, success and failure, youthful idealizations and prejudicial generalizations, new opportunities and ageist encounters, and virtual self-identity and marginalized social identities.

This rhetoric of ambivalence is also significant for Swedish social gerontological narratives in general, popularly called "the misery perspective" versus "the resource perspective."[1] In this chapter, I wish to introduce a series of contradictory images concerning the aging body. I will challenge many negative stereotypes of the aging body through empirical results gleaned from subjective experiences of the body obtained through a Swedish survey.

The youthful body has become a focal point for people's self-image. Daily, we are overwhelmed with "gerontophobic" messages of youthful ideals: how to stay young, how to get older without signs of aging, and how to "stop the clock." A majority of these messages are concerned with the female body and directed toward women. We are surrounded by pictures of slim, young bodies and are constantly reminded that individuals who work to take care of their bodies stay healthier, live longer, maintain their figure, and, in general, look "good." Television, film, and other visual media remind us that the slim and graceful body, with dimples in the attractive face, is the key to happiness—maybe even its essence (Featherstone 1994).

In the study on which this argument is based, I use Grogan's (1999) definition of body image. According to the author, body image is defined as "a person's perceptions, thoughts and feelings about his or her body" (p. 1). Our body image may in turn affect our ability to relate to others and will influence how others respond to us. Our body image is shaped not just by what we perceive our body should look like, but its place in wider societal and cultural discourses (Nettleton and Watson 1998). Thus, the biological changes that occur in the body through the "natural" aging process can be comprehended only within the cultural framework that exists to give them meaning (Hepworth and Featherstone 1998). Douglas ([1966] 1997) echoes these sentiments, explaining how the social body constrains the way that the physical body is perceived, for example, how the "same disease" can be experienced as an "illness" in varying ways in different cultural contexts. The physical experience of the body is always modified by the social categories through which it is known (see the proceeding for the different "liberation rhetorics" about the menopause).

Studies of the body are part and parcel of reasserting the significance of the day to day and the mundane in the aging experience. To a considerable degree, the days in everyday life are structured around the care of the body: getting up, dressing, washing, eating, excreting, and sleeping (Twigg 1999, 2000, chapter 5 in this volume). There is an emerging interest in the everyday experiences, in an "emic" or inner perspective of older people, that is not preoccupied with their health and potential frailty (Gilleard and Higgs 2000). Even the study on body image presented in the proceeding chapter is about the mundane and everyday experiences of the expressive and aesthetic body—not about health and illness. There has been little research concerning ordinary men's and women's personal bodily experiences, especially in an aging context. This study looks to contribute to this growing perspective on aging by its focus on how people perceive their own bodies through the life course.

The empirical study discussed here was performed in Sweden in 1998, a typical Western, late modern society and was based on a mailed survey to a random national sample of 1,997 men and women between the ages of 20 and 85 years. The response rate was 63 percent (1,250 respondents) and the respondent group was, in terms of age distributions statistically representative of the whole Swedish population within the corresponding age span. In terms of sex distributions, there was a small overrepresentation of women (55 percent among the respondents compared to 51 percent in the whole Swedish population in the corresponding age span). The results from this study will consequently be presented in the following text, integrated with theoretical discussions and results from other studies, and referred to as *our study* or *our Swedish study*.[2] All the results presented in figures are from our study. Methodological questions will also be presented throughout the text, mainly in the footnotes.

Self-Identity and Social Identity: A Disharmonious Relationship?

One source of contradictory images concerning the aging body is the noted discrepancy between self-identity and social identity. According to Erving Goffman (1972), *self-identity* refers to our own subjective view of ourselves, while *social identity* refers to the image of ourselves acknowledged through social interaction. In this section, I look to problematize the tension between these two identity concepts, central to the aging process, a tension between "outer" social images and inner experiences. Goffman notes that the body is a central medium in social interaction and mediates the relationship between an individual's social identity and self-identity.

The identity of body and self is challenged by bodily changes such as puberty, pregnancy, and menopause. According to Goffman we have a "shared language of bodily idiom" that guides people's perceptions of bodily appearances and provides us with a common schedule with which to classify embodied information. In this sense, the social meanings that are attached to particular bodily forms and performances may become internalized by an individual and therefore affect his or her sense of self. This has been documented by various studies of stigmatized bodies. The studies have made us acutely aware of the body as a political entity and central to self-identity (Synnott 1993). Indeed, we now see the self as an "embodied self." We know from Goffman ([1972] 1991) how appearance can be central to a person's social acceptability. To Goffman, it is the body-in-the-world. The body, as C. Wright Mills ([1959] 1985) might so eloquently term it, is most certainly both a public issue and a private matter.

Along with gender and ethnicity, our age roles are the principal determinants of our lives and practiced social identities. The concept of social identity also implies that people, as noted earlier, are classified by reference to their bodies. The body is a sort of mannequin that wears the signs of sex, power, and status. It is a construct that serves as the battleground for politics (Baerveldt and Voestermans 1998).

The difference between self-identity and social identity often becomes obvious in the aging process. In discussing social identity among elderly clients in community care, Julia Twigg (2000) writes that many caregivers experienced the old people as a fixed category, as if they had always been old, and though the workers knew intellectually that the old clients had once been young, they found it hard to grasp on an emotional and practical level. In the eyes of the caregivers, the old clients preferred to remain the people they always were, which by and large meant someone clothed, not naked, and capable of managing their own bodily functions. To our own self-identity, bodily experiences are central to memories of our own lives and, thus, in our own understanding of who and what we are (Nettleton and Watson 1998). Social identity, on the other hand, rests as a "frozen picture" lodged in present social interactions.

One theoretical concept building on the discrepancy between these two important identity concepts is *the mask of aging* (Featherstone and Hepworth 1991). This implies a negative identification—or disidentification—with the exterior body, but simultaneously offers a strategy for maintaining a positive and youthful self-concept. The mask refers to a gap between the exterior of the body, on the one hand, and the inner subjective feeling of self-identity, on the other—a gap that becomes more apparent as people age. Thus, the mask of aging implies a difference between *Feel-Age* (experienced age) and *Look-Age* (how old one looks). The outer body can be interpreted as a betrayal of the youthfulness of the inner self. This tension can be illuminated by quotations of age identification used in several texts, illuminating Sharon Kaufman's (1986) thesis in *The Ageless Self.* For example, listen to this aging man Eileen Fairhurst (1998) is referring to:

> I think you'll find yourself that you reach a stage where you don't grow any older inside. Outside you do but you're perpetually 28 or something or whatever it may be—wherever you stop. (P. 269)

In a biographical study conducted in Finland (Öberg 1996, 1997), informants were provided a mirror, instructed to gaze into the mirror, and asked to describe their reflection. An emerging way of describing the reflection was in accordance with the mask of aging theory, as proposed by Mike Featherstone and Mike Hepworth:

> I see a reflection of an ageing person, but who thus far is satisfied with his life. . . . One has changed a lot on the outside, not in the inside. As young in the inside as always (77-year-old man).

> It isn't a reflection of me. I know myself pretty well. . . . Spiritually I don't feel old, like "oh dear how old I am." But I can see it in the appearance (79-year-old woman).

This provides us with a useful example of a number of studies of older people where a discrepancy between social and self-identity is a central focus of the research. This raises a quite intriguing question, To what extent is the efficient marketing of youthful images reflected in people's phenomenological experience of aging, and to what extent do people see themselves as youthful?

In our Swedish study we measured *age identification* using three fill-in-the-blank questions: (1) "In my inner self I feel as if I am__years old." (2) "I would most like to be__years old." (3) "I think that other people see me as__years old." The first item addresses *Feel-Age;* the second, *Ideal-Age;* and the third, *Look-Age.* Means were calculated for the items on respondents' subjective ages. The experience of age reflects individual aging experiences and functional capacities, as well as social ages, age norms, and normative values in society. Feel-Age is about psychological functioning, Ideal-Age is about desired age, and Look-Age is about physical functioning and physical appearance (Uotinen 1998). Look-Age includes people's body images and the role physical appearance plays in the constitution of age identities. Previous studies have shown that older people tend to deny that they are "old" and maintain subjective age identities that are younger than their actual age (Goldsmith and Heiens 1992; Kastenbaum et al. 1972; Lehr and Puschner 1963; Linn and Hunter 1979; Montepare and Lachman 1989; Ruoppila 1992).

The maintenance of younger age identities is also confirmed in our study, where the vast majority (70 to 78 percent) of 20- to 85-year-old Swedes have lower subjective ages than their chronological age on all three studied indicators: Feel-Age, Ideal-Age, and Look-Age. The majority in all ages from 25 and above, thus, *feel* younger, *wish* to be younger, and *think that other people see them* as younger than they are. A minority (15 to 23 percent) report the same subjective as chronological age, and an even smaller minority (5 to 11 percent) report a higher subjective than chronological age (Öberg and Tornstam 2001).

However, even if people's subjective or experienced age is lower than their chronological age, figure 4.1 shows that the idea of an ageless self, or of the stopping of the clock, does not hold true as a general pattern among elderly Swedes. Even if the vast majority (as we see in figure 4.1) have lower subjective than chronological age, and this discrepancy grows by age, there is still a strong correlation between the two variables (see also Öberg and Tornstam 1999). One could, ordinarily, say that "the self seems to be aging, but not as fast as one's chronological age."[3]

Figure 4.1. The Discrepancy, for Respondents in Different Age Groups, between Chronological Age and (A) Look-Age, (B) Feel-Age, (C) Ideal-Age

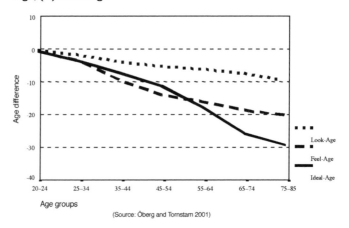

(Source: Öberg and Tornstam 2001)

Figure 4.1 displays how much younger than their actual age individuals *desire* to be, *feel* they are, and think they *appear to be* in the eyes of others. Discrepancies are nonexistent in the youngest age group, in which the ideal seems to be quite close to one's chronological age. However, the discrepancy grows with each subsequent age group for all three subjective variables. For respondents in their eighties, the general picture can be summarized as follows: they think they look like seventy, they feel like sixty and wish to be fifty.[4]

One central value and universal ideal in a late modern consumer society such as Sweden is youthfulness. A source of contradictory images is, as we have seen, a youthful self-identity acting in and through the aging body. According to Christopher Lasch (1981), central to a narcissistic personality is an orientation to the body as youthful, enduring, and constitutive of the self. The quintessentially modern person can be described as one who is young and never dies (Shilling 1993). Along these same lines, Featherstone and Hepworth (1991) have suggested that in late modern times the belief in eternal life has been replaced by the consumer culture's images of eternal youth.

Not surprisingly, among 65- to 85-year-old respondents in our Swedish study, four out of ten think that it is important to keep a youthful look and about half in this age group still consider themselves as youthful people (Öberg and Tornstam, 2001). In this sense, old people are *subjectively* younger than they are defined to be by society in terms of chronological age. To have a youthful age identity, to consider oneself younger than one's actual age, can be seen as a denial of aging and resistance to inclusion in the social stigma of old age.

Youth is now central to most of contemporary culture and to images in the "leisure industry."[5] And in the twenty-first century, those who actively contributed to the shaping of the postwar "youth culture"—the baby-boomer generation—are themselves approaching retirement age. The aging of the postwar youth culture generation is confounding and challenges the meaning of aging and old age. The creation of new methods for antiaging, such as increasing lifestyle aestheticization, exemplified by cosmetic surgery, is an exploding market that has originated largely from the baby-boomer generation (Gilleard and Higgs, 2000).[6] Marcene Goodman (1994) found that women who had undergone cosmetic surgery were satisfied with reconstructing their appearance so that it was now harmonious with their inner feelings of youthfulness, instead of resigning themselves to age-related bodily changes.

Hepworth and Featherstone (1982) have suggested that the new image of middle age is one whereby the battle against aging becomes a social duty. People in middle age, in "the new midlifestyle" are not expected to accept aging with resignation. A pioneer in the sociology of the body, Bryan Turner (1984), goes even further than this, arguing that "the new anti-Protestant ethic defines premature ageing, obesity and unfitness as sins of the flesh" (p. 251). Instead, this new midlife is presented as a chance for self-realization and personal growth. Now one can enjoy an endless "middle youth" (Featherstone and Hepworth 1991). We can now, through the consumption of lifestyles, realize different "possible selves" (Gergen 1991; Gilleard and Higgs 1996) and actively determine *how* to be old: what to wear, where to live, how to look, and so on. In our time, self-identity is the self as reflexively understood by the individual.

Questions like: How shall I live? Shall I continue my marriage? Shall I live together or apart with my partner? Shall I start a new job or a new education? Shall I have gray or dark hair? All must be answered through practical, day-to-day decisions about how to behave. An embodied identity is a negotiated process whereby the individual actively and creatively draws on cultural resources for making sense of who he or she is, who he or she was, and who he or she might become (cf. with Davis 1995). Along these same lines, for Giddens (1991), life "politics" is about the freedom of choice to create morally justifiable forms of life that promote self-actualization.

Elders today are active "consumers of leisure" rather than people who have retired from production and disappeared into the winter land of old age. A change has occurred. Retirement is now a "personal project." This "agentic" construction of identities also offers new possibilities for older people to break with stereotypical images and contribute to reforming new images more in line with one's inner experiences. It is necessary to recognize aging as something individuals have to engage in and make choices about—instead of seeing aging as something that just "happens" to people (Gilleard and Higgs, 2000). In this context, a developing new stage of life, the Third Age, represents a culturally new position in our increasingly age-conscious society. A time where the aged are offered new and exciting possibilities for a personal identity that is exiting, desirable, attractive, and consumable.[7]

The Performing Self

In the discussion of identities and images in consumer culture, the performing self, or the self on an arena for public display, has become central to sociological theorizing. According to Shilling (1993), the body achieves greater significance as a marker for self in high modernity.[8] When meaning is more privatized, as some have argued, people seek meaning at the individual, private level—through their bodies. The body has quickly emerged as a basic, experiential marker of self-identity. In a world dominated by visual representations, consumer culture is preoccupied with more "marketable selves." Important to this is the production of "perfect bodies" as vehicles for self-expression, pleasure, and display. The beauty industry impinges and intersects with the clothing industry, the hairdressing industry, the cosmetic surgery industry, the food industry, the fitness business, and the media and advertising industry (Synnott 1993), all focusing on bodily maintenance and its improvement.

It is perhaps the beauty industry that has prospered the most in light of our increasing attention to creating the attractive body, whether aged or not. In fact, the "ordering" of the surface of the body has led to a new science—cosmetology (Turner 1984). In the 1950s, creams and cosmetics for women focused on the face, certainly only one aspect of bodily care and its production. While women certainly aimed at having "attractive figures," many women achieved this through underwear that molded and concealed the body and clothing that hid the bodies. In later years, this changed drastically. By the 1980s, the bodies were dieted, toned, and exercised into the required shape. Now visible control and ordering of the body was extended much further than the face. It could all be changed! The 1980s saw a massive expansion in creams and lotions aimed at the body-as-a-whole (shower gels, body lotions, allover moistures, exfoliants, anticellulite creams, and so on).

This development also reflects new demands being made on the body, its appearance, and its representation (Twigg 2000). Cosmetic practices are indicative of the new presentational self, the Goffmanian self, in a society where the self is no longer lodged in formal roles, but validated in a competitive, public space. Unlike those who became pensioners in the immediate postwar era, women who were born after the First World War became accustomed to cosmetics as intrinsic to their public, social presentation. They were and are used for "putting on their face" (Gilleard and Higgs 2000).

Our present world is a highly visual one. We are bombarded with visual messages from the time we wake up to the time we go to sleep (Synnott 1993). Blaikie (1999a) talks of the rise of visual culture stemming from the great motion picture industry and the mechanisms that Hollywood, television, and market models have used to codify our assumptions about youthful beauty. Lasch (1981) echoes this sentiment, suggesting that we live in a "hall of mirrors" (p. 66). Within the consumer culture the body is both desirable and desiring. As noted in the previous discussion, the closer the physical body approximates the idealized images of youth, health, fitness, and beauty, the higher its exchange value.

> Self preservation depends upon the preservation of the body within a culture in which the body is the passport to all that is good in life. Health, youth, beauty, sex, fitness are the positive attributes that body care can achieve and preserve. (Featherstone 1982, 26)

In today's visual culture, a world abounding with "appearance junkies," experience and maturity have limited social capital (Bauman 1994). But are images, accentuating beautiful, youthful performances, corresponding to people's own experiences of the aging bodies? Influenced by sociological theorizing of the aging body, where "youth = beauty = health" (Featherstone 1994), we asked the respondents in our study, "In which age do you think you were/are/will be physically most attractive?" Means were then calculated for the item.[9]

Figure 4.2 shows that people, regardless of chronological age, seem to follow dominant messages in consumer culture. They are/were/will be at their highest level of physical attractiveness in a rather short period of their lives before entering middle age: women in the age span of 28–35 years, and men in the age span of 28–39 years.

However, even if people consider themselves as *most* attractive in this short period of time, they could, of course, still experience themselves as attractive and sexually appealing in different ages, though not to the same degree. Figure 4.3 shows that the proportion of both men and women who agree to the statement, "My body is sexually appealing," diminishes by each successive age group.[10]

Supporting the results in figure 4.2, the response pattern in figure 4.3 also shows a diminished experienced sexual appeal by age. For male

Figure 4.2. Level of Physical Attractiveness

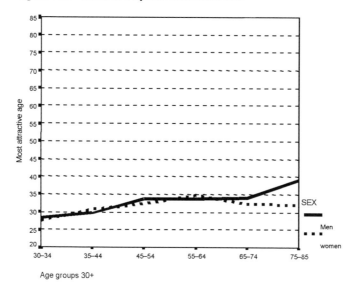

Age groups 30+

Figure 4.3. Sexual Appeal by Age

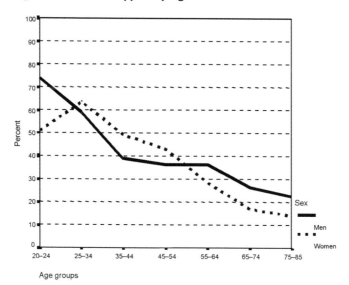

Age groups

respondents the proportion who think their body is sexually appealing diminishes from 74 percent among the youngest to 22 percent among the oldest (eta = .30, p<.001). For female respondents, the proportion is 51 to 14 percent (eta = .33, p<.001). Among the retirees (65–85), a much smaller minority, 25 percent of the male and 16 percent of the female respondents, evaluate their bodies as "sexually appealing." However, I suggest that age is only one explanation for the variation in experienced sexual appeal among different age groups. While there is variation, the difference between those 20–34 and those aged 35–64 is not remarkably striking. This leads us to consider what other variable might possibly be at work here.

So while the results, on the whole, seem to support a correspondence, or harmony, between age-resisting images in consumer culture and subjective experiences of youthfulness, there are certainly other cultural forces in play. In the next section I will concentrate on sexuality as an important formative aspect of body image and, in turn, discuss older people's experiences in relation to sexualized images of youth and desexualized images of old age.

Older People's "Silent" Experiences in a Sexualized Society

The cross-sectional data in figure 4.3 points us toward the hypothesis that aging implies an experience of decreased sexual appeal. Turner speaks of a "sexualization of society" by which we are forced to be sexually acceptable in order to be socially acceptable (Turner 1984). The "we" Turner speaks about seems to be only one "we"—those people who exist up to middle age. This places the aged in a bit of a quandary.

One possible interpretation of the effect of youthful, sexualized images in consumer culture could be that old people are marginalized and made "invisible" to people in general. The contrast becomes obvious in a culture where we value sexuality as a fundamental asset of younger people and simultaneously refuse to acknowledge it in older ones. However, this has led us to neglect an important aspect of it all—gender and masculinity. In *Older Men's Lives*, Thompson (1994) argues that gender studies on men have been "age blind." According to Twigg (2000), studies about masculinities have advocated a narrow "overphallusized" picture of man focusing on issues like violence, aggression, war, and sexuality (especially gay sexuality). The studies emphasize strength, violence, and virility, things that may not be relevant to the bodily experiences of older men.[11] As a contrast to this phallusized image, frail, old, and visible bodies may confront many late modern dreams of autonomy, boundedness, and youthful success. In discussing her study on bathing in community care, Twigg writes explicitly of this strange absence:

> Culture provides us with almost no images of the ageing body un-clothed, so when we do encounter the reality of such, it comes as a vi-sual shock. . . . We have little sense culturally of aesthetic pleasure in old flesh, or of what a beautiful old body might look like. . . . Older people thus experience their ageing bodies in the context of a profound cultural silence. (P. 46)

Thus, we have a contrast between highly prized images of young, slim, and sexual bodies in contemporary consumer culture and aging bodies, se-questrated from public attention (Shilling 1993). One example of the process of making elderly bodies invisible was the first national survey on sexuality in Sweden. In this study, the oldest studied age group was sixty-year-old people. This took place even though the sociologist involved in the study warned that "one obviously has to go higher up in the ages to es-tablish the point where sexual activity is ceasening" (Zetterberg 1969, 38).[12] A second example is a Swedish study of images in retirement greet-ing cards, where a dominant message is that the retiree is independent and in the position of choosing an individual style of life. In the retirement cards, the body is not at center of the cultural discourse, but is marginal-ized almost to symbolical invisibility. Indeed, at times the aged body is ex-changed with all types of animal bodies, such as ducks or elephants (Gaunt 1998). A third example is a study of senior dancing in Sweden, popularly called "raisins disco," "wrinkles disco," or "prostate dance," where Ronström (1998) describes the desexualization inherent to the dancing practice:

> What makes senior dancing different from most other forms of dance is that the bodily movements are so heavily undercommunicated. . . . The movement of the group is more important than the movement of the individual. . . . In Sweden in the 1990s originates new dancing

places around the country frequented by people in very mature age, on weekdays, during daytime, with all lamps on, where sobriety is a demand and scoring often is counteracted, where women have taken the leading position and where the dance and music is disconnected from Baccus and Venus and has changed into keep-fit activities for body and soul. (P. 251–57)

A fourth example of the marginalization of aging bodies is the invisibility or underpresentation of the elderly in mass media and popular film (Grogan 1999; Hajjar 1997; Huston et al. 1992; Markson, chapter 3 in this volume; Robinson and Skill 1995; Vernon et al. 1990). Older men are represented significantly more frequently than older women, and men in their fifties, even sixties, can still be portrayed on film as attractive and sexual (Grogan 1999; Markson and Taylor 2000). When older women are specifically portrayed in films, they usually embody ageist stereotypes (Markson and Taylor 2000)—represented as unattractive, without function, and perhaps even bored or boring. Older women are rarely portrayed as sexual, and sexual desire in older women is usually a point of ridicule: "Rarely are older women portrayed as capable and independent, never as sexually attractive" (Itzin 1986).[13] When old women are portrayed in sexual roles, they usually have a youthful appearance, and the director often avoids exposing the body of the actress by implying sexual activity, rather than displaying the body seminude or nude (Grogan 1999; Bildtgård, 2000).

To this point, the discussion in this section has concerned representations and images in consumer culture, often negatively ignoring or desexualizing elderly people. But another concern arises. Social gerontological discourse about aging and the aging self has been rather silent about sexuality in general and all the more so about the relationship between aging sexuality and masculine/feminine identities. One interpretation is, as Gilleard and Higgs (2000) suggest, that gender becomes a less salient source of social differentiation at older ages than it does at younger ages, because sexuality is expressed weakly—if at all—in old age.

However, this interpretation is not in line with arguments about *gendered ageism* (an issue touched on in the preceding paragraph about images of old people in popular film). According to "the double standard of ageing-thesis" (Sontag 1979) often touched on in social gerontological literature, bodily aging confronts women with the failure to maintain the standard of idealized feminine images. Therefore, many argue that the aging process affects older women much more than older men. According to Susan Sontag, women's power is embedded in perishable values of beauty and sexual allure, while men's power is embedded in more enduring values of status and wealth. Adams and Laurikietis (1976) argue that women are often ashamed of aging because aging is linked in the public mind with a lessening of attractiveness. Ginn and Arber (1993) write that the double jeopardy of aging causes great anxiety for women as the visible signs of aging increase inexorably:

> Because women's value is sexualised, positively in the first half of life, negatively in the second, . . . aware that loss of a youthful appearance brings social devaluation, women are vulnerable to immense pressure to ward off the signs of ageing with an armoury of cosmetic aids and, especially in the U.S., surgery. (Ginn and Arber 1993, 61)

According to Frida Furman (1997), a woman who does not invest in her appearance, who fails to "put on a face," and rebels against feminine practices can easily be seen as a deviant or "misfit." Being overweight represents the clearest failure in the maintenance of ideal femininity. Furman describes the experience of moral failure among older women who, though they try, are unable to meet normative ideals of femininity. In her study, older women's "reading" of their bodies was in constant tension with images of youth—their own, their friends, acquaintances, or public figures like actresses and models. The cultural elevation of youth and youthful ideals of attractiveness serve as the norm against which all women are evaluated, both by others and by themselves. As women grow older they acquire, according to Furman, a spoiled identity. This includes an inscribed invisibility through the loss of respected social roles and the perceived loss of femininity.

As part of the double standard of aging, women in several studies have been judged to enter middle and old age earlier than men (Bernard et al. 1995; Drevenstedt 1976; Hagestad and Neugarten 1985; Uutela et al. 1994).[14] In line with this, a Finnish survey in which respondents were asked what the important factors associated with aging were, a "change of looks" was evaluated as a much more important factor for women than for men (Uutela et al. 1994).[15] Miriam Bernard et al. (1995) speak of gendered ageism as having profoundly negative effects, both on attitudes toward old women and on women's own attitudes, beliefs, and behavior, stating that "women tend to look at their disadvantages rather than what they have to offer" (p. 63).

These arguments about gendered ageism imply that the aging process and age-related bodily changes have much more detrimental effects on women than on men. In our Swedish survey, we asked men and women about the experience of age-related changes in their appearance. The pattern in figure 4.4 shows that there is no significant variation between genders among all age groups to the question, "Are you disturbed by age-related changes in your appearance?"[16]

Among all respondents (30–85) there is a significant gender gap in the answers given. Only 22 percent of the male respondents are disturbed by age-related changes in their appearance compared to the double that (45 percent) among the female respondents. According to ageistic assumptions, one would have expected an increased percentage by successive age groups who are disturbed by age-related changes in their appearance as a part of an increased desexualization by age, especially among women. However, we do not find any such age correlation. The results seem to support sexist—but not ageist—values in society. The sexist values that lead women to believe that

Figure 4.4. Gender and Age-Related Changes in Appearance

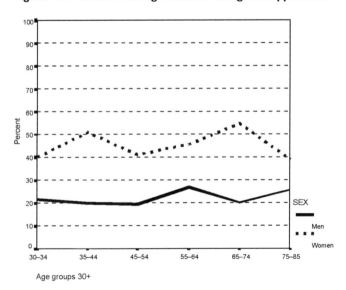

Age groups 30+

age-related bodily changes are much more damaging to a positive sense of self are the same among the young and middle aged, as among old people. This alerts us to the great importance of gender in phenomenological concerns of the relationship between body and self.

But the insecurity and threat of desexualization just discussed concerning older women also focuses our analytic attention on men. Middle age is marked by the onset of a bodily decline that challenges self-identity and makes the middle years a period of uncertainty for men as well, a transition termed *the male menopause* (Hepworth and Featherstone 1998). The analysis of the male menopause cannot take place outside the context of a society in which aging into old age is seen as problematic and in which relationships between men and women are undergoing significant changes. Just as the menopausal woman is a nonproducer of children, the menopausal man is seen as a nonproducer at work, in his sexual relationships, and personal relationships.

In *The Seasons of Man's Life* (1978), Levinson characterizes late adulthood in a discontinuous imagery, as if aging is a negation of masculinity. In a U.S. study in which people were asked to complete the sentence "An old man . . . ," the older men were depicted as sedentary. They were resting on a park bench, passing time, and asexual. Images of older men portrayed a diminished masculinity. In the literature on older men, two competing models prevailed: one based on the continuity of gender across the life span and another, discontinuous model, wherein the older man is emasculated because of aging (Thompson 1994). David Gutmann and Margaret Huyck (1994) studied old hospitalized male veterans. Their work showed that the greatest fear for these men, who had fought in wars, was their own emerging passivity and vulnerability to their newly assertive wives "when they become aware of the gender shifts in themselves and their wives, the dystonic dependent men felt castrated" (p. 69).

As opposed to these negative images of emasculated aging, Gutmann and Huyck (1994) argue, in line with the discontinuous developmental model, that in the transition to postparental life, men experience a reorganization of their sexual life and adopt new versions of manhood with broadened gender styles and new possibilities. Furthermore, changing technologies offer new and contradictory opportunities for multiple masculinities. Viagra has rapidly bypassed its role as a treatment for specific pathologies, to become the means for older men to "reverse" their aging and restore a synthetic youthful sexual performance (Gilleard and Higgs, 2000). Viagra is a way for men to perform important self-work, restoring a phenomenological sense of the youthful, sexualized self.

In our Swedish study we asked the respondents two questions: "Do you look masculine?" and "Do you look feminine?" The results are in figure 4.5 and in the following discussion. The proportion of men who think they look masculine diminishes with each successive age group (eta = .18, p<.01). There is no significant comparable change among women who believe they look feminine. Among male respondents in the youngest age group, 92 percent think that they look masculine compared to only 56 percent of the oldest ones. Among the female respondents, 91 percent of the youngest women think that they look feminine. Of the women in the oldest age group, 87 percent still feel this way. According to the hypothesis of the double standard of aging, one would expect the opposite result: that men subjectively stay masculine much longer, while women lose their femininity at a younger age. But the results of the experiences in our study on the contrary show a possible tendency for increased senses of lost masculinity among older men. Again, when looked at subjectively, the experience of the everyday practice of gender presents a much different picture than reported elsewhere.

Figure 4.5. Aging and the Appearance of Masculinity and Femininity

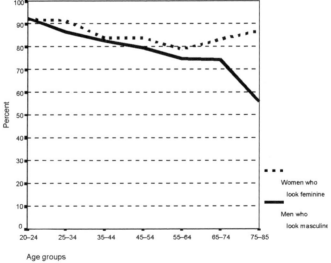

However, this is not to say that this always holds true. Other studies do seem to support Sontag's thesis of a gendered ageism and the "double standard of aging," with different gender norms for age-appropriate behavior throughout the life span favoring men. In line with the images in popular film previously discussed that allow men to perform sexual roles with (often) younger women, many studies have reported a higher degree of sexual activity among older men than women (e.g., Bruun Pedersen 1988; Lewin 1997; Ronkainen 1998). In our Swedish study we asked the respondents about their *own experienced* sexuality. As figure 4.6 points out, the proportion of both men and women who agree to the statement "To be sexually active is important for me" diminishes by each successive age group. For male respondents the proportion diminishes from 77 percent among the youngest to 33 percent among the oldest ones (eta = .31, p<.001) and for female respondents from 73 percent to 11 percent (eta = .41, p<.001). In this figure, the difference between men and women is interesting, especially among the aged. When 52 percent of the young-old (65–74) and 33 percent of the old-old (75–85) male respondents agree to the statement, the comparable percentages among older women are only 15 percent and 11 percent.[17] Thus, these data suggest that the sexualized body is a paramount body for men and not so much for women. In their own subjective concerns,

Figure 4.6. Aging and Sexual Activity

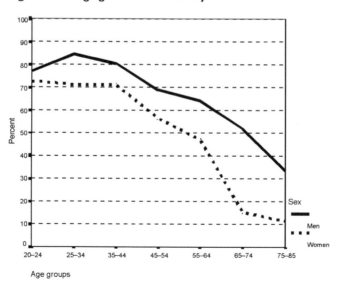

men hold on to this in greater numbers than women, seeing their body as discursively constructed around and through sexual practices.

This figure displays significant gendered discrepancies among the retirees based on sexualized or desexualized identities. In line with the previous discussion, only 14 percent of the older women (65–85), but still 45 percent of the older men, think that it is important for them to be sexually active. These gender differences in the response patterns can, and probably are, strongly affected by generational differences.[18] Gender "inequality" can be an effect of different moral standards, where the men who are old today have had more sexual freedom than today's older women. A cohort emphasis provides us with an intriguing new area of study as we continue to investigate the subjective body.

The Aging Body as the Enemy

From the preponderance of gerontophobic images concerning youthful performances and self-presentations, we could logically deduce a fear of growing old, an issue I discuss in this last section of the chapter. Gilleard and Higgs (2000) argue that aging in late modernity represents an ever-present risk to the success of identity projects based on choice and negotiation. Resisting not just old age, but aging itself, is becoming an integral component of many adult lifestyles. Physical exercise, self-control, dieting, and other techniques of bodily discipline are vibrant methods of this resistance.

But awareness of aging serves as an ever-present premonition that such aspirations are, in the end, beyond our reach. In this sense, the aging identity is increasingly framed through resistance—an identity of staying young, of choosing not to grow old, that the results in age identification in the preceding may indicate. The desire to feel young is effectively internalized and expressed in terms of the entrance into midlife as an awareness of the onset of age as a profoundly ... welcome experience (Hepworth and Featherstone 1998). Thus, we return to the tension, or "struggle," mentioned in the beginning of this chapter: success and new opportunities on one hand, risk of failure on the other. In our study, we asked the respondents if "they look forward to growing old" (figure 4.7). It is certainly not surprising at all that it seems to be a small minority of people who actually look forward to the "new opportunities" growing old might offer.

Figure 4.7. Percentage of Men and Women in Different Age Groups Who Agree with the Statement: "I Look Forward to Growing Old"

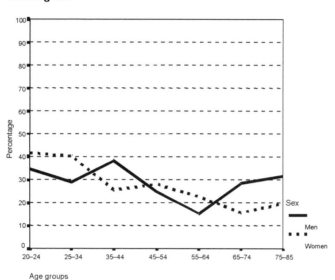

Age groups

Only 28 percent of the men and 29 percent of the women look forward to growing old. And it is only a negligible minority, 5 percent of the male respondents and 4 percent of the female respondents, who "agree to a high extent" to the statement. Among women, only in the two youngest age groups (20–34) more than 40 percent look forward to growing old, and then the proportion diminishes (eta = .19, p<.001). Among the male respondents, the proportion who look forward to growing old varies greatly between age groups, from 15 percent to 38 percent (eta = .16, p<.05), but there is no significant difference between men and women concerning this issue. One would assume from the gendered ageism thesis concerning the detrimental effects on women's aging that this would certainly not be the case, yet subjectively we find this argument does not hold.

The aging body is rapidly becoming an important element in late modern uncertainty over what constitutes the normal body. One can, as Gilleard and Higgs (2000) do, ask, is it ageism that causes people to undergo cosmetic surgery—or is it ageism that prevents or restricts the accessibility of such surgery? This interesting question tells us much about the relationship between the current social world and the body. According

to Chrisler and Ghiz (1993), it may be difficult for people to feel comfortable about aging in a culture where older people are made invisible,
and those who are seen are celebrated primarily for their "youthful" good
looks. As noted earlier, Fairhurst (1998) found that women worried more
than men about their image in the coming old age and worked to maintain their youthful appearance. The aging body is an uncomfortable entity.

A great fear associated with aging is the fear of "bodily betrayals."
That the body becomes an unpredictable force stigmatizing the person
through "destructive information" and constructing a bodily production
where it is impossible for the individual to present him or herself in a fa-
vorable light (see Featherstone and Hepworth 1990; Frank 1991; Öberg
1996). We asked the respondents about these potential fears of bodily aging. Figure 4.8 displays the percentage of respondents in different age
groups who agree to the statement, "I am worried that my body will fall
into decay when I grow older."

The responses show no significant variation by age. However, gender
seems to have a stronger influence. Among all respondents, 25 percent of
the men agree to the statement compared to 36 percent of the women.
Worries about bodily changes generally seem to affect women more than

**Figure 4.8. Percentage of Men and Women in Different Age
Groups Who Agree with the Statement: "I Am Worried That My
Body Will Fall into Decay When I Grow Older"**

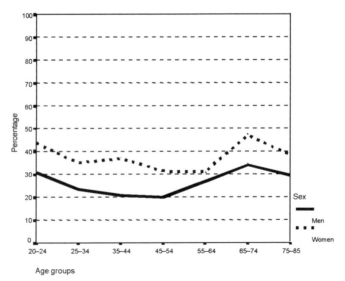

men, even if the difference is statistically significant only in age groups between 25 and 54 years. These worries about bodily decay when growing older do not support any sense of gendered ageism. Instead, different standards are affecting women more negatively than men—*regardless* of age. In the end, gender as practically experienced is the dominant force here, not the theoretically supposed age.

There is, in prospect, a substantial majority who generally do not look forward to growing old and a substantial minority that express worries about bodily changes in the future. But despite this fact, at present, the majority of the respondents, regardless of age, are satisfied with their bodies. Figure 4.9 shows the percentage of respondents in different age groups who agree to the statement, "I am satisfied with my body."

Among all respondents, 74 percent of the women and 88 percent of the men are satisfied with their bodies. In the *youngest* age group, 92 percent of the male respondents and only 63 percent of the female respondents are satisfied with their bodies. Among the oldest respondents, the corresponding difference has diminished to 84 percent for male and 76 percent for female respondents. The difference between men and women is significant in all groups up to sixty-four (except for 35- to 44-year-old

Figure 4.9. Percentage of Men and Women in Different Age Groups Who Agree with the Statement: "I Am Satisfied with My Body"

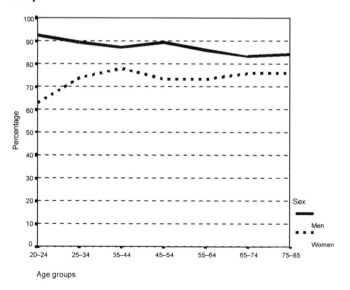

respondents), but among older people it ceases to be statistically signifi-cant.[19] So even if the aging body often may be represented as an enemy, the majority do not seem to experience their body in that way.

Discussion

In this chapter, I have introduced a series of contradictory images con-cerning the aging body. These images are discussed in the context of the consumer culture in our late modern society. They are gerontophobic in their presentation of youthful sexualized images, an image market in which older people are marginalized and older bodies made invisible. As a consequence, our Western culture has become increasingly visual (see Baudrillard 1983) and new demands are made on the body and its public appearance. In sociological theorizing, this is described by concepts such as performing selves, selves on public display, marketable selves, bodies as vehicles for self-expression, and bodies for pleasure.

In our contemporary landscape, people are also increasingly classified by references to their bodies and the manner in which these things affect their social identity. The "reading" of our bodies is in constant tension with im-ages of youth. The process of aging has been described as representing an ever-present risk to the success of long-term identity projects. One aspect of these negative, or gerontophobic images, is gendered ageism. In a society where there are different standards for men's and women's aging, the aging process is seen as having a detrimental effect on older women, who in the public mind are becoming less attractive with a femininity rapidly disap-pearing. The suggested "victimization" of female aging has also affected men's aging as well. Concepts such as the male menopause, in which aging represents a threat in the form of decreased masculinity and desexualisation, point us toward an arena of study that is rapidly increasing.

All these varied arguments alert us to the importance of the social world and its claims on the body. We "read" our bodies through interpre-tive lenses that are the direct reflection and construction of the culture and society we inhabit. The interesting question here is *how* the cultural im-ages and stereotypes of aging and old people may affect this reading. One hypothesis is presented in the "mask of aging" argument, suggesting a growing discrepancy between social identity and self-identity. However, we know little about how these images affect the individuals' *experience* of growing old. One risk with a cultural studies approach to the body and aging is that dominant social values are possibly considered as synonymous with subjective experiences of aging. Thus, we should distinguish between images of the aging body in popular and consumer culture and individuals' subjective experiences of their own bodies and their own aging. This is a very important switch in focus to the lived experience of the aging body.

My intention in this chapter has been to use the empirical results from our Swedish study to document subjective claims and how these relate to wider, theorized claims. Often contradictory images are presented. A possible theoretical explanation to these contradictory images concerns new and increasing positive images of aging and new possibilities for aging identities represented by the development of the Third Age. Images are, of course, important enough to be studied in "their own right," independent of how well or poor they correspond to people's experiences. But we must not forget our elders' own voices as they experience the aging body in everyday praxis. By acknowledging the importance of this as an arena of study, our understanding of the aging process only increases as another piece of the puzzle, as it were, is found (see Gubrium and Holstein 1999, chapter 7 in this volume).

The results from our study in Sweden show that men and women—of all ages—have internalized these images of youthfulness. A majority of the respondents report younger subjective ages than their chronological age, and roughly half of the old (65+) still consider themselves to be "youthful persons." In accordance with this, the respondents thought that they were/are/will be physically most attractive in the rather short age span between 28 and 39 years. The older the respondent, the less he or she thought that their body was sexually appealing. Differences by age were also shown concerning the sexualized body. The proportion who think that it is important to be sexually active decreased by each successive age group, with the data suggesting that older people—especially older women—are much more marginalized from this social arena than other age groups. An unexpected finding concerning gender was that older men reported a decreased masculinity while older women did not report this same concern with femininity.

The hypothesis of the "double standard of aging" received support from some of the results, but certainly not all. These results display a variation—both according to age *and* sex. In short, women report more negative experiences than men and also show an increase in negative experiences by each successive age group. This was especially true in the responses in figure 4.6, where it was much more important to be sexually active for older men than older women. However, data gathered from other studies support the argument that we can expect this gap to decrease in the future.

However, many results did not show any variation by gender (see figure 4.1). This includes the subjective experience of one's most attractive age and the experience of being sexually appealing. This was also the case concerning the attitude to one's process of growing old. If the result about the experience of masculine/feminine look is suggesting any gendered ageism, this is not concerning women—but men. So, though gendered ageism is an important issue, we should be aware of projecting oversimplified, victimizing, negative images on older women. Again, we must attend to the aging experience, not simply its representation.

The results to several questions on body image indeed show this to be a more "problematic" and "disturbing" issue for women than men—in many cases regardless of age. In all ages, women are much more disturbed than men by age-related bodily changes, and young and middle-age women are more worried than men about projected bodily decay and presently less satisfied with their bodies. When the results do show differences by gender, but not age, we should be quite careful not to mix, or confuse, ageism with sexism. One jeopardy does not necessarily, by definition, mean double jeopardies.

It should also be noted that the results from our study on body image and experiences of the aging body are based on cross-sectional survey data. This is discussed in relation to the results in figure 4.6 but could be discussed concerning all results. The strengths of this type of data are that it makes generalizations possible in reference to a large population of men and women of different ages. Empirical studies of the body are often focused on very special groups of the population with only one gender represented and rarely in an aging perspective or context. There are, of course, many limitations with surveys. This includes the "fact" that we cannot know for sure the *meaning* of the responses.

The meaning of "growing old" will very likely be different for respondents in their twenties from those in their sixties. We can also assume that sexuality, sexual activity, and desexualization can have different meanings in different periods of the life cycle. According to Peck (1968), the physical and sexual should be toned down and be subordinated to the spiritual in order to achieve a successful aging. The results in figure 4.6, where only a small minority of older people think that it is important to be sexually active, should, according to Peck, not be interpreted as any form of marginalization, but rather a manifestation of successful aging, where older women seem to be much more successful than older men (for contradictory discourses and interpretation of the meaning of sexuality, see also note 19).[20] In this case, more qualitative studies are needed to identify different meanings of the aging body.

In conclusion, the results from this survey on body image are in accord with a variety of other studies concerned with attitudes toward aging. This, like many other social gerontological studies, shows that general ascribed problems to old age—loneliness, low life-satisfaction, retirement trauma, and so on—do not correspond to old people's own experiences. From the growth of gerontology as a discipline, the field has been dominated by a "misery perspective" focusing on "problems of aging." However, we know that it is often only a minority of older people who experience these difficulties, as subjectively defined, in their everyday life. And if young and middle-aged people, as well, are included in the studies, the minority experiencing problems in their everyday life is often as significant as among older people. So despite youthful self-images in relation to bodies, the majority of elders seem to be rather satisfied with their own bodies, a quite opposite finding to what we might expect from the images of aging presented to us everyday.

Notes

This work has been stimulated by seminars within the Social Gerontological Group at the Department of Sociology, Uppsala University. The Social Gerontological Group is composed of, in addition to the author, Gunhild Hammarström, Ph.D., professor; Lars Andersson, Ph.D., associate professor; Marianne Winqvist, Ph.D.; Fereshteh Ahmadi, Ph.D.; Sandra Torres, Ph.D.; Torbjörn Bildtgård, B.A.; and Karatu Kiemo, M.SSc. In addition, the research was funded by The Swedish Council for Social Research and the Faculty of Social Science, Uppsala University. The home page of the Social Gerontology Group is at www.soc.uu.se/research/gerontology/.

1. The ambivalent attitudes toward aging stated in the preceding are also, according to Synnott (1993), characteristic of attitudes toward the body in general. From the Pauline teachings we know that the body should be bruised, but honored; mastered, but hallowed; crucified, but glorified; and it's an enemy, but also a temple and a member of Christ, and these "double messages" have continued throughout the centuries. They are evident even today in a deep ambivalence toward the body in general and sexuality in particular.

2. This study is a continuation of a research project about aging and body image carried out together with Professor Lars Tornstam (see Öberg and Tornstam 1999, 2001; Öberg 2000).

3. There is a strong correlation by age group for the age difference in relation to chronological age in the figure; for Look-Age (eta = .45, p< .001), for Feel-Age (eta = .53, p< .001), for Ideal-Age (eta = .68, p< .001). If we do not compare the *difference*, but instead compare the chronological age and Feel-Age, this correlation is even much higher (see also Öberg and Tornstam, 1999).

4. The results in this figure are not presented separately for men and women because there is no significant gender difference in terms of Feel-Age and Ideal-Age, and only a small difference in Look-Age, where older men thought that other people viewed themselves as younger than older women do.

5. The struggle against old age is, of course, not any new historical phenomenon, but rather a phenomenon that has taken different expressions in different times. According to the historian Riitta Oittinen (1994) the *commercial* youth culture broke through after the First World War. In Finland, a Nordic neighbor to Sweden, the first advertising agencies were established in the 1920s, and in 1930, products like skin creams and perfume soaps were rarities in the Finnish countryside. Even in the capital of Helsinki, there were only three beauty salons at that time. Though bodily care, as well as rejuvenation, wasn't a new issue, it lost its connotation with a luxurious life only for the upper class and started to become— or at least was marketed as—a duty for all social classes. In commercials for Nivea soap, it was said that a smooth, nonwrinkled face did not only belong to the upper class, but was necessary for everyone (p. 213).

6. There are no national statistics on the development or use of cosmetic and aesthetic surgery in Sweden, even if we do know that this is a growing medical branch. In our Swedish study, a negligible minority, 2 percent of the men and 3 percent of the women, responded that they had actually undergone cosmetic surgery. However, among the women, 28 percent "would consider having cosmetic surgery in order to get a more beautiful body," 21 percent "would consider having cosmetic surgery in order to get a more beautiful face," and 16 percent "would consider having cosmetic surgery in order to achieve a younger appearance." The corresponding figures among male respondents were 10, 10, and 8 percent (Öberg, 2000).

7. The Third Age represents—like adolescence—transition phases in which individuals are considered to be out of the previous age category but not yet into the next. This late midlife crisis—as well as teenage trauma—provides the social license to experiment with norms, values, and personal conduct (Blaikie, 1999b).

8. By the late 1920s, sunbathing, which previously had been considered a treatment for tuberculosis, became widely fashionable. The beach transformed itself into a site for mass exposure, and for the first time, sunbathing on the beach brought together large numbers of people in varying degrees of undress, legitimating the public display of the body (Featherstone, 1999).

9. The sample in this study was 20- to 85-year-old Swedes. However, some questions in the survey were asked only of respondents in the 30+ age. This is the case for the results presented in both figures 4.2 and 4.4.

10. In *our survey*, the responses to most attitudes were measured by statements with four response alternatives: "Agree to a high extent," "Agree to a moderate extent," "Hardly agree," and "Do not agree at all." In the figures, the percentage of the respondents who agree to a "high" or "moderate" extent to the statements are grouped together and shown, differentiated by age group.

11. According to Blaikie (1999b), the field of cultural sociology has been characterized by a generational bias that has clearly privileged youth over age. Youth has occupied a center stage in both popular culture and sociological investigation since the 1960s. Cunningham and Jacka (1997; cf. Blaikie, 1999b, 131) sees in cultural studies the presentation of a "skewed sense of culture as merely modern, youthful, fashionable, MTV-vise, consumerist. . . . It is life, the self, the culture as one long *Saturday Night Fever*. Lad life, girl power." The same critique has been directed against feminist research. Woodward (1995) criticizes feminism's concerns for displaying ageism.

12. In the latest national Swedish survey on sexuality, the age span was broadened to 74 years, and the study showed that more than a half of 70- to 74–year-old Swedes had had sexual intercourse during the last year (Lewin, 1997).

13. One example of this "radicalization" can be the appearance of older people's sexualization in jokes and comic stories. In a Swedish study of images of elderly in folklore, old women were described as old hags, whose sexuality was dangerously increasing, while old men were depicted as becoming impotent (Eklund, 1998).

14. Historically, Hepworth and Featherstone (1998) explain that due to the inability to produce children in middle age, women were considered to age earlier than men, who did not lose their virility until well into old age.

15. The response alternatives were a certain age, decreased health, children leaving the home, weakened work capacity, menopause, birth of grandchildren, weakened sexual capacity and desire, retirement, and change of looks (Uutela et al. 1994).

16. This question was only asked to respondents whose age was 30+. The response alternatives were (1) "Yes, to a high degree," (2) "Yes, to a certain degree," (3) "Hardly not," and (4) "No, not at all." Figure 4.4 shows the percentage of respondents who have answered "Yes, to a high degree" and "Yes, to a certain degree." Response alternatives 1 and 2 are grouped together.

17. To make the text more readable, I use the concepts *young-old* for 65 to 74, and *old-old* for 75- to 85-year-old respondents, even though one could argue that old-old today often means at least 80+. When I speak of these two groups together (65–85), I use the term *retirees* or just *older people*.

18. In a Finnish study of sexual autobiographies, Haavio-Mannila and Roos (1998) identify three different "sexual generations" writing three different types of stories. For *the generation of sexual repression* (born 1917–1936), sexual matters were taboo in childhood and not to be discussed openly. The fear of pregnancy limited sexual intercourse and double moral standards gave more sexual freedom to men. Thus, there was a wide gender gap in sexual behavior. For *the generation of sexual revolution* (born 1937–1956), new contraceptive methods made it possible to engage in sexual relations. Sexual liberation was part of gender equality and other radical social movements in the 1960s and 1970s. For *the generation of sexual ambivalence* (born 1957–1973), individualization and gender equalization, as well as the AIDS epidemic and efficient sex education at school, made this generation's sexual attitude and behavior ambivalent and not coherent.

19. In a previous study among 2,002 Swedes in corresponding age groups, the response pattern was similar with one exception: the proportion of women who were satisfied with their bodies increased with age (Öberg and Tornstam, 1999). But this study showed no significant variation by age, neither for men nor women.

20. The desexualization of old women has been interpreted through two opposite frames or models by different female representatives, both claiming to be emancipatoric. The first model interprets desexualization negatively and necessary to avoid, including recommendations to continue a sexualized identity, to stay "feminine forever," and where the elimination of menopause has been described as the way to liberation and the second biological revolution for women. The second model interprets desexualization positively and celebrates the "asexualism" of aging embodied by the menopause, as one source of women's liberation (Gilleard and Higgs, 2000).

References

Adams, C., and R. Laurikietis
1976 *The Gender Trap: A Closer Look at Sex Roles*. London: Sage.

Baerveldt, C., and P. Voestermans
1998 The Body as a Selfing Device. In *The Body and Psychology*. Edited by J. S. Henderikus, 161–81. London: Sage.

Bauman, Z.
1994 Från Pilgrim till Turist. *Moderna Tider* 5(47): 20–34.

Bernard, M. et al.
1995 Gendered Work, Gendered Retirement. In *Connecting Gender and Ageing. A Sociological Approach*. Edited by J. Ginn and S. Arber, 56–68. Buckingham, U.K.: Open University Press.

Bildtgård, T.
2000 The Sexuality of Elderly People on Film—Visual Limitations. *Journal of Ageing and Identity* 5(3): 169–83.

Blaikie, A.
1999a *Ageing and Popular Culture*. Cambridge: Cambridge University Press.
1999b Can There Be a Cultural Sociology of Ageing? *Education and Ageing* 14(2): 127–39.

Baudrillard, J.
1983 *Simulations*. New York: Semiotext(e).

Bruun Pedersen, J.
1988 *De Ældre og Seksualiteten. Mediemyter og Realiteter*. Stencil. Roskilde: Roskilde Universitetscenter.

Cunningham, S., and E. Jacka
1997 Neighbourly Relations? Cross-Cultural Reception Analysis and Australian Soaps in Britain. In *Media in Global Context: A Reader*. Edited by A. Sreberny-Mohammadi et al. London: Arnold.

Drevenstedt, J.
1976 Perceptions of Onsets of Young Adulthood, Middle-Age, and Old Age. *Journal of Gerontology* 31: 53–57.

Davis, C.
1995 *Reshaping the Female Body. The Dilemma of Cosmetic Surgery*. Routledge: London.

Douglas, M.
[1966] 1997 Renhet och fara. *En Analys av Begreppen Orenande och Tabu*. Falun: Nya Doxa.

Eklund, C.
1998 Kåta Kärringar och Impotenta Stålmän. In *Pigga Pensionärer och Populärkultur*. Edited by O. Ronström, 96–124. Stockholm: Carlssons.

Fairhurst, E.
1998 "Growing Old Gracefully" as opposed to "Mutton Dressed as Lamb": The Social Construction of Recognising Older Women. In *The Body in Everyday Life*. Edited by S. Nettleton and J. Watson, 258–75. London: Routledge.

Featherstone, M.
1982 The Body in Consumer Culture. *Theory, Culture and Society* 1: 18–33.
1994 *Kultur, Kropp, Konsumtion*. Stockholm: Symposion.

Featherstone, M.
(ed.) 1999 *Love and Eroticism*. London: Sage.

Featherstone, M., and M. Hepworth
1990 Images of Ageing. In *Ageing in Society: An Introduction to Social Gerontology*. Edited by J. Bond and P. Coleman, 250–75. London: Sage.
1991 The Mask of Ageing and the Post-modern Life Course. In *The Body: Social Process and Cultural Theory*. Edited by M. Featherstone, M. Hepworth, and B. S. Turner, 371–89. London: Sage.

Frank, A. W.
1991 For a Sociology of the Body: An Analytical Review. In *The Body, Social Process and Cultural Theory*. Edited by M. Featherstone, M. Hepworth, and B. S. Turner, 36–102. London: Sage.

Furman, F. K.
1997 *Facing the Mirror. Older Women and Beauty Shop Culture*. London: Routledge.

Gaunt, D.
1998 Natur och Kultur. Människor och Djur. In *Pigga Pensionärer och Populärkultur*. Edited by O. Ronström, 197–229. Stockholm: Carlssons.

Gergen, K.
1991 *The Saturated Self: Dilemmas of Identity in Contemporary Life*. New York: Basic Books.

Giddens, A.
1991 *Modernity and Self-Identity*. Cambridge, U.K.: Polity Press.

Gilleard, C.
1996 Consumption and Identity in Later Life: Toward a Cultural Gerontology. *Ageing and Society* 16(4): 489–98.

Gilleard, C., and P. Higgs
2000 *Cultures of Ageing: Self, Citizen and the Body.* London: Prentice Hall.

Ginn, J., and S. Arber
1993 Ageing and Cultural Stereotypes of Older Women. In *Ageing and Later Life.* Edited by J. Johnson and R. Slater, 60–67. London: Sage.

Goffman, E.
1972 *Stigma. Den Avvikandes Roll och Identitet.* Stockholm: Rabén och Sjögren.
[1959] 1991 *Jaget och Maskerna. En Studie i Vardagslivets Dramatik.* 2nd Swedish ed. Simrishamn: Rabén och Sjögren.

Goldsmith, R. E., and R. A. Heiens
1992 Subjective Age: A Test of Five Hypotheses. *The Gerontologist* 32(3): 312–17.

Goodman, M.
1994 Social, Psychological and Developmental Factors in Women's Receptivity to Cosmetic Surgery. *Journal of Aging Studies* 8: 375–96.

Grogan, S.
1999 Body Image. *Understanding Body Dissatisfaction in Men, Women and Children.* London: Routledge.

Gubrium, J., and J. Holstein
1999 The Nursing Home as Discursive Anchor for the Ageing Body. *Ageing and Society* 19: 519–38.

Gutmann, D., and M. Hellie Huyck
1994 Development and Pathology in Postparental Men: A Community Study. In *Older Men's Live.* Edited by E. H. Thompson, Jr., 65–84. London: Sage.

Haavio-Mannila, E., and J.-P. Roos
1998 Love Stories in Sexual Autobiographies. *The Narrative Study of Lives* 6: 239–74.

Hagestad, G. O., and B. L. Neugarten
1985 Age and the Life Course. In *Handbook of Aging and the Social Sciences.* 2nd ed. Edited by R. Binstock and E. Shanas. New York: Van Nostrand Reinhold.

Hajjar, W. J.
1997 The Image of Aging in Television Commercials: An Update for the 1990s. In *Cross Cultural Communication and Aging in the United States.* Edited by H. S. N. Al-Deen, 231–44. Mahwah, N.J.: Lawrence Erlabaum Associates.

Hepworth, M., and M. Featherstone
1982 *Surviving Middle Age.* Oxford: Basil Blackwell.
1998 The Male Menopause: Lay Accounts and the Cultural Reconstruction of Midlife Age. In *The Body in Everyday Life.* Edited by S. Nettleton and J. Watson, 276–301. London: Routledge.

Huston, A. C. et al.
1992 *Big World, Small Screen: The Role of Television in American Society.* Lincoln: University of Nebraska Press.

Itzin, C.
1986 Media Images of Women: The Social Construction of Ageism and Sexism. In *Feminist Social Psychology.* Edited by S. Wilkinson, 119–34. Milton Keynes, U.K.: Open University Press.

Kaufman, S. R.
1986 *The Ageless Self: Sources of Meaning in Late Life.* Madison: University of Wisconsin Press.

Kastenbeum, R. et al.
1972 "The Ages of Me": Toward Personal and Interpersonal Definitions of Functional Aging. *Aging and Human Development* 3: 197–211.

Lasch, C.
1981 Den Narcissistiska Kulturen. Stockholm: Norstedts.

Lehr, U., and I. Puschner
1963 Studies on the Awareness of Aging. In *Age with a Future.* Edited by P. F. Hansen. Proceedings of the Sixth International Congress of Gerontology, Copenhagen.

Levinson, D.
1978 *The Seasons of Man's Life.* New York: Ballentine Books.

Lewin, B., ed.
1997 *Sex i Sverige. Om Sexuallivet i Sverige 1996.* Uppsala, Sweden: Uppsala Universitets Förlag.

Linn, N. W., and K. Hunter
1979 Perception of Age in the Elderly. *Journals of Gerontology* 34(1): 46–52.

Markson, E. W., and C. A. Taylor
2000 The Mirror Has Two Faces. *Ageing and Society* 20: 137–60.

Mills, C. W.
[1959] 1985 *Den Sociologiska Visionen*. Malmö: Arkiv förlag.

Montepare, J. M., and M. E. Lachman
1989 You Are Only as Old as You Feel: Self-Perceptions of Age, Fears of Aging, and Life-Satisfaction from Adolescence to Old Age. *Psychology and Aging* 4(1): 73–78.

Nettleton, S., and J. Watson
1998 The Body in Everyday Life: An Introduction. In *The Body in Everyday Life*. Edited by S. Nettleton and J. Watson, 1–24. London: Routledge.

Öberg, P.
1996 The Absent Body: A Social Gerontological Paradox. *Ageing and Society* 16: 710–19.
1997 Livet som Berättelse. Om Biografi och Åldrande, Acta Universitatis Upsaliensis, *Comprehensive Summaries of Uppsala Dissertations from the Faculty of Social Sciences 62*.
2000 Att Åldras i ett Estetiserande Konsumtionssamhälle, En Studie om Kroppsbild. *Gerontologiska skrifter* 8: 7–31.

Öberg, P., and L. Tornstam
1999 Body Images Among Men and Women of Different Ages. *Ageing and Society* 19(5): 629–44.
2001 Youthfulness and Fitness Identity Ideals for All Ages? *Journal of Aging and Identity* 6(1): 15–29.

Oittinen, R.
1994 Vanhuuden "Välttäminen" Viime Vuosisadan Lopulta Toiseen Maailmansotaan. In *Muuttuva Vanhuus*. Edited by A. Uutela and J. E. Ruth, 201–20. Tampere, Finland: Gaudeamus.

Peck, R. C.
1968 Psychological Development in the Second Half of Life. In *Middle Age and Aging: A Reader in Social Psychology*. Edited by B. L. Neugarten, 88–92. Chicago: University of Chicago Press.

Robinson, J. D., and T. Skill
1995 The Invisible Generation: Portrayals of the Elderly on Prime-Time Television. *Communication Reports* 8(2): 111–19.

Ronkainen, S.
1998 Ikä ja Seksi: Katveesta Seksuaalitutkimuksen Kohteeksi. In *Muuttuva Vanhuus*. Edited by A. Uutela and J.-E. Ruth, 184–200. Tampere, Findland: Gaudeamus.

Ronström, O., ed.
1998 *Pigga Pensionärer och Populärkultur*. Stockholm: Carlssons.

Ruoppila, I.
1992 65–84-vuotiaiden Asennoituminen Ikään ja Vanhenemiseen. *Gerontologia* 6(1): 3–21.

Shilling, C.
1993 *The Body and Social Theory*. London: Sage.

Sontag, S.
1979 The Double Standard of Aging. In *An Aging Population: A Reader and Sourcebook*. Edited by V. Carver and P. Liddiard, 72–80. New York: Holmes and Meier.

Synnott, A.
1993 *The Body Social. Symbolism, Self and Society*. London: Routledge.

Thompson, E. H., Jr.
1994 Older Men as Invisible Men in Contemporary Society. In *Older Men's Lives*. Edited by E. H. Thompson, Jr., 1–21. London: Sage.

Turner, B. S.
1984 *The Body & Society*. Oxford, U.K.: Blackwell.

Twigg, J.
1999 The Spatial Ordering of Care: Public and Private in Bathing Support at Home. *Ageing and Society* 21: 381–400.

Twigg, J.
2000 *Bathing: The Body and Community Care*. London: Routledge.

Uotinen, V.
1998 Age Identification: A Comparison between Finnish and North-American Cultures. *The International Journal of Aging and Human Development* 46(2): 109–24.

Uutela, A. et al.
1994 Vanhenemiseen Liittyvät Mielikuvat. In *Muuttuva Vanhuus*. Edited by A. Uutela and J.-E. Ruth, 7–26. Tampere, Findland: Gaudeamus.

Vernon, J. A. et al.
1990 Media Stereotyping: A Comparison of the Way Elderly Women and Men Are Portrayed on Prime-Time Television. *Journal of Women and Aging* 2(4): 55–68.

Woodward, K.
1995 Tribute to the Older Woman: Psychoanalysis, Feminism and Ageism. In *Images of Aging. Cultural Representations of Later Life*. Edited by M. Featherstone and A. Wernick, 79–96. London: Routledge.

Zetterberg, H.
1969 Om Sexuallivet i Sverige: Värderingar, Normer, Beteenden i Sociologisk Belysning. SOU 1969: 2.

Part Two

EVERYDAY EXPERIENCE

CHAPTER FIVE

THE BODY AND BATHING:
HELP WITH PERSONAL CARE AT HOME
Julia Twigg

To write about the body is to write about the mundane and the everyday, for that is what the body is: something that is with us always and everywhere—both our constant companion and our essence. Nothing could be more mundane or day to day than the processes of body care. These actions punctuate our daily lives in the forms of dressing, shaving, showering, combing, washing, eating, drinking, excreting, and sleeping, providing us with a rhythm and pattern to the day. The bodily rhythms provide a basic experiential security in daily life. We are, however, mostly acculturated to ignore these patterns, at least at the level of polite speech. The processes of body care are assumed to be both too private and too trivial for comment, certainly too trivial for traditional academic analysis. They belong with those other aspects of bodily life that we are socialized to pass over in silence. Though such bodily processes form the bedrock of daily life, they are bedrocks assumed, rather than reflected on. So long as they are there, functioning correctly, we have no need to comment.

But for many older people this easeful state of bodily ignorance and transcendence is no longer available. Their bodies force themselves into the front of their thoughts, posing a mass of practical problems. The body assumes new prominence by virtue of its inability to do things. Among those things can be the tasks of body care such as washing, showering, and bathing. This chapter explores what happens when older people can no longer cope with these aspects of life but need assistance in doing them. In particular, it focuses on the situation of older people living at home receiving help with personal care, typically washing and bathing.

While a discussion of the everyday activities of washing and bathing is, by definition, concerned with micro-processes, these actions are not outside wider discursive concerns. Bathing is located in a wider set of discourses than the simple discussion of hygiene that tends to permeate accounts in the area. In this chapter, I will explore how far the provision of help does indeed draw on these wider discourses and how far it remains located in a narrower set of preoccupations. Help with bathing also entails negotiating the management of the body; it involves touch and nakedness and at times verges on the taboo. I will explore how older people feel about this, and who they prefer to help them in these areas. Before doing so, however, I will discuss briefly the paradoxical neglect of the subject of the body in relation to the support of older people.

The Neglected Body of Social Care

Though body care lies at the heart of service provision, this has not been emphasized in accounts of the sector. There are three primary reasons for this: The first derives from a concern within gerontology to resist the dominant discourses of medicine and popular accounts of aging that present it in terms of inevitable bodily decline. The excessive focus on the body is seen as damaging—endorsing ageist stereotypes in which older people are reduced to their aging and sick bodies, which visibly mark them as old. Progressive gerontology by contrast aims to present a more rounded account of age: one that gives due weight to social rather than just bodily elements in the structuring of its experiences. The "political economy" approach, in particular, that has dominated social gerontology in Britain and North America since the 1980s, emphasizes the degree to which old age is the product of social structural factors such as retirement age, pension provision, and ageist assumptions (Phillipson and Walker 1986; Estes and Binney 1989; Arber and Ginn 1991). From this perspective, factors like the differential access to resources or social exclusion primarily determine the social experience of old age not bodily decline. Close, analytic attention to the body from this perspective is thus regarded as a step backwards.

The second reason for the neglect of the body derives from the way in which the field of community care has traditionally been conceptualized within the debate on aging. "Community care" is the term commonly used in Britain and elsewhere for the support of older and disabled people enabling them to live in the community, typically in their own homes, and it is the principal policy objective in most advanced industrial societies.

Community care is not, however, predominantly conceptualized in terms of the body. Partly this is because the dominant professional group in the field is social work, which concentrates on questions of interpersonal and social functioning and whose remit tends to stop short of the body. This territory is traditionally handed over to the care of medicine. As a result, though community care is inherently about the body and its day-to-day problems, this fact is not emphasized in accounts of the sector. The evasion is further compounded by the increasing influence of managerialism in the sector. Managerial discourse, constructed as it is out of the disciplines of economics, business studies, organization, and methods, embodies an abstract and distancing form of theorizing that is far from the messy, dirty realities of bodily life. When community care is discussed, it is done so in a manner that largely dismisses the body, rendering it invisible as a site of concern.

The third reason for neglect comes from work on the body itself. Since the 1980s there has been an explosion of writing in this area (Williams and Bendelow 1998), but its focus has been on younger, sexier, more transgressive bodies. The roots of much of this literature in feminism, queer theory, and cultural studies have not encouraged it to venture into the territory of old age. Indeed, these approaches have displayed a significant degree of ageism in their assumptions about what is interesting and important. More recently, however, new work has begun to address bodily issues in relation to later years (Öberg 1996; Tulle-Winton 2000; Gilleard and Higgs 2000). Some of the best of this work has—belatedly—come out of feminism (Woodward 1991, 1999; Andrews 1999; Furman 1997, 1999). It has been marked by a sense of agency and a desire to emphasize the subjective, meaning-making experiences of people as they engage in the aging process. Often these ideas are linked to concepts of the Third Age.

The Third Age represents a postretirement period of extended middle age in which people who are no longer confined by the labor market and are free from direct responsibility for children can pursue leisure interests, develop aspects of their personalities, and enjoy the fruits of later life. The emergence of this new social space is often linked to theories about identity and selfhood in postmodernity, particularly ones that emphasize self-fashioning. It is open, however, to the familiar critique that such optimistic accounts of the Third Age are only possible by virtue of projecting the negative aspects of aging into a dark Fourth Age, a period of declining health and social loss, sometimes also termed "deep" old age. As Gilliard and Higgs (2000) note, accounts of the Third Age emphasize agency and subjectivity and are described from the perspective of the optimistic self. But accounts of the Fourth Age focus on dependency and are written from the outside. A macro-level perspective dominates this literature. In such accounts, older persons are rarely seen as agents at all but are often presented as the "other."

Physical decline is frequently presented as marking the point of transition between the Third and Fourth Ages, and receiving personal care of a close and intimate kind is a key marker in this transition. In this chapter we focus on just such a personal care situation. In doing so I am thus attempting to extend the analysis in terms of the body to a group who until recently has been excluded from such a perspective. The literature on the body and aging that has emerged of late has tended to focus on the earlier optimistic stage of the Third Age, exploring the ways in which people negotiate issues of bodily aging as they make the transitions from middle to later life. Relatively little work focuses on the body in the Fourth Age, precisely because this Fourth Age is perceived to be *all* about the body and to be dominated by bodily issues of a discouraging kind. One of the moral tasks of literature on the Fourth Age has been to retain some of the sense of the person *behind* the body. Here, I hope to continue to do this, but in a way that acknowledges the significance of bodily experiences in the later stages of life and in doing so extends the literature on the body to this previously excluded group.

Personal Care as a Social Marker

Why is personal care such a marker of social states? The reason lies in the profound social symbolism that relates to the body and its management. This means that receiving help in these areas erodes the personhood and adult status of the subject. Personal care means being helped with precisely those tasks that as adults we do for ourselves: getting washed and dressed, moving, eating, and excreting. However rich we are, these are things that—at least in the modern West—we do for ourselves, typically alone or in the company of intimates. Body care of this type thus marks the boundary of the truly personal and individual in modern life. Having to be helped in these areas transgresses this boundary and undermines adulthood. Only babies and children are helped in this way, and this underwrites the profoundly infantalizing tendencies of "care."

The effect is particularly strong if the person suffers from incontinence. As Lawton (1998) argues, to have an unbounded body in the context of modern expectations of the clearly bounded, individually defined body is to have one's autonomy and personhood questioned. Incontinence is for many people the last frontier of the social life; the point beyond which it is no longer possible to engage actively and equally in society.

Personal care also involves nakedness. Nakedness is not, largely, part of ordinary social interaction. It is a special state reserved for certain situations and relationships, and it is a marker of close, typically sexual, intimacy. To be naked in a social situation, as recipients of personal care are, is therefore to be put in a disjunctive context. It is made all the more so by the fact that the nakedness is asymmetrical: the recipient is naked, while the helper is fully clothed. To be naked in this way is to be exposed and vulnerable, and it inevitably creates a power dynamic in which the helper, usually younger and stronger, is clearly the dominant party.

Personal Care and Bathing

Personal care has become an increasingly significant issue for social care agencies across the Western world as a result of widespread social and political policies aimed at supporting frail elders living at home. Home care in Britain and elsewhere is no longer primarily a matter of housework and shopping, but of personal care, in which washing and bathing form an important aspect. Historically, in Britain such help was primarily provided by the community nursing service but is now largely provided within a home care system. This same shift in home care can be detected in other Western welfare systems.

The principal driver behind it has been cost reduction, with the desire to move the provision of home care away from the relatively expensive health care sector where staff are trained and where the provision of personal care is often free to the recipient, into the less expensive social care sector where staff are typically untrained and where recipients are often required to fund their care. The shift has, however, also arisen from concerns about the overmedicalization of older people's lives. Home care services are seen as embodying a potentially more sympathetic and caring approach than that of medically directed ones.

This chapter draws on a study of help with washing and bathing provided to older and disabled people living at home in Britain (Twigg 2000a). The study was based on interviews with recipients, caregivers, and managers. In the research, elders received help with bathing from a variety of sources: the local authority home care service; voluntary sector or for profit agencies; or a specialist voluntary sector bathing service (the last is unusual in Britain). Depending on their income, users either received such help free or were expected to meet some or all of the costs.

The Meanings of Bathing

Within public welfare services, washing and bathing tend to be presented narrowly in terms of a discourse of hygiene and cleanliness. The broader meanings of bathing in terms of luxury, pleasure, and well-being are not emphasized. There are a number of reasons for this: Partly it arises from a narrow concern with health and physical functioning, which is regarded as a particularly legitimate aim for such interventions. Bathing in this context is presented as a concern for hygiene; though in reality, dirtiness has to be extreme before health is genuinely threatened. Partly it comes from long-established political pressures to ensure that the remit of public welfare remains limited in scope and extent; and this is linked to a related puritanism that regards ideas of bodily pleasure in connection with public provision as—at the very least—discordant. Such tendencies are reinforced by the recent dominance of managerialism, which, as we have seen, tends to present the sector in a distant and disembodied way. Recipients are categorized in terms of their "personal hygiene deficits," and accounts of the work sanitized and confined within the discourse of hygiene. The body—the width of its experiences and feelings—has little part to play in this discourse.

But bathing has much broader meanings. While there is certainly not space here to explore the history of washing and bathing and of the various practices and discourses that have led to its construction (see Twigg 2000a for such a discussion), I will, however, refer briefly here to four recurring strands in that history to suggest some of the ways in which bathing is located in a wider set of discourses than just those of hygiene.

Historically, bathing has long been connected with luxury, pleasure, and to some degree, eroticism. For the Romans, bathing was a social activity associated with relaxation, exercise, conviviality, and pleasure (Yegül 1992). During the Middle Ages it was recurringly presented in connection with images of feasting and courtship (Vigarello 1988). These meanings narrowed by the nineteenth century, when bathing lost its social dimension and became a more private affair, more closely connected with the tasks of getting clean, though the sense of luxury and pleasure that derived from abundant hot water remains (Wilkie 1986; Bushman and Bushman 1988). During the twentieth century, luxurious bathrooms, whether presented in the celebratory imagery of Hollywood or the dreams of real estate promoters, continued to draw on this discourse of pleasure and luxury and only barely suppressed eroticism (Kira 1967).

Bathing is also located in a wider discourse of well-being. Again, this has been so since Roman times, when baths were seen as part of a general regimen of health and well-being. Baths have also been prominent in the alternative medical tradition from hydrotherapy to nature cure, and they remain a central element in the recent revival of spa culture, often in association with diffuse concepts of "Eastern" medicine, which has become a feature of modern Western lifestyles or at least aspirations. Spa treatments are presented as an antidote to stress and others ills of modern living. Through all of this, well-being is the key concept; and the focus is on the experiential body, not the medical body.

The third theme concerns the frequent use of baths and water as markers of social transitions. This is clearest in relation to classic rites of passage, such as Christian baptism, but it also operates in secular contexts like prisons, schools, and hospitals, where people are commonly compelled to have a bath as part of the initiation into the institution, marking their transition from the status of a citizen outside to that of an inmate inside (van Gennep 1908; Goffman 1961; Fitzgerald and Sim 1979; Littlewood 1991). Individuals also draw on such symbolism in their daily lives, clearly marking out the transitions of the day or week through bodily practices such as bathing and showering. The bedrock of body care punctuates the day, providing a framework of time and of social states in terms of eating and drinking, washing and dressing, and sleeping and rising. No small part of our sense of ontological security is derived from these practices.

Last, bathing also contains darker themes. Baths have been widely used as part of coercive cultures, particularly within institutions. For example, cold plunges, sudden showers, and shockingly cold water have all been used as part of the history of the treatment of the insane. Though the justification for such techniques has often been in terms of shocking the patient back into reason, a clearly coercive, even sadistic, element is also often intensified by the use of machinery or the enforcement of humiliating bodily postures. Though Michel Foucault does not write of baths in particular, there is a strongly Foucauldian element in such treatments with their emphasis on the disciplining and control of bodies, as well as on the exercise of bio-power by key actors, including welfare professionals. Though these four themes are not in general articulated within the context of community care, all resonate at some level with the practice of bathing in the wider community and society.

The Adaptibility of the Old

Before exploring what people feel about receiving help, it is worth reflecting briefly on the adaptability of the old. Accounts of older people often present them as inflexible and unable to cope with change. In fact, the changes imposed on people in their later lives are enormous. No amount of jet travel, adaptation to new information technology systems, or learning to appreciate new music can remotely compare with the changes that older people have to learn to become accustomed to on a day-to-day basis. The aged may lose their lifetime companion; may have to move to a new home, town, or region; and may have to learn to live in an institution among random strangers in a collective way that is wholly at odds with their earlier lives and under the auspices of a staff whose background and worldview may be completely alien to them.

In all of this, bodily experiences can be among the most significant: not being able to move freely, to speak clearly, or to manage your bodily functions present major changes in life. Having to receive help with personal care, in particular, breaches some of the most profound of social expectations, requiring people to cope with new situations and new relationships. As we shall see, some of the respondents expressed dismay at what they had to face, but it is testimony to their adaptability that they did indeed manage to cope. The majority approached old age with stoicism, concentrating on the day and trying to make the best of it. Some developed ingenious and innovative ways to circumvent their physical difficulties.

What Does Bathing Mean in This Context?

Within the British tradition, the predominant ways of getting clean have been baths, in the sense of bathtubs, and washing at a basin. This is in contrast to Continental and American traditions where showering established itself much earlier as the main alternative to strip washing at a basin. Showering is now common among younger people in Britain, but is still largely unfamiliar or disliked among this older age group. Few people in the study had showers in their homes. In the context of drafty houses and feeble flows of hot water, showers do not warm the body in the way that hot baths do. One or two respondents of Continental origin did prefer showers, sharing the mainland European view that baths are not an adequate way to clean oneself.

People varied in how important baths were to them. Some respondents had never been great bathers and relied instead on a strip wash. For others, a daily bath was a long-established habit and one that they greatly missed. As Mrs. Fitzgerald (all respondents' names have been changed) explained, she loved bathing and continues to see it as a vital part of the day: "All my life, up in a morning, throw open the bed, into the bathroom—that's the way I lived. . . . It's always been terribly important to me. And that's when I got panic-stricken when I thought I wasn't going to be able to have any baths."

The care people actually received from the bathing service was not always in line with their hopes. Some individuals did indeed have a "proper bath," in the sense of being placed directly under the water, with all the warmth and buoyancy that this could bring. But for many, "bathing" really meant sitting on a board over the bath while the caregiver helped them to wash and poured warm water over their bodies. This was enjoyable, but it was not a proper bath, and many regretted this. Mrs. Kennelly, whose severe Parkinson's meant that she could no longer have a bath, remembered the experience with a sense of nostalgia, "I'd love to be able to get in the bath. Just lay there and splash it over . . . wallow in it. Lovely." Mrs. Bridgeman tells of how wonderful it would be to just once receive a proper bath, "I *long* to get my bum in the water. It would be bliss you know."

The problem was that many recipients did not have sufficient flexibility to get down into the tub or the strength to get up, and very few homes had the kind of expensive equipment that would allow for this. Workers were forbidden by Health and Safety legislation from lifting the clients out of the bath (though sometimes they still performed the task). This meant that many had more in the way of an assisted wash than a bath. By and large, recipients were resigned to these limitations and grateful for what assistance they received, but problems did occasionally arise, particularly if clients rebelled and attempted to preempt the situation by sitting down fully in the bath. In these cases, the caregivers were instructed to tell the person that they would not help them up, but would instead ring for an ambulance. The potential humiliation of this was sufficient to keep most clients in line.

The Experience of Bathing

For some individuals, bathing did remain a pleasurable, even luxurious, experience. Mrs. Fitzgerald, who had most feared the loss, now saw the coming of the bathing service as "the rose of [her] week." Mrs. Napier also relished the experience as something that brings back pleasurable memories of the past, explaining how "we have nice foamy shower gel. . . . It's lovely, like being a baby again." Baths were also a source of pleasure because of the number of aches and pains that many older people suffer from. The warmth and buoyancy of the water restored lightness to limbs that had become heavy, giving back something of the easy, youthful, bodily experience of the past.

Baths also retained their capacity to wash away more than just dirt. For some, they had always been both a source of renewal and a marker of social transitions. As Miss Garfield explained, baths are "part of, sort of washing the day away and all the bothers and troubles, and you're there and it's all very comfortable and nice." But the experience of bathing was inevitably strongly affected by the presence of the caregiver in the room. For most people, bathing is a private affair, a time apart, when individuals can attend to themselves and not worry about others. But the presence of the worker changes that to some degree, disturbing the ease. Their presence in the room inevitably refocuses the event on tasks to be accomplished, rather than a state to be experienced; recipients were no longer free to control the timing of the event as they had been in the past. Workers needed to get the job done, and this sometimes meant that time was now of the essence, not pleasure. This acted to limit the nature of the experience, removing luxury, and centering it instead on cleaning of the client.

Having a worker in the room also removed much of the spontaneity of bathing; it was no longer possible to draw a bath when you simply felt like it. With this also went much of the capacity of baths to act as personal rites of passage or markers of social transitions. Body care still marked out the rhythm of people's days, in the sense of dressing, washing, and eating, but baths now had to be taken at the times they were scheduled; this could mean otherwise "meaningless" times, such as eleven-thirty in the morning, that disrupted rather than underwrote social patterns. For some people this was less disruptive than expected. This was because those who received such bathing assistance were often among the most frail and dependent, people who rarely if ever left the house. For them, the world of conventional timings had become less significant. To quite an extent, they had reordered the pattern of their lives *around* the provision of care. Caregiving had come to operate as a social structure in itself.

The Gaze of Youth

Much of the recent work in gerontology has emphasized the ways in which we are aged by culture—by the meanings that are ascribed to bodily aging, rather than the aging process itself. Gullette (1997) has described the subtle and omnipresent means by which such meanings are conveyed. We inhale this atmosphere daily, imbuing doses of its toxicity wafting from cartoons, billboards, birthday cards, coffee mugs, newspaper articles, fiction, and poetry: "The system is busy at what ever level of literacy or orality or visual impressionability the acculturated subject is comfortable with" (p. 5). Consumer culture, with its emphasis on youth, is particularly saturated with such messages (Featherstone 1991; Gilleard and Higgs 2000).

The dominant theme in all of this work is that old age is constructed as a negative entity and the bodily process of aging is seen in the same light. Aging represents a form of Otherness, on to which culture projects its fear and denial. As Woodward (1991) argues, our cultural categories here are essentially reducible to two, youth and age, set in a hierarchical arrangement. We are not judged by how old we are, but by how young we are not. Aging is a falling away, a failure to be young. Like disabled people, the old are evaluated as "less than." The bodily realities of aging thus create a version of Erving Goffman's spoilt identity, something that people are, at some level, ashamed of and marked in terms of.

We are accustomed to the idea of the medical gaze in the context of professional power, or the phallic gaze in the context of gender relations, but there is also a gaze of youth. It, too, is an exercise of power in which the "other"—in this case older people—are constituted under its searching eye. Nowhere is the gaze of youth more evident than in relation to bathing care. Here the bodies of older people are directly subject to the gaze of younger workers. From the workers' perspective, this sometimes presents them with a shock. Modern culture, though saturated with visual images of young perfect bodies, rarely permits old imperfect ones to be on display. As a result, the way in which the body looks in old age was something that the younger workers were unprepared for. As one worker explained, seeing old people naked was "weird, and I just had to stop myself staring at people, because I hadn't really seen . . . because you don't really see people naked."

At times this element of gaze was itself part of the professional task. Nurses who do bathing work often comment how the activity is useful in assessing the general state of the older person, in terms not only of illness and physical condition but also in a more extensive way. To be bathed is indeed to be made subject to—very directly subject to—the professional gaze. It is indeed a kind of developed, intimate surveillance.

So how did older people feel about this? It was certainly the case that many respondents appeared to have internalized the wider cultural denigration of the bodies of the old. They constituted their own bodies under the gaze of youth, presenting them as something that it might be unattractive, even distasteful, for people to see or handle. As Mrs. Fitzgerald once remarked of the caregiver, "They're so young and beautiful, it must be awful for them to have to handle old, awkward bodies." At the same time, she added that "they're wonderful people. . . . I must say, I mean they must have something inside them because—it's not the sort of thing—I don't know when I was young whether I would have wanted to have looked after old people." For some, the contrast between their aging bodies and the youthful flesh of the workers was painful to see and experience:

> Mrs. Kennelly: I say to them, "I feel sorry for you, getting up in the morning and this is the kind of job you've got to do." You know, not very nice. . . . This young girl, Amanda it was, came in—twenty-eight, beautiful girl. She's very pretty. And there's the ugly lump. Oh dear!

To be caught within the youthful gaze was disturbing, and many of the elders had turned its corrosive force back on themselves, in turn disciplining their own bodies in the course of assisted practice.

Embarrassment

Receiving help with bathing was potentially embarrassing, but respondents varied in the degree to which they experienced it as such. Some never lost this sense of unease, but the majority adapted. As Mrs. Elster once explained:

> Mrs. Elster: Well, at the beginning I didn't like being personally washed of course, but after six years I haven't got any more hold ups about that, you know. You just get on with it. Get clean is my main thing.
> Interviewer: Right so you get used to it or you just have to learn to put up with it?
> Mrs. Elster: Well pretty well learn to put up with it. And really you do put up with a helluva lot.

The exchange once again points to the adaptability of the old. Mrs. Elster had been literally confined to her bed for six years and was determined to remain independent. She had learned to accept what could not be changed.

For many, the experience of being in the hospital had been a watershed in their feelings about their bodies. After being pulled and pushed about on the wards, they had lost any sense of modesty. Mr. Wagstaff once commented that "once you've been in hospital for a while, all ideas of privacy disappear straight down the drain." In these cases the sense was less one of bodily ease than of detachment and distancing of the self from the body, its pain, and embarrassment.

Some elders, however, seemed genuinely unbothered by the new situation they now found themselves in. One caregiver recounted that "most of them aren't shy at all, they just come in and take their clothes off and walk around, they don't really mind." Mrs. Napier said that she was never embarrassed in front of the caregiver, stating, "Oh gracious no, I've walked round in my birthday suit without any trouble at all." Listen as one caregiver described how a client still loved to show off her zest for living:

> [She] just stands up in the bath and goes like this, you know, does a little dance. . . . The whole thing is kind of a pursuit in proving how agile and full of life she is. . . . It's that kind of love of just being in that little wicked body of hers, and doing a dance with a towel right in the middle of the bath.

Parts of the Body

The body is a landscape onto which meanings are inscribed. These are not, however, evenly distributed over the body, and certain parts come to be more heavily freighted with significance than other bodily parts. In general, there is a familiar privacy gradient whereby certain parts of the body are deemed more personal and private. Access to them by sight or touch is socially circumscribed and varies according to relationship and situation (Jourard 1966; Jourard and Rubin 1968; Henley 1973; Whitcher and Fisher 1979). Areas of the body such as the upper arms and back are relatively neutral and can be touched by a range of people. Knees and thighs are less so. Breasts and genitals are in general off-limits in all but erotic relations. Touch is also a vector of status and authority with the powerful accorded more leeway to touch than the less powerful. There is a gender dimension, with women more likely to receive touch than men. Within a service provision context, women are more likely to interpret touch from a service provider in a positive way, while men are more inclined to see it negatively, interpreting it as a marker of inferiority and dependency. In addition, men are also more likely to see touch as sexual.

These sensitivities affect the experience of bathing. Receiving hands-on help with soaping, rising, and washing is more tolerable in relation to some parts of the body than to others. Arms, legs, feet, and hair are all fine. Matters become more sensitive, however, in relation to what is often termed "down below": the genital and anal areas. In practice nearly everyone in the study could manage to wash these parts themselves, at least with some indirect assistance, and a number of respondents expressed relief that they were able to do so. Having to be washed in these areas was seen as humiliating and embarrassing, yet another twist in the spiral of dependency. Maintaining one's independence in relation to these intimate areas was an important part of self-esteem. Caregivers were also reluctant to involve themselves with these parts of the body, which they, too, regarded with a certain amount of ambivalence. In general, bathing was practically managed in such a way as to limit direct contact in relation to more sensitive bodily parts.

Conflict sometimes arose, however, in a small number of cases in which male clients attempted to "try it on" and get caregivers to touch their private parts. One female caregiver recounted how when she was new to the work, one man "was always trying to get us to wash his private parts . . . and I think I did it the first time, [because] I was quite new." But her manager explained such "help" was rarely necessary, telling the caregiver that "he could do it, and I realised this when he turned the shower on. I thought, if he can do that, then he can do it. He's just trying it on." Attempts of this sort are usually met by refusal or transferred to a male caregiver.

There was one part of the body that was recurringly mentioned in the interviews by both recipients and workers: this was the back. In the context of bathing and the ambivalent intimacies it creates, the back has a special meaning, coming to stand for the body in general, or at least for an acceptable version of the body, one that has a certain neutrality about it. In the interviews, the back was the only part of the body that was spontaneously named by recipients, and they sometimes talked about the process of bathing as if it were confined to the process of washing the back. The back was also the one part of the body where pleasure in touch was openly acknowledged.

A number of recipients described how much they enjoyed having their backs scrubbed. Expressing pleasure in this form of touching was acceptable. Caregivers agreed with this account. One in particular commented that "they do enjoy it, that you know, a lot of people really, 'Oooh,' you know, 'give my back a good rub.'" In general, expressing pleasure in touch was something that recipients were reluctant to do. It seemed to suggest in their eyes something that was not quite right, an ambivalent element that did not belong in this context of relative strangers and of public provision. Presenting bathing in terms of scrubbing the back was one means of deflecting an otherwise disturbing intimacy onto a relatively neutral and public part of the body.

The back is also significant in the bath encounter in that it is the part of the body that is both offered to the gaze of the worker and also used to shelter more private and sensitive parts. It stands in for the public presentation of the body in the context of an otherwise discordant intimacy. The back also offers a safe setting for the expression of affection and closeness. Putting an arm across the back while giving the recipient a hug fits in easily with the way bathing disposes the body, while at the same time providing a relatively neutral form of physical contact. Touch could thus be used to express closeness, but in a manner that does not transgress social codes.

Bounded Relationships and Access to the Body

Bathing makes for a strange relationship: in one sense intimate and close, involving physical contact, nakedness, and access to the private dimensions of life; yet in another, it is a meeting of strangers in which the worker is paid to do a job and may never have met the recipient before. The intimacy, moreover, occurs in a context that is forced. It arises from disability, not choice. The closeness is imposed, not sought. As a result there is an inherent discordance in the relationship. It is transgressive of normal social codes, and effort is needed on both sides to define the character of the relationship and to put limits on the nature of its intimacy.

How the relationship was experienced was clearly affected by who the helper was. What were people's preferences in this regard? Did they, for example, prefer to be helped by close relatives? An assumption of this sort is often made, resting on the idea that kinship closeness renders the negotiation of bodily closeness easier. While this can certainly sometimes be so, often it is not. We have evidence from other studies (Parker 1993; Daatland 1990) that suggests that while people may like to receive more neutral forms of help from relatives, personal care is different. In these cases many people prefer the formal service system. The reason is that bodily care threatens the nature of a relationship. In particular it erodes the status of the recipient and with that their identity in the relationship. What older people fear is that the person that they once were—and in their own eyes still are—will be lost, and that person, by and large, is someone with their clothes on, managing their own bodily functions and relating to their families in a sociable way. We should not thus make any easy assumptions about kinship closeness translating unproblematically into bodily closeness.

Even less do people want friends to perform this activity. It is in the nature of friendship that it rests on equality and reciprocity, and few friendships survive marked change in circumstances when these occur on only one side of a valued relationship. Intimate care represents just such a change. Lawler (1991) notes how nurses experience similar unease if cared for by a friend and colleague. Though recipients wanted the care worker to be "friendly," they were quite clear that this was a different and defined sort of relationship. These were not friends in the full sense of the word. As Mrs. Ostrovski said to me, "Friend is a very big word."

Bath work involves a kind of intimacy, though it is of a different nature from that of kinship or friendship. What recipients want is a bounded intimacy, something that is close, but in a specialized and limited way. For these reasons they preferred someone whom they had got to know in these particular circumstances and where the relationship was defined by them. This is not to say that that it was not close, friendly, or based on a kind of trust. In most cases it was all of these, but the relationship was of a special kind, in which bodily closeness played a part but was defined and limited.

At the same time, recipients disliked the experience of having to deal with strangers. Bathing involves both a literal and a psychic unwrapping of the self. Having to participate in this process repeatedly with strangers was exposing and dispiriting. Recipients wanted the ease that comes with familiarity; they did not want constantly to have to readjust to a new person. But agencies could not always be relied on to send the same person, and indeed the constant staff turnover that is characteristic of low-wage sectors in cities like London meant that it was quite difficult for them to do so. Some recipients subverted the problem by refusing to have a bath if an unfamiliar worker was sent, diverting them into other household tasks rather than facing the unwelcome process of self-disclosure. What recipients wanted, therefore, was someone they knew, who was friendly and sensitive and who would offer emotional support, but who understood the limits of the relationship.

Among formal service providers, it is sometimes thought that nurses are the most appropriate people to do this work since they are the group traditionally associated with the direct management of the body and the negotiation of interventions involving bodily fluids, nakedness, and other sorts of bodily vulnerability. With their sacralising uniforms and professional manner, they are well placed to deal with the profanities of the body in a neutral way (Wolf 1988; Lawler 1991). Perhaps surprisingly, older people in the study did not endorse this view. By and large they preferred to have ordinary care workers. Some indeed held negative views of nurses who were seen as bossy, interventionist, and hurried. Many had had bad experiences in hospitals where their bodies had been pushed and pulled about by nurses in the course of the diagnosis and treatment. Although holistic accounts of nursing (Lawler 1997) stress the importance of body care and the role of nurses in integrating the object body of medicine with the experiential body of the individual, the realities of nursing care on busy wards with an increasing division of labor, as well as the invasive and unpleasant nature of many hospital procedures mean that the body in nursing is largely the object body of biomedicine.

The body in social care is different. As I noted at the start of this chapter, within social care there is no consciously articulated language of the body. Indeed the discourses of community care and of aging that have constituted the field have traditionally avoided the subject. However, there is most certainly a body within social care. It is a version of the social body that is managed to some degree, as we have seen, within discourses of sociability and personal relationships, tempered by conscious attempts to limit and neutralize the connection. The body within social services is managed within a more homely discourse than that of nursing, one in which uniforms and titles are not used as distancing techniques and where familiarity replaces professional authority in the negotiation of intimacy.

The social body is, of course, also a gendered body, and gendered assumptions affect the negotiation of social care. Issues of gender profoundly affect care work. Like nursing, the job is effectively constructed around gendered identities in which qualities associated with women in the private, domestic sphere are carried over into the public world of work. Care work is archetypally women's work, and this underpins a number of its key features: the unbounded character of the work and its links to the ethic of care; its association with the body and with emotion; society's schizoid valuation of it, at the same time inestimable and yet discounted; and the ways that it is naturalized in the persons of women. So what is needed to do the work is "good" women, rather than trained or qualified workers, with the financial and other rewards that such workers can command (Hochschild 1983; Waerness 1987; Bates 1993; Tronto 1993; Davies 1994; Skeggs 1997; Twigg 2000b).

The recipients also made assumptions about gender. This invariably focuses on who was appropriate to do the care work. Responses varied according to whether the person was a man or woman. In general, women-to-women care was regarded as "natural" and unproblematic. Issues arose, however, in relation to cross-gender tending and, to some extent, in relation to same-sex male tending.

What underpinned this asymmetrical pattern were wider assumptions about the meaning and management of the body. Within Western culture, men's and women's bodies have traditionally been treated differently (Young 1990; Connell 1995; Brook 1999; Watson 2000). Women's bodies tend to be regarded with greater circumspection. Access to them, both physical and visual, is more guarded. They are seen as more private, something that is secluded and hidden. Women's bodies are also often presented as more sexual, indeed often coming to represent the principle of sexuality more widely within culture. Women's bodies are also subject to greater control. There is more constraint over what they may do and express. Men's bodies are, by contrast, presented as more public and neutral in character. They tend to embody active principles rather than the passive ones circumscribed on the female body. They desire, rather than are constituted by the desire of others.

These cultural patterns underwrite responses to bathing help. In general women preferred not to have a male worker, and some expressed their feelings very strongly in this regard, "Oh, no. I wouldn't have a man. No thank you!" This was not universal, and some said that they would not mind. But in practice this situation only rarely arose. The majority of workers are female, as are the clients, and this "naturally" delivers a pattern in accord with dominant values. Most agencies also have a policy against men giving personal care to women in their own homes, partly out of respect for client's assumed preferences and partly to avoid accusations of abuse. Running through attitudes toward male care workers was a set of assumptions about the nature of male sexuality as something that is active and potentially predatory. This is in contrast to the assumptions that are made about women. They are presented as passive or asexual in this context, dominated by the values of maternity, not sexuality.

For men, the experience of receiving cross-gender tending was, by its very nature, different. Men are accustomed to being helped by women from childhood onwards, and many saw such assistance in old age as a natural extension of that. Such care contained no sense of threat. Indeed, for many men the idea of being helped by a woman was pleasant. As one manager remarked: "A lot of the men quite enjoy having a woman. And honestly I think, you know, specially a nice young girl come to help them have a bath, they like it. You know, not in any sort of perverted way, just, just in a you know, they like the attention."

As Mr. Lambert said, provided the women were married—that is where women were accustomed to seeing men naked—there was no difficulty in cross-gender tending. Mr. Wagstaff concurred with this sentiment:

Interviewer: Did you find it embarrassing at first or . . . ?

Mr. Wagstaffe: Well not really. I thought it might be more embarrassing for *them* than for me, but they don't seem to mind a bit.

Interviewer: Why did you think it would be more embarrassing for them?

Mr. Wagstaffe: Well, the first girl I had she was only about eighteen I think. She was a sort of punk, she'd got bright red hair and earrings in her eyebrows. Sort of girl that a person of my age looks at and thinks Gawd Almighty. But she was absolutely sweet, she was a lovely girl. It turns out that they nearly all live with their boyfriends or something, so I don't bother about it now. . . . And young ladies in their early twenties these days are rather different from when I was the same age.

For men, therefore, cross-gender tending contains no sense of threat. The issue is one of managing the encounter in such a way as to avoid embarrassment, in which they had some remaining sense of responsibility for not disturbing the innocence of the young. Even in old age, men experience a residual sense of the power of the phallus.

For men being cared for by men, the assumptions were slightly different. In many cases this occurred without comment or problems. But for some men the idea was unwelcome. Men construct other men as sexually predatory in relation to themselves (Connell 1995). Intimate care by a man raises the possibility of a homosexual encounter, a concern reinforced by ideas that caregiver was not proper work for a man at all.

The Discourses of Bathing Revisited

How far does bathing provided at home embody the wider discourses of bathing that I referred to at the start of this chapter? With regard to luxury and pleasure, we saw that these experiences are, to some degree, found within the service, particularly the service as provided by the specialist bathing project. They were slightly less characteristic of the provision of personal care located within a general home care service where bathing had to be fitted in as possible and where the worker came to clean both the house and the person. Luxury was also somewhat limited by the nature of what was offered, and as we have seen throughout the chapter, bathing often fell short of the desire of recipients for a "proper bath." This was further complicated by the character of many older people's bathrooms. These were often cramped and old-fashioned. For those who were well housed, however, as a result of either their own money or some form of social housing, bathing could be a source of bodily pleasure. How far it could be articulated as such was, however, much more questionable. Many recipients seemed inhibited in expressing such hedonistic thoughts in the context of public provision.

Eroticism was present, but only in a muted form, and more as a shadow than an active principle. Some of the difficulties around nakedness, embarrassment, and intimacy clearly had their roots in the potentially erotic nature of the exchanges, and some of the boundary maintenance work that went into defining the relationship was concerned with resisting or limiting these meanings. The element of the erotic was most strongly present in relation to questions of cross-gender tending and the differential construction of this between men and women. On occasion such issues did emerge overtly, and dealing with unwanted sexual expression is one of the minor tasks of caregiving. By and large, however, the erotic was more present in its exclusion than its action.

With regard to well-being and wider concepts of health, it was certainly the case that the provision of bathing, though officially justified in terms of hygiene in a fairly narrow way, was in practice provided on a broader basis that acknowledged its significance in a larger sense of well-being. Cleanliness of a strictly medical kind could have been achieved by more limited interventions, and most people who received a bath did not require one by the narrow criteria of health. Care managers recognized that baths were sources of bodily well-being that went beyond this and were willing to allocate them on that basis.

Baths also act as rites of passage and markers of social transitions. As we have seen, they retain something of this aspect even when provided within a service context. What is lost, however, is the capacity to control the timing in such a way that underwrites transitions. Too many people are forced to have baths at "meaningless" times, and certainly the element of spontaneity is lost. For some, however, the provision of help itself comes to form the basis for a new framework for the temporal and social organization of the week.

Last, bathing has sometimes been located within a discourse of power and domination, and these elements are in some degree present whenever someone is taken and given a bath—where the bath is something that is done to them. The bathing encounter certainly contains aspects of this, in potential at least. The client is naked, weak, and seated, while the worker is clothed, strong, and above the client. The situation enshrines a powerful dynamic of subordination in which bodies are potentially observed, corrected, and disciplined, according to the principles of Foucauldian biopower. That the clients did not feel that this was in fact how they were treated was in large measure a tribute to the kindness and good practice of the workers who went to considerable efforts to ensure that they were accorded respect and dignity. In doing so, however, they had to override what was a powerful dynamic inherent in the exchange.

Conclusion

Throughout this chapter, I have argued that bathing and washing exemplify day-to-day and mundane activities of the old. As a result they have received little in the way of academic attention, often considered too practical and too banal to be of interest. But it is in these ordinary and banal patterns that much of the texture and meaning of life exists. The life of the body is the bedrock on which our existence rests. Tending, caring for, managing our bodies, and using and presenting them in a social life are central to our day-to-day experience, though it is not often brought to the front of our consciousness. Until, that is, some disruption in these taken-for-granted activities forces them and the existential life of the body into conscious consideration. Old age is one such source of disruption. Though we are indeed aged by culture as some theorists suggest, we are also aged by our bodies. The body can impose its own constraints, as we have seen concerning the practical difficulties some people experience in relation to personal care. The ways in which personal care is managed, the meanings it contains, and the discourses that encode it significantly affect how these bodily constraints are experienced.

Among the discourses within which personal care is encoded are those relating to bathing. As we have seen, the official account of service provision presents the activity in a narrow, utilitarian way—as the achievement of adequate standards of hygiene. The discourse of social welfare is a constrained one in which the scope of interventions are limited and in which health and hygiene have a privileged status. But as we have seen, baths and bathing are about more than this. They touch on other matters; their meanings are wider and more diffuse, and the experiences they offer more various. Bathing is part of the experiential life of the body and as such is drawn into a variety of discourses and sets of meanings around pleasure, luxury, eroticism, renewal, initiation, and power. Echoes of these wider meanings reverberate through the experience of bathing in the community. Hearing them enables us to set community care in a broader social and cultural context and thus to rescue it from too narrow a policy context. It also allows us to hear something of the voices of some of the most disabled older people, people whose bodily experiences have received little analytic attention in our overarching focus on the body.

References

Andrews, M.
   1999 The Seductiveness of Agelessness. *Ageing and Society* 19: 301–18.

Arber, S., and J. Ginn
   1991 *Gender and Later Life: A Sociological Analysis of Resources and Constraints*. London: Sage.

Bates, I.
1993 A Job Which is "Right for Me?": Social Class, Gender and Individu-
alisation. In *Youth and Inequality*. Edited by I. Bates and G. Riseborough,
14–31. Buckingham, U.K.: Open University Press.

Brook, B.
1999 *Feminist Perspectives on the Body*. Harlow: Pearson.

Bushman, R. L., and C. L. Bushman
1988 The Early History of Cleanliness in America. *Journal of American History* 74: 1213–38.

Connell, R. W.
1995 *Masculinities*. Cambridge, U.K.: Polity.

Daatland, S.
1990 What are Families For: On Family Solidarity and Preference for Help.
Ageing and Society 10: 1–15.

Davies, K.
1994 The Tensions between Process Time and Clock Time in Carework:
The Example of Day Nurseries. *Time and Society* 3: 277–303.

Estes, C. L., and E. A. Binney
1989 The Biomedicalization of Aging. *The Gerontologist* 29: 587–96.

Featherstone, M.
1991 The Body in Consumer Culture. In *The Body: Social Process and Cultural Theory*. Edited by M. Featherstone, M. Hepworth, and B. S. Turner,
170–96. London: Sage.

Fitzgerald, M., and J. Sim
1979 *British Prisons*. Oxford, U.K.: Blackwell.

Furman, F. K.
1997 *Facing the Mirror: Older Women and Beauty Shop Culture*. New York:
Routledge.
1999 There Are No Old Venuses: Older Women's Responses to Their Aging Bodies. In *Mother Time: Women, Aging and Ethics*. Edited by M. U.
Walker, 7–22. Boulder, Colo.: Rowman & Littlefield.

Gilleard, C., and P. Higgs
2000 *Culture of Ageing: Self, Citizen and the Body*. London: Prentice Hall.

Goffman, E.
1961 *Asylums: Essays on the Social Situations of Mental Patients and Other Inmates*. New York: Doubleday.

Gullette, M. M.
1997 *Declining to Decline: Cultural Combat and the Politics of Midlife*. Charlottesville: University Press of Virginia.

Henley, N. M.
1973 The Politics of Touch. In *Radical Psychology*. Edited by P. Brown. London: Tavistock.

Hochschild, A.
1983 *The Managed Heart: The Commercialisation of Human Feelings*. Berkley: University of California.

Jourard, S. M.
1966 An Exploratory Study of Body Accessibility. *British Journal of Social and Clinical Psychology* 5: 221–31.

Jourard, S. M., and J. E. Rubin
1968 Self Disclosure and Touching: A Study of Two Modes of Interpersonal Encounter and Their Inter-Relation. *Journal of Humanistic Psychology* 8: 39–48.

Kira, A.
1967 *The Bathroom: Criteria for Design*. New York: Bantam.

Lawler, J.
1991 *Behind the Screens: Nursing, Somology and the Problem of the Body*. Melbourne, Australia: Churchill Livingstone.

Lawler, J.
(ed.) 1997 Knowing the Body and Embodiment: Methodologies, Discourses and Nursing. In *The Body in Nursing*. Melbourne, Australia: Churchill Livingstone.

Lawton, J.
1998 Contemporary Hospice Care: The Sequestration of the Unbounded Body and "Dirty Dying." *Sociology of Health and Illness* 20: 121–43.

Littlewood, J.
1991 Care and Ambiguity: Towards a Concept of Nursing. In *Anthropology and Nursing*. Edited by P. Holden and J. Littlewood, 170–89. London: Routledge.

Öberg, P.
1996 The Absent Body: A Social Gerontological Paradox. *Ageing and Society* 16: 701–19.

Parker, G.
1993 *With This Body: Caring and Disability in Marriage.* Buckingham, U.K.: Open University Press.

Phillipson, C., and A. Walker
1986 *Ageing and Social Policy: A Critical Assessment.* Aldershot, U.K.: Gower.

Skeggs, B.
1997 *Formations of Class and Gender: Becoming Respectable.* London: Sage.

Swenarton, M.
1977 Having a Bath: English Domestic Bathrooms, 1890–1940. In *Leisure in the Twentieth Century: History of Design,* 92–99. London: Design Council Publications.

Tronto, J. C.
1993 *Moral Boundaries: A Political Argument for an Ethic of Care.* London: Routledge.

Tulle-Winton, E.
2000 Old Bodies. In *The Body, Culture and Society.* Edited by P. Hancock, B. Hughes, E. Jagger, K. Patterson, R. Russell, E. Tulle-Winton, and M. Tyler. Buckingham, U.K.: Open University Press.

Twigg, J.
2000a *Bathing: The Body and Community Care.* London: Routledge.
2000b Carework as a Form of Bodywork. *Ageing and Society* 20: 389–411.

van Gennep, A.
[1908] 1960 *The Rites of Passage.* Translated by M. B. Vizedom and G. L. Cafee. London: Routledge & Kegan Paul.

Vigarello, G.
1988 *Concepts of Cleanliness: Changing Attitudes in France Since the Middle Ages.* Cambridge, U.K.: CUP.

Waerness, K.
1987 On the Rationality of Caring. In *Women and the State: The Shifting Boundaries of Public and Private.* Edited by A. Showstack Sassoon, 207–34. London: Hutchinson.

Watson, J.
2000 *Male Bodies: Health, Culture and Identity*. Buckingham, U.K.: Open University Press.

Whitcher, J. S., and J. D. Fisher
1979 Multidimensional Reaction to Therapeutic Touch in a Hospital Setting. *Journal of Personality and Social Psychology* 37: 87–96.

Williams, S. J., and G. Bendelow
1998 *The Lived Body: Sociological Themes, Embodied Issues*. London: Routledge.

Wilkie, J. S.
1986 Submerged Sensuality: Technology and Perceptions of Bathing. *Journal of Social History* 19: 649–54.

Wolf, Z. R.
1988 *Nurses' Work, the Sacred and Profane*. Philadelphia: University of Pennsylvania Press.

Woodward, K.
1991 *Aging and Its Discontents: Freud and Other Fictions*. Bloomington: Indiana University Press.

Woodward, K.
(ed.) 1999 *Figuring Age: Women, Bodies, Generations*. Bloomington: Indiana University Press.

Yegül, F.
1992 *Baths and Bathing in Classical Antiquity*. Cambridge: MIT Press.

Young, I. M.
1990 *Throwing Like a Girl and Other Essays in Feminist Philosophy and Social Theory*. Bloomington: Indiana University Press.

CHAPTER SIX

THE HOMOSEXUAL BODY IN LESBIAN AND GAY ELDERS' NARRATIVES
Dana Rosenfeld

Theorists have expressed a long-standing concern with the sexual body. Psychoanalysis' very epistemological foundations, for example, are constructed along a sexuality/society dualism. Freud, perhaps more than we have realized (Williams and Bendelow 1998), was primarily concerned with the social construction of the body *via* its production and regulation by societal controls on sexual action.[1] The sexual body also figures, however vaguely, in classical sociological theory: Engels (1972), for example, connected the sexual order to the organization of production, and Weber (1958) "recognized that sexual abstinence was a significant component of Puritanism and capitalism" (Turner 1996). But it was Michel Foucault who provided us with the most powerful—and explicitly theoretical—tool for understanding the relation between the body, sex, and society (Featherstone, Hepworth, and Turner 1991). His philosophical concern with the relationship between power and knowledge and discursive formation turned to the sexual body in his three-volume study on *The History of Sexuality* (1979, 1987, 1988), in which, by unpacking the "series of restrictions, prohibitions, censorships, and taboos on the 'sexual' body" (Williams and Bendelow 1998, 30–31) in seventeenth-century Europe, he deconstructed the very technologies through which sex (and, in turn, sexual bodies) is discursively produced.

Beginning in the 1990s, however, sociologists began to criticize Foucault on phenomenological grounds (see Featherstone, Hepworth, and Turner 1991 [1995]; Nettleton and Watson 1998), noting that, while his latter works increasingly attended to the "active individual," his abiding, primary concern with a bodily power whose activity resides only in its discursive construction effectively excluded an active body that experiences and responds to everyday life (Williams and Bendelow 1998). In Jackson and Scott's (2001, 10) words, while "Foucault legitimized the study of the body . . . his focus on governance and surveillance de-emphasized individual agency except in so far as it was engaged in resistance." Moreover, that Foucault's focus was the construction of the body over *historical time*, not the experience of the body in the individual's *lifetime*, provided little room for considering how the body is formulated, experienced, and managed across the life course, or aging sexual bodies.

This latter consideration finds its home in life course theory, which examines actors' differential engagements with social structure and social change based on their age and life course locations at the time of those changes (see Hardy and Waite 1997; Settersten 1999; Elder 1995; Rosow 1978; Ryder [1965] 1997). In contrast to the medicalized depiction of aging as a biological process of maturation and decline,[2] this tradition approaches aging as the movement through—and experience of—time and, thus, of both individual and collective engagements with and experiences of social change. While life course theory has not explicitly focused on the body, these changes clearly include how the appetites, capacities and limitations, habits and foibles, and rights and responsibilities (indeed, the very nature) of the body itself are seen and experienced. While my work has engaged life course theory by exploring the implications of late-twentieth-century gay and sexual liberation movements for the identity work of lesbian and gay elders (see Rosenfeld 1999, 2003; Pollner and Rosenfeld 2000), this chapter will focus on the implications of these movements—and of my subjects' distinctive relation to them—for their vision of the appropriate bodily enactment and expression of homosexuality.[3] In so doing, I suggest a conceptualization of the aging sexual body unavailable through a strict application of Foucault's framework—as an inherently active one embedded in, but not completely constructed by, the discourses of both aging *and* sexuality.

There are a number of intersecting dimensions on which my subjects invoked and moralized about the homosexual body. The first is the *division of everyday life into public and private worlds* that has characterized the move to modernity and the related increasing relegation of bodily functions, desires, and conditions to the private world. This movement into everyday concerns is, as Nettleton and Watson (1998) note, an important step away from "simply" theoretical concerns with the body. Citing

Bakhtin, Turner (1999, 66) notes that the premodern world, in which "the 'open' body [was] linked to the public world through ritual and carnival," gave way to a modern world in which "the 'closed' body of individualized consumer society" was sequestered in the private realm of the home. As a result, "Desires are now inscribed in private bodies separated from the hygienic space of the public world." This split sets the public world of the "formality, impersonalism, neutrality and universalism of work" against the "informality, particularism and affectivity of the private home," which, in turn, attends to the emotional and physical needs of intimates, and where private bodily needs and desires are expressed and pursued. In such a society, sexuality is contained within the body and expressed in exclusively private arenas such as the home, and the public expression of sexuality is strictly regulated by a range of social agents, including private citizens who sanction the breaching of these divisions in everyday interaction as, in Mary Douglas' ([1966] 1991) words, "matter out of order" and thus as "defilement."

The second is the tension between two competing *typifications of homosexual people* that prevailed throughout my informants' lives. In the early twentieth century, a gender-based system of sexual-classification-associated homosexuality with gender "inversion"—or the assumption of sex-opposite roles, manifested in both personality and bodily appearance—since gender identity, rather than sexual identity, was the basis for the categorization of actors into the ranks of the normal or the abnormal (Chauncey 1994; Newton 1985). It was not until the Freudian invention of homosexuality as a question of sexual object choice rather than of gender inversion was embraced by the new medical-state alliance during the Second World War (and imposed on both the military and the civilian populations, which found themselves subject to a new focus of surveillance and control—see Berube 1990 and D'Emilio 1983) that the new category of sexual "pervert" became a serious challenge to the gender-based discourse of homosexuality.

This new construction was also embraced by a new group of middle-class homosexual men and women, who saw this new identity as providing a coherent sexual self and a community of others that honored the middle-class commitment to constraining sexual desire within the normal body and enacting it in exclusively private settings (Valocchi 1999). These two homosexual "types" complicated the symbolic and practical field in which homosexuals negotiated their identities and their daily lives, since, because same-sex activity on the part of gender-conforming bodies was no longer seen as normal, these bodies began to be scrutinized for evidence of "perversion." Indeed, it was because the "pervert" was not easily identifiable that she or he became a dangerous figure in the popular imagination (hence, the postwar sex panic—see D'Emilio 1983). While the first construction posited homosexuality as a corporeally evident abnormality, the second posited it as an internal, private desire that was corporeally felt and enacted, but not necessarily corporeally evident. Passing as heterosexual therefore involved more than mere gender conformity—rather, it involved controlling biographical information,[4] the movement between heterosexual and homosexual arenas and contexts and homosexual associations themselves.

The third is the dimension of *stigma*. If "we can . . . think of the body as an outer surface of interpretations and representations and an internal environment of structures and determinations" (Turner 1999, 66–67), then the relationship between these two is further complicated by the stigmatized nature of homosexual desire. When this desire becomes evident in this "outer surface" within the public realm, homosexuality—or, indeed, any stigma—endangers both the stigmatized actor's social status and the interaction order itself. Stigma is embodied, by virtue of either the nature and source of the stigma (i.e., physical deformities and disabilities) or its expression (i.e., sexual nonconformities)—stigmas can thus be either inscribed on the body or contained by it.

In the first case, the person bearing the stigma is always already discredited, at least in the eyes of actors who recognize the stigmatized quality as discrediting. In the latter case, the bearer of the stigma is merely discreditable, committed, in Erving Goffman's (1963) view, to keeping that discreditable quality hidden from all but her fellow-stigmatized through the use of information-control devices designed to help the stigmatized actor pass as "normal." Whatever the nature of the stigma, it is expressed or silenced by the body and communicated or suppressed in interaction between bodies. Passing as a member of a nonstigmatized group centers on normalizing the presented self by manipulating or reframing the body and its expression in interaction.

This potentiates the secondary stigmatization of actors unable to differentiate between private and public realms, or unable or unwilling to honor that distinction. For those who understand and embrace the construction of homosexuality as a stigmatized (discreditable) aspect of self, then those whose homosexuality is known to heterosexuals is explicable by reference to two orders of homosexual incompetence (I define homosexual competence as the appropriate enactment of homosexuality). The first is a temporary, correctable—and ultimately corrected—incompetence born of ignorance, and the second is an intractable incompetence born of an informed flaunting of the informed refusal to honor the distinction between public and private realms.

As this chapter will show, subjects invoked homosexual others' incompetent management of their homosexuality while presenting their own actions and orientations as competent; indeed, some pointed to their own past incompetencies as a backdrop for their present, corrected and correct approach to managing their homosexual desires.

The final dimension is that of *discursive change.* During my subjects' middle age, a new discourse of homosexuality emerged that introduced new criteria for homosexual competence. While the history of homosexuality—and, indeed, all sexualities—in the twentieth century is complex, clearly the increasingly severe stigmatization of homosexuality as a shameful and essentially private condition was the dominant discourse of homosexuality before the Stonewall uprising of 1969 (Duberman 1994) galvanized the lesbian and gay liberation movements of the late 1960s and early 1970s. These movements constructed homosexuality not as a source of personal stigma, but as a source of political status, and the homosexual as an accredited rather than a potentially or actually discredited person (see Faderman 1991; Stein 1997; Nardi and Sanders 1994).

The liberationist claim that homosexuality was an essential self to be enacted in public as well as in private realms rather than an aspect of self to be exclusively enacted in private constructed those who adopted the latter and stigmatized formulation as ignorant or morally weak or both. While the invert and the pervert were both *stigmatized* identities, constructing homosexuality as a discreditable aspect of self, the liberationist discourse created a new *accredited* homosexual identity, constructing homosexuality as an essential and global self that could not be contained within the body without damaging the actor's authenticity and integrity.

The lesbian and gay liberation movements therefore called on all homosexuals, regardless of age, to embrace both this new identity and their call for its open display as essential to honoring the authentic homosexual self and to abandon the previous policy that homosexuals had adopted in order to survive in a hostile heterosexual world, namely, passing as heterosexual. (For the initial responses of middle-aged homosexuals to these demands, see Grube 1990.) To pass, the new discourse claimed, was to collaborate not only in the oppression of a valid community but in the continuous suppression of an authentic, global sexual self that could only be honored through both individual/private and collective/public celebration.

Stigma thus remains a theoretical backdrop for the post-Stonewall discourse of homosexuality, which adopted as its core properties the rejection of the properties of the previous, stigmatizing discourse. But it also remains a lived backdrop for the identity work of lesbian and gay elders, who spent the first half of their lives experiencing in a context that provided only a stigmatized formulation of same-sex desires and relations. When gay liberation's claims were made, my subjects were aged thirty-nine to sixty-three, and most had adopted and enacted stigmatized homosexual identities for decades. A smaller group, however, adopted an accredited homosexual identity through the properties of the lesbian-feminist and gay liberationist discourse.[5] My analysis thus uncovered the existence of what I termed as two "identity cohorts," each composed of actors who identified themselves as members of a particular category of person in the same historical era bearing a distinctive discourse of self—in this case, the pre-gay liberation (1920–1970) era that stigmatized homosexuality and the era of gay liberation and lesbian-feminism (1969–present) that destigmatized it, constructing it instead as a source of status.

For the people I interviewed, the implications of membership in one identity cohort or another were far reaching. They ranged from the nature of the threat heterosexuals posed to homosexuals in general, to relations with heterosexuals and homosexuals alike, and to (of greatest relevance here) how they understood the relation of homosexuality to the body. In this chapter, I explore how these subjects understand, manage, and assess the body as a sexual signifier in light of their ideological commitments to one of these two discourses through which they continue to conduct their identity work. This chapter will uncover two competing formulations of the body as a communicator of sexual identity, each centering on three overlapping issues: the division between public and private realms, the informing character of copresent sexualized bodies, and the embodiment and communicative significance of gender inversion.

176

The chapter will demonstrate that while my informants understood homosexuality to be manageable within the confines of the body—hidden from heterosexuals who were incapable of recognizing homosexual bodies as such unless the latter embodied or disclosed their homosexuality—they read the implications of this protective feature very differently. Specifically, those who had identified themselves as homosexual through the properties of the pre-Stonewall stigmatizing discourse saw it as strengthening their ability to enact their homosexuality appropriately—in private—and thus to achieve homosexual competence, while those who identified themselves through the properties of gay liberation saw it as discouraging the commitment of all homosexuals to publicly enact—and disclose—their homosexual identities.

The point is that these actors, having committed themselves to one of these discourses, experienced their lives and their movement through time through discursive properties, currently and in the past. The chapter examines how subjects view their early actions and orientations from the vantage point of their current identities and ideologies and shows that their narratives express a set of obligations that they either maintained despite the discursive change alluded to in the preceding or replaced because of it. Accordingly, I present past actions (i.e., passing devices) not to suggest that actors engage in them in exactly the same way and under the same conditions in later life (and different times), but to highlight their retrospective assessments of these actions as expressing homosexual competence or incompetence. Clearly, many of the constraints and dangers my informants cite as reasons for their past actions no longer exist (i.e., police harassment), but the underlying realities to which past actions were designed to respond do, in subjects' views, endure (i.e., the homosexual body as essentially unreadable by heterosexuals). The challenge, then, lies in attending to deep assumptions about the world, the body, and the self that are expressed through accounts of past and present actions and orientations.

Readable and Unreadable Sexual Bodies

Underlying the division between inverts and perverts is the assumption that homosexuality can be contained within the body and that heterosexuals are incapable of reading homosexual bodies as such unless they are provided with specific cues, most notably, of course, gender inversion. Indeed, heterosexuals' inability to read the gay body was seen as so intractable that subjects' lives were sometimes constrained by it. Rodney (75, D),[6] for example, was attracted to a heterosexual man whose ignorance of gay culture and courtship made it difficult for Rodney to communicate his attraction to him without breaching certain "limits":

> I'd love to have a connection with him but he doesn't know that I'm gay, I guess. My god, the things that I have said, within limits, you would think that you would have tumbled long ago, but I don't think he's tumbled to the fact that I'm gay.

These "limits" also prevented Rodney from asking his doctor how to have safe sex with the object of his romantic interest should he manage to connect with him. Because homosexuals are "not part of the mainstream," he explained, "you hesitate even if you wrote a professional person. My doctor doesn't know that I'm gay. I've mentioned earlier this young [man]—if he were available I would like to go to the doctor and say, 'Is there any way that we could make contact that's gonna be relatively safe?'"

Others described receiving unwanted attention from heterosexuals that they found difficult to refuse without making their homosexuality known. Manny (77, D) described being the object of women's "crushes" at the local Jewish senior center—attention from which he protected himself by feigning ignorance as to the nature of the inquiries. "The women don't know that I'm gay," he explained, "and two of them have a terrible crush, but I act like I don't know what they're doing." Brian (74, D) had married and divorced a lesbian when both were in their twenties—a marriage designed to facilitate public heterosexual identities—and found his heterosexual friends' assumption that he was lonely because he had not remarried to be troubling but did not see how he could convince them that he was not, in fact, lonely without undermining the heterosexual façade he had constructed:

> I think now they think of me as being lonely, more so than—they don't know I'm gay. And there's no reason to let them know. I'm not going to get into that. It's just they [think], "Oh, he's been divorced, had an unfortunate marriage and now he's lonely" or something. So they do nice things for me. It's all right, and we have a good time, but they bother me. I think sometimes they're feeling sorry for me because I'm divorced,

don't have a wife now, I'm alone. It bothers me that they do, because it doesn't bother me like they think it bothers me.

Note, however, that none of these subjects—or, indeed, any other members of the discreditable identity cohort—saw these negative consequences of passing as anything other than the minor costs attached to the most central project of their homosexual careers: passing as heterosexual while in the company of heterosexuals. Indeed, even when telling me how "bothered" he was by his friends' unnecessary concern, Brian stressed that there was "no reason to let them know" he was gay; thus, being the object of pity as a presumed heterosexual was preferable to being the object of derision as a known homosexual, just as, for Manny, being considered a socially inept (even sexless) heterosexual was preferable to being recognized as a homosexual.

Obtrusive Homosexual Bodies

Despite the new, unreadable homosexual body provided by the Freudian pervert, the association of homosexuality with gender inversion remained strong among heterosexuals and homosexuals alike, and aware of the existence of homosexuals who adopted this gender-based construction on the one hand and of heterosexuals who maintained this gender-based formulation on the other, most subjects described having concealed their homosexuality by achieving bodily appearances that conformed to dominant gender norms. For the female subjects, this involved managing the tension between their desire to wear pants and the consequences of being seen thus attired by heterosexuals. They did this by dressing "normally" in heterosexual contexts and wearing pants only in homosexual ones. Abby (70, A) "would wear slacks down in the Village, but I would never wear slacks in mid-town Manhattan. It just wasn't the thing to do." For the male subjects, this involved achieving a heterosexual image by using exclusively "masculine" gestures and mannerisms. George (75, D) worked to break his youthful "habit" of holding his hands in a stereotypically feminine way, which he defined by turning his hands palm-down and making his wrists limp, and Julius (89, D) altered his gait to conform to a typically masculine style of walking:

> Kids always liked me, and two or three of them would be walking down
> the street with me and they would say "Julius, take longer steps," and

these would be kids that were twelve, thirteen years old. And one of them would say, "Julius, be careful, you use your hands quite a bit, you should not do that." I think that they sensed that I was gay, but they didn't want me to show it. It made a lot of changes with me, because I took it seriously when they would say these things. At the moment it wasn't serious, but later you think about it, you think about these things. So I learned to take longer steps.

These subjects also strongly condemned those who failed or refused to achieve gender-appropriate appearances—indeed, they condemned all homosexuals who made their homosexuality obtrusive in the presence of heterosexuals. Rhoda (89, D) characterized as "stupid" those homosexuals who openly embodied their gender inversion despite the "ridicule" they "endured." She explained that "the majority of the society didn't accept it, especially the ones that were butch looking. It might be what they wanted and yet—they would want it and be that way and endure the ridicule." According to these subjects, the appropriate way to handle one's homosexuality was to decline to use the body as a signifier of homosexuality when in the company of heterosexuals—a policy these informants glossed under the term "keeping it private." Thus, Lillian (69, D) described herself as having "always been very closeted about my lifestyle," defining being "closeted" as a refusal "to announce my sexuality to the world" and a commitment to "not wearing a sign on my back." Declaring her sexuality to be "my business, it's none of your business," she did not "go walking around and telling who I am and what I am."

Lillian's statements invoke the clear and unequivocal marking of the body as homosexual—wearing a sign—and thus displays an assumption that anyone can "read" the body as homosexual should it exhibit certain homosexual qualities. Moreover, her use of the term "walking around and telling what I am and who I am" invokes the image of randomly traversing space and indiscriminately displaying an essentially private desire to an anonymous (and presumably heterosexual) public. This implies that such an act would express either an inability to distinguish between public and private worlds or a refusal to honor that distinction.

Flaunting—in Goffman's (1963, 107–8) words, "flamboyantly or pitifully acting out the negative attributes imputed to" the stigmatized group of which she is a member—was even more universally—and strongly—

condemned as an extreme and unnecessary form of embodied obtrusiveness that was damaging to all homosexuals, including the subjects themselves. By publicly marking hitherto unreadable bodies as homosexual, they improved the heterosexuals' semiotic literacy and alerted them to the existence of other "invisible" homosexuals, thus endangering the latter's ability to pass. Also, when the stereotyped behavior of homosexuals was exaggerated, those who flaunted did not only call attention to homosexuals but reproduced the heterosexuals' sense of them as driven by their sexual desires and unrestrained in their pursuit. Patricia (77, D) explained that should homosexuals feel the need to assemble and march *en masse*, they should do so while dressing "normally," as "ladies and gentlemen"—in other words, while publicly displaying their commitment to self-restraint and to the containment of sexual desire within private bodies. Thus, it is not the public assembly to which she objects, but the public embodiment and display of stereotyped homosexual qualities and behaviors, which extrude the facticity of sex, which rightly belongs "behind closed doors," into public space and public view:

> Some of them go around and push their lesbianism or homosexuality down everybody's throat. When you have your gay parades and the men grab their balls and say "Hey, hey, we're gay!"—I don't feel that that's necessary. If they could only learn to be gentlemen and ladies people would accept us much more easily. They can go do their parades and dress up normally. What we do behind closed doors is up to us, we don't have to flaunt it.

Another drawback of flaunting, other subjects emphasized, is that it makes heterosexuals' acceptance of homosexuals less likely. Gabrielle (78, D) and her lover "don't go to any gay things, gay parades" because "the media picks out the worst" images to transmit. Rodney (75, D) explained that "I don't like to see a lot of the [actions] of some of the gay guys and I'm not too keen on dykes on bikes. I think these are the extremes, I think they give the whole community a bad name." Similarly, Julius (89, D) claimed that "parades and marching" would not, in fact, grant homosexuals the civil rights they sought, since these public actions led young people to associate homosexuals with "transvestites or floozies" rather than with the larger, more legitimate group of "straight gay people" with which he identified.

This stance was also adopted by members of the accredited identity cohort; Marilyn (66, A), for example, said it was "unfortunate that some people feel they have to go running around without any clothes on hardly in gay and lesbian parades." Although she had engaged in similar activity while at a lesbian-feminist commune in the 1970s, that, she explained, "was for ourselves, and not in a public parade [with] TV and cameras that are nation-wide that say, 'Oh, look at these terrible things that gays [do].'" Indeed, Leonard (72, A) associated some homosexuals' declination to participate in his program for gay seniors with their fear of being linked to extreme members of the gay community such as ACTUP, a political AIDS organization that "can be terribly embarrassing if you want to do some nice little thing and here they come marching by with signs and throwing things or something of the sort."

Contextually Obtrusive Bodies: Gay Bodies in Space

Declining to exhibit or flaunt one's homosexuality was not, however, enough to pass as heterosexual, since heterosexuals, while unable to "read" homosexual bodies as such, could discern an actor's homosexuality through her bodily position in relation to homosexual regions and to other, more recognizable homosexual bodies. Thus, while adopting a typically "heterosexual" (read: gender-appropriate) deportment was sufficient enough to pass as heterosexual while in direct interaction with heterosexuals, it did little to cover observed interactions with other homosexuals, such as passing as heterosexual while entering or exiting gay space (managing the movement between heterosexual and homosexual regions), and while in the company of other homosexuals who could discredit each other by association (managing associations). These became practical problems.

Managing the Movement between Regions

While recent historical research has belied our sense of the pre-Stonewall gay world as necessarily isolated and isolating, it has also shown that the veritable carnival of gay expression and sociality that characterized much of urban gay life in the early part of the twentieth century was suppressed during the post-Prohibition years (see Chauncey 1994). As a result, the gay world in which my subjects immersed themselves before the late 1960s was generally limited to cruising areas (such as parks), bars, and private homes. Despite being subject to raids, the former two places were dangerous because people seen entering or exiting them were tagged as homosexual.

Several subjects who patronized gay bars spoke of having committed themselves to covering their movement from spaces in which bodies are read as heterosexual to ones in which they are not. Abby (70, A), for example, explained that, because "it was an outlaw society in those days, you slunk around, you checked before you walked into a place to see if there was anybody that you could *possibly* know that would see you going into any of these places." Indeed, several subjects avoided gay bars completely, socializing in private homes instead; Barbie (67, D) did this in the 1950s, when she was a teacher, because "somebody from the school board might have their policeman out or something, trailing you."

But this sensitivity to context so essential to maintaining the presentation of a heterosexual front in public had implications for the embodiment of homosexuality in private as well, since subjects had to change their image back to a heterosexual one before they entered public space. Val (74, D) noted that while she "could dress the way I wanted" (in men's clothes) at the home of a friend, "nowhere else could I dress that way, nor could I travel back and forth that way." Similarly, Sharon (66, A) described packing her "men's outfit, men's suit and all" in a suitcase on Saturday nights and riding the bus to a "mixed gay and lesbian and straight cocktail lounge," where she would change, then "go out and have a good time with the gay guys."

Managing Associations

According to Goffman, the stigmatized are caught between the need to associate with other members of their stigmatized group (in this case, of course, homosexuals) and the need to pass as normal. The difficulty of balancing these lies is that associating with "their own," if seen and recognized as such by normals, can be discrediting in itself, since actors identify others based, in great part, on their associations. In Goffman's (1963, 47) words, "[T]he issue is that in certain circumstances the social identity of those an individual is with can be used as a source of information concerning his own social identity, the assumption being that he is what the others are." Subjects were, in fact, aware of the heterosexuals' ability to read stereotypically homosexual bodies as homosexual and to extrapolate their homosexual identification to copresent others and saw gay men and lesbians who exhibited or flaunted their homosexuality as threats to their own ability to pass as heterosexual. As a result, they avoided publicly associating with easily identifiable homosexuals, limiting their public associations to those who passed.

George (75, D) told me he wanted to have a gay man as a roommate, but "not a nelly person" because "the neighbors pick up on it," and Lillian (69, D) avoided "women who look gay":

> I don't like to be around a woman who looks gay. I don't want to be walking down the street *per se* with someone that's—you know what I mean? I don't want anyone turning around and pointing their finger: "Oh, look at those two."

The precautions discreditable subjects took to avoid being seen in the company of "obvious" homosexuals did not, however, prevent heterosexuals from intruding into homosexual space. Manny (77, D) was "ruined" when his coworkers, who had entered a gay bar to see the drag show, saw him there as well:

> This gay bar, a lot of the boys would be in drag, and it was a big thing, where the straight people would come. And at that time I was out of the garment trade, and one time the buyer from the dress department came. They came in a crowd of five or six, but two of them were the big buyers, and of course [they] saw me, so I was *ruined*, absolutely *ruined*. Well, you know, it's a terrible thing. I was just *there*.

Clearly, then, being seen by heterosexuals in a recognizably gay space was severely discrediting—unless, of course, those who were seen there could account for it in such a way as to repair the rift between, in Goffman's terms, their virtual and their actual social identities. Val (74, D) did this when she encountered a fellow police officer at a gay bar in her neighborhood; when he asked what she had been "doing at a place like that," she asked him the same question, only to be told that he and his partner "were about to make a bust." Having determined that he was not homosexual himself, she explained that she was showing her out-of-town friends "the other side":

> I said "I live not far from here, and my friends that I worked with at North America were coming up to visit, and to see what goes on, on the other side. I said I would join them." "Well, you were dancing with girls!" "Well, it's all the same group, and that's what you do in a place like that, what else do you do in a place like that?" So he said, "Forget it."

Another repair technique was to distance oneself from the other homosexuals in the area by joining one's heterosexual contacts in ridiculing them, thus displaying a condemnation of homosexuals that was, presumably, read as evidence of heterosexuality. Ryan (81, D) spoke of having done this whenever an "obvious" homosexual entered the supermarket where he worked. When he and his coworkers saw "some real nelly thing come in the store, we'd all laugh at him when he went out. I didn't want to be that type of a person. I didn't want people laughing at me. So I stayed away from it." Marge (81, D) said that when she was among people who "considered everybody [else] straight" and "made derogatory remarks [about] gay people," she had joined in the derogation because "you couldn't let them know how you felt about things."

Avoiding being seen in the company of "obvious" homosexuals and accounting for instances in which this was unavoidable did not, however, preclude informants' homosexual connections, which they limited to homosexuals who declined to embody their homosexuality in public and who thus did not threaten the public heterosexual identity subjects worked to achieve. Patricia (77, D), for example, described having dined at restaurants with a large group of gay men and women who dressed in gender-appropriate fashion and thus passed as heterosexual, a project that was furthered strengthened by the mixed-sex composition of the group. Marge's (81, D) husband did not know she was a lesbian even though she held social events for her lesbian and gay friends at their apartment (a group that included her female lover) because these friends dressed in gender-appropriate fashion. Although she eventually told him she was gay:

> At first [my husband] didn't know what was going on, he thought we were just really good friends and although he didn't drink he used to buy alcohol for my friends who were mostly all gay, the guys were so manly.

Passing, then, entails managing one's relations with other homosexuals, limiting them to those who neither flaunt nor exhibit their "private" desires and to those who thus recognize and honor the distinction between the public realm of work and anonymous association, on the one hand, and the private realm in which "private" (read: bodily) needs and desires can be expressed and pursued, on the other. This, again, was designed to avoid situations in which the sexual semiotic abilities of heterosexuals—part of the repertoire of what Goffman (1963, 50) terms actors' "decoding capacities"—could be used to read homosexual "obvious" bodies and to conclude that copresent bodies, whether "obviously" homosexual or not, were homosexual as well.

Subjects saw this practice as a rational and justifiable way to insulate themselves from the embodied obtrusiveness of incompetent homosexuals. Indeed, Maria (64, D), the one subject who was herself avoided because of her gender-transgressive homosexuality, described this avoidance as reasonable, citing the fact that her friends, who were "not *out* out" (read: not open about their homosexuality to heterosexuals) were not to be blamed for limiting their public associations to actors whose bodies could not be read as homosexual by heterosexuals:

> She picks her friends very carefully. And I don't think I seek her [out] because she's not *out* out, you know, and I'm a very obvious lesbian. And I find that a lot of lesbians don't wanna [hang] too much with [obvious lesbians.] They're not *out* out. And so there are functions that they attend that they would never ask you to go to, because I just don't fit in. And I don't blame them. I'm not, you know, I understand that there's places where I just don't fit in, because of the way I am, my attire and everything else.

Some of the accredited had, of course, engaged in this and other passing devices when they were living as stigmatized homosexuals, before they distanced themselves from this discourse and identified through the properties of gay liberation or lesbian-feminism or both. But their current, accredited homosexual identities and criteria for homosexual competence required them to retrospectively reformulate these past practices as homosexually incompetent.

Thus both Abby and Marilyn contrasted their (relative) comfort with associating with other gay women in public with their past declination to do so. "For the first time in my entire life," Abby explained, "I am so comfortable with being who I am. I never even think about it anymore. It feels great! I never worry about what other people think." She characterized this as "a major step": while she doesn't "walk around the street, or walk into the market, and say, 'Oh by the way, I'm a lesbian,'" she is "not uncomfortable with it anymore. I never worry about who I'm with, what they look like or *anything*." At a recent outing with other members of a social club for lesbian seniors, Marilyn was surprised to have

> found myself talking about being gay and lesbian without any thought about it until I stopped and looked around—I said "Hmm!" But here I was in public talking about being gay and lesbian. I might not have done that at one time, but I felt comfortable doing it on Sunday and I didn't care—well, I mean, it was easy to do and not something I censored myself doing, which at one time I might have.

For the discreditable, though, these passing devices remain abidingly rational. Ryan's (81, D) assessment of his life spent managing associations with other homosexuals stands in stark contrast with Abby's and Marilyn's statements:

> I oftentimes think if I had my life to live over, I would probably do it about the same as I did because I think I've been smart to stay away from it and not make myself obvious. When you were working you had to be very careful that way. We would have some people come into work, we would hire them, why, I don't know, because it was obvious they were gay. And they would get them in there and just make fools out of them. They'd try to make them do the dirtiest work and the hardest work. Well, they didn't pull that on me. And I think it was because they weren't sure about me.

Again, to discreditable subjects, these complex and time-consuming passing devices were—and continue to be—necessary because according to the stigmatizing discourse through which these informants identified (and continue to identify) as homosexual, homosexuality is an essentially and exclusively private aspect of self whose public embodiment or disclosure or both are severely discrediting and unnecessary. But informants' narratives uncovered another reason for the validity and utility of passing: not only does it provide several benefits, but it carries few, if any, costs (except for the type of minor inconveniences that Brian and Manny described—see the preceding).

While heterosexuals are constructed as incapable of reading the homosexual body as such, other homosexuals have that ability, and it is this ability that enables homosexuals to recognize—and approach, and associate with—each other without, as it were, tipping their hand. This ability is critical to the project just described: connecting with other homosexuals without identifying oneself as homosexual to heterosexuals, a matter of obvious concern when in mixed (gay and straight) contexts. In direct contrast to Manny's unfortunate "outing" incident (see previous discussion), for example, Rhoda would routinely socialize with other gay men and women in a "gay bar" that heterosexuals attended to observe the female impersonators, but relied on the heterosexuals' inability—and homosexuals' ability—to recognize "normal-looking" homosexual bodies (such as her own) as homosexual.

It Takes One to Know One

Given the importance of the homosexuals' ability to read unobtrusive homosexual bodies as homosexual, it is not surprising that most subjects described it as "natural," since to see it as the product of concerted effort would be to articulate a complex range of communicative devices—a task few, if any, social actors can accomplish. The range of cultural codes through which we determine the sexual orientations, needs, and designs of another thus fall under the category of "taken for granted background knowledge" of which, as Garfinkel (1967) has demonstrated, we only become aware in those rare instances in which social order—and our ability to negotiate it—has been breached. Thus, Barbie (67, D) explained that while she had never spoken of her lesbianism to her "other lesbian friends," they knew she was gay because "there's just something about it, it takes one to know one." Similarly, Sharon (66, A) characterized this ability as a "sixth sense" that helped her connect to the gay world when she was still in high school and saw a "swishy" man reading a book entitled *The Gay Years*. "For some odd reason," she said, "the words gay, gay years," inspired her to think, "I gotta be gay, that's me." Susan (75, A) said that she can't conceive of just going up to somebody and saying, "You know, I'm gay." It's just that you seem to fall into meeting other people, and you're comfortable with them, and there's no *denying* it. That's the way I think about it.

Others, however, described this "natural" ability as a skill they developed by being exposed to and immersed in the homosexual subculture, a process that took time and that they remembered by virtue of situations in which, ignorant of the basic cultural, conversational, and sexual codes of homosexual life, they had failed to recognize other bodies—and desires— as homosexual. Dan (70, A), for example, while aware of his desires for other men, had not yet identified himself as homosexual or learned about homosexual life when a man subtly propositioned him, a gesture he misread at the time:

Looking back you note things, but I didn't know. When I worked in New York, the storekeeper had an assistant that was a real butch man that used to screw all these actresses and everything, and he asked me if I wanted to go along with him to watch or be part of it. Looking back, I think he wanted me alone in the room, but I didn't know that at the time. I was completely oblivious. I was drafted at nineteen into the Army. I used to hear the beds squeak all around me, but I didn't know what was happening, I wasn't aware.

Similarly, Tex (72, A), who had had same-sex desires for years, recognized neither what he now realizes were another man's intimations of homosexuality (e.g., "talking about the latest shows") nor yet another man's homosexual overtures to him. "In retrospect," he said, "a lot of people were trying to show me, but I didn't know, I guess I didn't *want* to know. One fellow I even went *home* with him and I still didn't get the idea, we played records! That's about as far as it got. He was always talking about the latest shows, but nothing sunk in."

Deborah (74, D) was most explicit about this ability being learned, describing her relatively recent ability to read other homosexual bodies as such as evidence of her own maturation as a lesbian:

All of a sudden I was aware of knowing whether somebody was or not without knowing them. You know what I mean? I mean just by me walking down the street. It must have sort of grown on me gradually and first I wouldn't be aware and then—it really surprised me, I would look at this person and then we'd click: "Oh, there's one!" In the market place, walking along the street—it wasn't that I was looking for anybody, it was just a recognition. Sometimes it was mutual and sometimes not. Mostly not. I just thought, "Well, you are growing up a little more now."

Interestingly, that homosexual bodies are "naturally" read as such by homosexuals skilled in the codes and ways of the homosexual world marks gay men and women who cannot do so as incompetent, and their explicit efforts to communicate their own homosexuality to other homosexuals— or to divine that of others—is both unnecessary and insulting, since it displays an assumption that the interpolated homosexuals are themselves devoid of the "sixth sense." This incompetent assumption is thus, in the final analysis, itself an assumption of incompetence; moreover, not only does it make homosexuality obtrusive by making it a topic, it dishonors the delicate balance between passing among heterosexuals and connecting with homosexuals that other homosexuals have fashioned and make available to competent homosexuals at large. Consider the outrage with which Bernie, a lesbian with whom Kate (76, A) and her then-lover Jan (68, D) had socialized "for years" in the 1950s, exhibited when Kate broached the subject of Bernie's long-term lesbian relationship with Marianne:

> We were friends with them for nine years approximately. And after Jan and I broke up I continued teaching at Adams Clay and Marianne was teaching there even at the time when I retired. And several years after I retired I met her at some party or function or dinner or something. And I decided hey, it really is time to come out to this one, time to get this thing clear. And I said something to her about "Bernie, I really should ask you what's your formula. You did a hell of a lot better than Jan and I did." And she looked at me sort of blankly as if she didn't understand or I'd suddenly started speaking to her in Esperanto and I said, "After all, you've been together how long now?" And she said, "I don't know what you're talking about." And I said, "About your being together so successfully!" And she said, "You know, I think you're insulting me!" And she glowered at me, and she has never spoken to me since. Go figure.

To recap: For all my informants, the homosexual body is unreadable as homosexual by heterosexuals unless the latter are provided with specific cues, but it is readable as such by competent homosexuals and is thus readily amenable to safe passage through heterosexual space and through interactions with heterosexuals. But these facts resonated differently for members of each identity cohort who saw them as calling forth different, even competing obligations: for the discreditable subjects, to maintain a heterosexual persona in any and all interactions with heterosexuals by refusing to disclose their homosexuality to them, and for accredited subjects, to embrace disclosing their homosexuality to heterosexuals in any and all situations that called for such disclosure. For the discreditable informants, then, that the homosexual body is innately unreadable as such provides an opportunity that homosexuals are obliged to embrace, while for the accredited, this same fact creates a new obligation: to disclose one's homosexuality—in other words, to invoke bodily desires—using venues other than the body itself.

The Promise and Perils of Unobtrusive Bodies

Promise: The Discreditable Identity Cohort

Again, members of the discreditable identity cohort fashioned their understanding of homosexual desire as an essentially private matter that can be contained within the body into a moral stance that should be so contained, and they committed themselves to passing in the presence of heterosexuals, condemning homosexuals who failed or refused to do so as incompetent and, often, as endangering the tenuous standing of competent homosexuals. Given this, they viewed the post-Stonewall practice of "coming out"—voluntarily disclosing one's homosexuality to heterosexuals—as the pinnacle of incompetence, since, not only did it breach the divide between public and private worlds, but it did so in the face of successful passing. After all, their accounts implied, only those whose homosexuality was not already evident would feel the "need" to verbalize their homosexuality to others. "Coming out" was thus an unnecessary invitation to negative sanctions on the part of homosexuals whose bodily deportment was competent and who were thus capable of reaping the rewards of having balanced public and private interests, specifically, enjoying both a safe and stable life in a heterosexual world and fulfilling relations with homosexuals.

Lillian (69, D), for example, was "astounded" at the naïve tendency of young gay men and women to come out as a matter of course—"by these kids who tell their bosses they're gay and then in the next breath they

wonder why they're fired." They are fired, she explained, "because this society, this era that we live in, is not ready to accept homosexuality as a
lifestyle." Similarly, Ryan (81, D) depicted a typical coming-out scenario,
in which a child voluntarily—and unnecessarily—discloses his homosexuality to his assembled family, as usually resulting in negative sanctions:

> They come out to their family—sit at the table, big dinner, big enter-
> tainment, something like that, and they'd say, "I've got something I want
> to tell you and I want to tell everybody at once: I'm *gay*." And some of
> the family would say "What does that mean?" and they'd have to tell
> them the truth and that's the way it would be. And some of them would
> explode and kick him out and disown him and others say, "Well, if you
> are, you're still our son and we'll accept you" and things are fine. But it
> was seldom that that had worked out that way.

In Ryan's account, the child's homosexuality had been unknown to the
family, and the source of the family conflict was not the child's passing as
heterosexual, but the child's declination to continue to do so. (Moreover,
the account implies that the child's homosexuality was not—and presumably would not become—a source of tension in and of itself; again, it is not
the existence but the obtrusiveness of the "private," bodily desire that creates havoc.) Ricardo (66, D) also invoked the negative effects of coming
out—telling his family about his "private affairs"—on the family as the
reason for his continued passing:

> I don't think I would ever come out. In other words I feel [having] come
> out is mainly still in telling your family "I'm gay." That's crucial to say a
> person really is out of the closet. I don't think I feel comfortable in my
> family telling them my private affairs. And that's the main reason why I
> will say I will never come out.

Indeed, discreditable subjects only told family members they were gay
to correct or preclude an actual or an imminent relational crisis. The most
obvious situations in which this issue arose were marriages in which the
homosexuality of one partner was becoming such an impediment to the
marriage that the marriage was doomed to failure; thus, both Susan (75,
D) and Tex (72, A) told their respective spouses of their new-found
homosexual identities in the course of asking for divorces. (These mar-

riages must, of course, be distinguished from marriages of convenience such as Brian's, in which both spouses knew of the homosexuality of one or both partners.) But two discreditable subjects disclosed their homosexuality to siblings to avert family crises. Jan (68, D) described having chosen to preempt her sister's inevitable discovery of her lesbianism when her sister was moving in with her. Here, the disclosure was not fully voluntary, but a considered and measured response to an extraordinary set of circumstances in which the disclosure would have occurred anyway and was taken to prevent, rather than to cause, trouble in the home:

> My youngest sister, the one who died and with whom I was so close, between husbands she came to live with me. This was about eight years ago I guess. She lived with me for two years. When she appeared I said—I had just met Carol—"I want to discuss this with you. You're going to be living here."

Similarly, Franz (86, D) told his sister he was gay because she was concerned about his mental health after he moved in with her when he immigrated from Israel at the age of forty. The move was so difficult that he became depressed, and when she questioned him about the source of his depression, he chose to tell her that he missed his lover and his gay friends rather than to have her question his overall condition:

> I was very depressed the first day, because I left a guy and I left a lot of friends. I left a whole community—we were sticking together, for instance Friday nights we went to one guy's apartment on the roof, and all the gays were meeting each other. So I missed it, I said, "Who am I here? A stranger." So my sister forced me to—"What's wrong with you?" So I told her that I'm gay.

Here, again, disclosure of homosexuality in the context of successful passing was justified by reference to extraordinary circumstances, reaffirming the routine necessity of passing with heterosexuals, including intimates. Moreover, these accounts reproduce the subjects' sense of the ultimate goal of passing as maximizing the quality of interaction with heterosexuals—should the quality of these relations be undermined by passing (an unlikely occurrence, as we have seen), then disclosure would (and should) be undertaken in the interests of salvaging the relationship.

Perils: The Accredited Identity Cohort

Accredited subjects, however, saw disclosure to heterosexuals—particularly heterosexual intimates—as a routine obligation rather than an unusual, even rare, demand. Again, the accrediting (liberationist) discourse through which they identified themselves as homosexual depicts passing as an inauthentic, even duplicitous, suppression of the essential self that undermines both personal and relational authenticity; thus, Tex (72, A) felt that

> if you are or believe in one way, and you project a belief or an idea what you are contrary to that, then you're not being honest with yourself or them, because you do have to interact with other people. I mean you can't have it both ways.

By characterizing passing homosexuals as trying to "have it both ways," Tex foregrounds the immediate and global salience of homosexuality for a range of social contexts and experiences, including, of course, relating to others. Because homosexuality implicates the entire self, it cannot be contained within either the body or the private realm without damaging both personal integrity and the integrity of social relationships. In this account that "you do have to interact with other people" makes disclosure of homosexuality imperative; this stands in clear contrast to Ricardo's (66, D) account, in which he cites the importance of his relationships with others as the reason for his decision not to disclose his homosexuality to them:

> I'm not a single person that acts individually. We are in the society and therefore family has something to do also with my affairs and my business. And therefore I could not affect them in any way if I'm behaving in [keeping with] I guess *their* beliefs or their way of conducting themselves.

The importance of disclosure to the quality of relationships with heterosexuals was a consistent theme in accredited subjects' accounts. Marilyn (66, A), for example, echoed Tex's equation of passing with dishonesty (or, as she put it, "deception") when she described the issue of disclosure as a "moral problem" centering on the honest and "complete" presentation of self in interaction. This problem, she explained, affected both the quality of the relationship and her experience and assessment of personal integrity:

It's also a moral problem that I've struggled with for some time, about coming out, because of being deceptive with other people if I'm not entirely myself. When I have somebody as a friend, it's somebody that I would talk over issues that are close to me. So if I have a straight friend I can enjoy their presence in going out and being social, but I wouldn't be completely *me* if I'm not out to that person.

While these statements are clearly global ones designed to express a commitment to disclosure as a guarantee of personal and relational authenticity, this commitment was not designed to be pursued in all contexts, since to do so would be to impose a trans-situationally relevant homosexuality onto specific, idiosyncratic situations. As Sharon (66, A) explained, "to me coming out is being able to say 'I'm a homosexual' to the people close to you in your life, wherever it's [so] important that it's a necessity." Clearly, whether one's homosexuality is so important that it requires disclosure is a matter of interpretation, not only on the part of the homosexual herself, but on the envisioned part of the heterosexual recipient of the information as well. After all, although Marilyn and others stated that they wouldn't be, in Marilyn's words, "complete" while interacting with heterosexuals as presumed heterosexuals, they did not suggest that it was essential that they be "complete" in all interactions with heterosexuals. Disclosure, then, becomes necessary in contexts in which the completeness of the homosexual interactant is necessary—for the homosexual and/or for the heterosexual recipient(s) of the disclosure. According to accredited informants' accounts of instances in which they came out to heterosexuals, disclosure should occur when it is made either relationally or conversationally relevant.

Sharon (66, A), for example, made it a point to tell her brother that she was a lesbian, even though he declined to tell her he was gay himself—a failure Sharon characterized as "unbelievable." Again, the contrast between discreditable and accredited informants is clear. While Jan (68, D) and Franz (86, D) only disclosed their homosexuality to siblings to avert an impending crisis, Sharon did so as a matter of course; for her, the crisis that emerged hinged on her own brother's failure to do the same:

He has never said anything to me about being gay. *Ever.* Can you believe it? And he and I were just this close, we grew up like twins, there was a year difference. We were very close, he and I were raised very close. Yet he will not tell me he's gay.

For Marilyn, the decision to disclose her lesbianism to a friend hinged on the quality of the friendship itself: on whether the person in question was sufficiently "humanitarian" to receive the information without "terminating the relationship." Her disclosure, then, becomes both a test and an assurance of her ability to determine the integrity and open-mindedness of particular heterosexuals. "You get to know them," she explained, "who they are and how humanitarian they are." The *relational relevance* of homosexuality was thus assumed in the context of close relationships, in stark contrast to discreditable subjects, who saw their homosexuality as a private matter that only concerned friends or family in certain rare crisis situations. Indeed, while accredited informants judged the closeness of their relationships with heterosexuals on whether the latter knew of their homosexuality, discreditable subjects often named heterosexuals who did not know they were gay as the people to whom they were the most close.

Accredited informants understood their homosexuality to be *conversationally relevant* in one of two contexts. The first is that of a question whose answer would be incomplete or would present a false or distorted self without the disclosure of the actor's homosexuality. An example was provided by Mary (66, A), who described having disclosed her lesbianism to the person interviewing her for her current job:

> I know some older people who say, "Well, yes I'm out," but what they mean is they're out among their friends, which to me is not being out. When I interviewed for this job that I have now, they said, "Oh, so you haven't worked in five years, what have you been doing?" And I said, "Well, I do community work." And then they said "Well, what kind of community work?" And I said, "Well, I'm co-chair of the Black Lesbian and Gay Party." And went right on with the rest of the interview. So to my way of thinking, I can't think of any other answer. Now if I were *not* out, I could probably have said uh . . .
> DR: Church.
> Whatever. You know. But that to me is being out.

The second context is produced by statements by heterosexuals that are so insulting or misrepresentative of homosexuals "in general" that they require correction. An example is Kate's (76, A) disclosure of her lesbianism to her aunt, who had described other family members' "disappointment" that their child was gay, as evidence of the fact that homosexuality is not necessarily a "tragic" condition:

> What made me decide on the spur of the moment to do it, over supper she was talking about problems that a niece and nephew of hers are having. One kid was on drugs and that was a problem, and another kid was a homosexual and that was a disappointment. And I said, "Well, it's not always a tragedy," and she said, "I realize [that] but they were unhappy." And I said, "You realize of course that I'm a lesbian." And she said, "No! Are you?" And I said, "Yeah." And she said, "Oh."

Note that in neither instance were the disclosures planned or seen as inappropriate. On the contrary, they were treated as reasoned and reasonable responses to situated demands for technically and morally correct information and demonstrated the relevance of the actors' individual homosexual desires and histories for their work (in the case of Mary) and families' (in the case of Kate) lives. These disclosures are not, therefore, what Mary Douglas (1991) termed "matter out of order," but successful attempts to make the world orderly by providing information that clarifies the matter at hand and by locating the self within the sexual, social, and (by honoring the essential homosexual self) moral orders.

Indeed, while discreditable subjects pointed to their having collaborated in the ridiculing of homosexuals as a legitimate passing mechanism, accredited informants pointed to their own failure to disclose their own homosexuality while correcting heterosexuals' misconceptions about homosexuals as evidence of failure, as can be seen in Abby's (70, A) account of her failure to disclose her lesbianism while defending homosexuals as a group as a "cop-out":

> Somebody did say something at a family gathering once and I jumped right in. I said, "I don't want to hear anything like that about my two close friends who are gay. I have a lot of gay friends." And that was a copout because that would have been a perfect opportunity to say, "You're talking about me."

Conclusion

This chapter has approached the aging sexual body as the product of the actor's distinctive historical location in society's changing discourse of the sexual body itself. Subjects' narratives express tensions between different formulations of the nature of the body and desire and their "natural" place in the social order that emerged over time. The increasing privatization and regulation of bodies in general and sexual desire in particular; the tensions between gendered and sexual identities and their implications for the embodiment and management of homosexuality; the stigmatization and destigmatization of homosexualities; and the emergence of different homosexual identities and standards for homosexual conduct—all these describe the descriptive and prescriptive accounts subjects produced in the course of recounting their past and present lives. Whether the homosexual body should be used as a signifier of homosexual identity and/or invoked as the locus and the means of fulfilling same-sex desires in public as well as in private realms; how, if at all, these should be done, under which specific circumstances, and to what ends; what, if anything, is gained or lost by doing this or declining to do this; and why; in short, the connection between bodily and social needs are practical and moral matters that subjects negotiated throughout their lives and throughout periods of substantial social change.

While all subjects, regardless of identity cohort membership, agreed on certain key issues (i.e., the innate unreadability of homosexual bodies by heterosexuals and the collective implications of flaunting), identity cohort membership colored their sense of the implications of these "obdurate realities" as the discourses of homosexuality, and the homosexual identities they adopted through their properties, provided competing guidelines for the place of the homosexual body in public space and in interaction with heterosexuals. Lesbian and gay elders' distinctive location in, and engagement with, the historical changes outlined in the preceding thus produced a new set of tensions—between those who believed that homosexual desire was an essentially private affair whose extrusion into the public (heterosexual) sphere was an incompetent act and those who saw homosexual desire as both a private and a political matter whose selective invocation in public contexts was both competent and necessary.

Aging sexual bodies are thus bodies in time (the product of macrohistorical shifts on the one hand and personal histories on the other) and space (managed in relation to other bodies according to precepts developed in relation to these historical shifts and personal histories). Clearly, this also has implications for nonsexual bodies, as standards and conditions for human health, hygiene, fashion, and living arrangements change over time, and for heterosexual and bisexual bodies, as standards and conditions for family composition (e.g., reproduction) and marital versus premarital sexual codes are equally historically contingent. That the larger historical context in which lives are lived and sexual bodies are constructed has a direct impact on the embodiment of sexuality suggests that future research would do well to approach the sexual body in later life as a historical, as well as an interactional, project.

Notes

1. Psychoanalysts such as Gilles, Deleuze, Lacan, Irigaray, and Kristeva have expanded on Freud's initial thoughts on the sexual body. Perhaps the most notable expansion is the controversial feminist direction taken by Irigaray and Kristeva in their criticisms of Lacanian psychoanalysis.

2. For a deconstruction of the medical and media enterprises' claims about the decline of sexual desire or capacity or both that are so strongly embraced by elders and middle aged alike, see, for example, Friedan 1993, Lorber 1997, and Gullette 1998.

3. I conducted open-ended, in-depth interviews with my 37 subjects (19 women and 16 men), in Los Angeles in 1995, when they were aged 64 to 89, contacting them through social groups for lesbian and gay elders and "snowballing" (Bailey 1994) from these initial contacts. Subjects' average age was 72.5, and 46 percent of the sample is 75 and older (13.5 percent being 80 and older). Their annual income ranged from below $10,000 to over $100,000; seven women and three men had been married (two women and two men have children); and over 75 percent lived alone. Two subjects are African American, and four are Latino/a. While all have been given new names, I have tried to capture as many details of their lives as possible, and only changed information that would be clearly identifying.

4. I do not attend to the control of biographical information in this chapter, since it does not invoke the body in as direct a fashion as do the other two passing techniques mentioned in the preceding. But the control of biographical information underlies the passing techniques and concerns I do attend to.

5. Some did this having adopted and then rejected stigmatized homosexual identities, some did this having deferred such identifications until the accrediting

discourse emerged, and one did this having only begun to discover her attraction to women during the 1970s. For how subjects came to adopt one or the other homosexual identity, see Rosenfeld 2003.

6. All subjects are identified by their age at the time of the interview and by their identity cohort membership—"D" for discreditable, and "A" for accredited.

References

Bailey, K. D.
1994 *Methods of Social Research*. New York: Free Press.

Berube, A.
1990 *Coming Out Under Fire: The History of Gay Men and Women in World War Two*. New York: Free Press.

Chauncey, G.
1994 Gay New York: Gender, Urban Culture, and the Making of the Gay Male World, 1890–1940. New York: Basic Books.

D'Emilio, J.
1983 *Sexual Politics, Sexual Communities: The Making of a Homosexual Minority in the United States*. Chicago: University of Chicago Press.

Douglas, M.
[1966] 1991 *Purity and Danger: An Analysis of the Concepts of Pollution and Taboo*. London: Routledge.

Duberman, M.
1994 *Stonewall*. Middlesex, U.K.: Plume.

Elder, G. J., Jr.
1995 The Life Course Paradigm: Social Change and Individual Development. In *Examining Lives in Context: Perspectives on the Ecology of Human Development*. Edited by P. Moen, G. H. Elder, Jr., and K. Luscher, 101–39. Washington, D.C.: American Psychological Association.

Engels, F.
1972 *The Origin of the Family, Private Property and the State*. Moscow: Progress Publishers.

Faderman, L.
1991 *Odd Girls and Twilight Lovers: A History of Lesbian Life in Twentieth-Century America*. Middlesex, U.K.: Plume.

Featherstone, M., M. Hepworth, and B. Turner
1991 *The Body: Social Process and Cultural Theory.* London: Sage.

Foucault, M.
1979 *The History of Sexuality: An Introduction.* Vol. 1. New York: Pantheon Books and Harmondsworth, U.K.: Penguin.
1987 *The History of Sexuality: The Use of Pleasure.* Vol. 2. Harmondsworth, U.K.: Penguin.
1988 *The History of Sexuality: The Care of the Self.* Vol. 3. Harmondsworth, U.K.: Penguin.

Friedan, B.
1993 The New Menopause Brouhaha. In *The Fountain of Age,* 472–500. New York: Simon & Schuster.

Garfinkel, H.
[1967] 1984 *Studies in Ethnomethodology.* New York: Prentice Hall.

Goffman, E.
1963 *Stigma: Notes on the Management of Spoiled Identity.* Upper Saddle River, N.J.: Prentice Hall.

Grube, J.
1990 Natives and Settlers: An Ethnographic Note on Early Interaction of Older Homosexual Men with Younger Gay Liberationists. *Journal of Homosexuality* 20: 119–35.

Gullette, M. M.
1998 Midlife Discourses in the Twentieth-Century United States: An Essay on the Sexuality, Ideology, and Politics of "Middle-Ageism." In *Welcome to Middle Age! (And Other Cultural Fictions).* Edited by R. A. Sweeder, 3–44. Chicago: University of Chicago Press.

Hardy, M. A., and L. Waite
1997 Doing Time: Reconciling Biography with History in the Study of Social Change. In *Studying Aging and Social Change: Conceptual and Methodological Issues.* Edited by M. A. Hardy. Thousand Oaks, Calif.: Sage.

Jackson, S., and S. Scott
2001 Putting the Body's Feet on the Ground: Towards a Sociological Reconceptualization of Gendered and Sexual Embodiment. In *Constructing Gendered Bodies.* Edited by K. Backett-Milburn and L McKie, 9–24. Basingstoke, U.K.: Palgrave.

Lorber, J.
1997 If a Situation Is Defined as Real . . . Premenstrual Syndrome and Menopause. In *Gender and the Social Construction of Illness*, 55–69. Thousand Oaks, Calif.: Sage.

Nardi, P. M., and D. Sanders
1994 *Growing Up Before Stonewall: Life Stories of Some Gay Men*. London: Routledge.

Nettleton, S., and J. Watson
1998 *The Body in Everyday Life*. London: Routledge.

Newton, E.
1985 The Mythic Mannish Lesbian. In *The Lesbian Issue: Essays from Signs*. Edited by E. Freedman et al., 7–25. Chicago: University of Chicago Press.

Pollner, M., and D. Rosenfeld
2000 The Cross-Culturing Work of Gay and Lesbian Elderly. In *Advances in Life Course Research: Identity through the Life Course in Cross-Cultural Perspective*. Edited by T. Owens. Vol. 5. Stamford, Conn.: JAI Press.

Rosenfeld, D.
1999 Identity Work among Lesbian and Gay Elderly. *Journal of Aging Studies* 13: 121–44.
2003 *The Changing of the Guard: Identity Work of Lesbian and Gay Elders*. Philadelphia: Temple University Press. Forthcoming.

Rosenfeld, D., and Eugene B. Gallagher
In Press. The Life Course as an Organizing Principle and a Socializing Resource in Modern Medicine. In *Advances in Life Course Research*. Vol. 7. *New Frontiers in Socialization*. Edited by R. Settersten, Jr. and T. Owens. Stamford, Conn.: JAI Press.

Rosow, I.
1978 What Is a Cohort and Why? *Human Development* 21: 65–75.

Ryder, N.
[1965] 1997 The Cohort as a Concept in the Study of Social Change. In *Studying Aging and Social Change: Conceptual and Methodological Issues*. Edited by M. A. Hardy, 66–92. Thousand Oaks, Calif.: Sage.

Settersten, R. A., Jr.
1999 *Lives in Time and Place: The Problems and Promises of Developmental Science*. New York: Baywood Publishing.

Stein, A.
1997 *Sex and Sensibility: Stories of Lesbian Generations.* Berkeley: University of California Press.

Turner, B.
1996 *The Blackwell Companion to Social Theory.* Oxford, U.K.: Blackwell.
1999 *The Body and Society: Explorations in Social Theory.* 2nd ed. London: Sage.

Valocchi, S.
1999 The Class-Inflected Nature of Gay Identity. *Social Problems* 46: 207–24.

Weber, M.
1958 *The Protestant Ethic and the Spirit of Capitalism.* Translated by Talcott Parsons. New York: Scribner.

Williams, S., and G. Bendelow
1998 *The Lived Body: Sociological Themes, Embodied Issues.* London: Routledge.

CHAPTER SEVEN

THE EVERYDAY VISIBILITY
OF THE AGING BODY
Jaber F. Gubrium and James A. Holstein

I t has been a decade since Chris Shilling (1993) alerted us to the "absent presence" of the body in social theory. It has been longer still since Bryan Turner (1984) made the body a primary concern in his discussion of contemporary social life. Until recently, Shilling notes, social theorists had conceptualized the self, identity, and other social forms without explicit reference to the material body. For the most part, the body was simply taken for granted as a background feature of life. As Turner (1992) and others have noted, classical sociology traditionally adopted a disembodied view of its subject matter, providing little or no basis for understanding how social organization related to the somatic groundings of experience.

Many commentators have since heeded these admonitions. The body currently stands center stage in feminist, postmodern, postcolonial, discursive, and critical theoretical discussions of the self and experience. This has made the body more visible than ever as a sociological phenomenon. At the same time, however, other critics such as Hallam, Hockey, and Howarth (1999), believe that the body is currently being located too prominently in the conceptual scheme of things. They ask whether social theory is now overextending the place of the body in experience. In this view, while the body should be acknowledged as a significant social entity, its presence in life cannot be taken for granted. Rather, as Schilling reminds us, the body is an *unfinished* experiential entity. Its presence is always subject to socially organized interpretation.

Shilling (1993) argues that "the body is most profitably conceptualized as an unfinished biological and social phenomenon which is transformed, within *certain limits*, as a result of its entry into, and participation in, society"

(p. 12, emphasis added). This chapter addresses the body in terms of Shilling's reference to both "unfinished" business and "certain limits." On the one hand, the body is an interpreted object of meaning-making actions and, as such, is a continuous project of everyday life. On the other hand, the body also is a concrete set of intrusions into life, an obdurate presence that must be accounted for, placing limits on the free play of meaning-making actions. If the body and its meaning are constructed through the interpretive ebb and flow of everyday experience, it also is a material condition within that same process.

This chapter is concerned, in particular, with the everyday visibility of the aging body. The aging body is continuously unfinished business; it is never simply open to view as patently old and decrepit, remarkably youthful, or resilient despite its shortcomings. This stance is contrary to that held by many gerontologists, who tend to view the body in static terms. Even in the later years of life, there are countless interpretive lenses between the body and the eyes of its beholders. Everyday contingencies shape interpretations and meanings, bringing the aging body to light in highly variegated ways. At the same time, the body's physical, material intrusions into life are matters individuals take into consideration as the body enters into experience under its own momentum.

To start, we discuss the visibility of the aging body in relation to two perspectives: the objective body with its intrusive, obdurate presence, and the more variable—even ephemeral—yet ubiquitous everyday body of lived experience. After briefly outlining the perspectives, we turn to the practical management of the presence and meaning of the aging body, considering how visibility can be empirically restricted, almost to the point of elimination or separation from everyday consideration. Still, if this is true in fact, it is too extreme to be the foundation of a more general analytic framework. Accordingly, we attempt to reestablish limits on interpretations of the body that acknowledge its material presence as well as the circumstances that influence interpretation. Ultimately, we conclude that the objective and interpreted bodies are inextricably intertwined in the practice of everyday life.

The Objective Body and the Everyday Body

From one perspective, the body is an object that imposes itself on life. Whether young or old, this is an *objective* body—a material entity with a physical presence that cannot be totally ignored. It is quite different from the mind, the self, and the emotions, for example, we take them to be more or less hidden behind or inside the body and only represented by gestures and other somatic activities. In contrast, the objective body is "there" for all to behold. It can be observed, evaluated, and responded to, as one might engage other physical entities.

Herbert Blumer (1969) often refers to the natural and evident features of life as "obdurate" realities. The body as a physical entity falls into this category. It is a relatively constant and concrete presence in experience. Distinguishing features of the body are taken as definite, tangible evidence of its status as an object in the world. In this context, the associations and meanings attached to the body are as objectively present as is the body itself. Important characteristics such as gender, age, and race are confidently read from bodily composition, configuration, suppleness, and pigmentation, among many other apparently "unmistakable" signs. Such characteristics form the foundation for the attributed personhood that is necessary for everyday interaction (see, for example, Kessler and McKenna 1978).

The objective body is appraised for a wide array of qualities. As Michel Foucault (1988) and, more recently, Nikolas Rose (1998) argue, an assessment industry has emerged to evaluate the array. Much of this focuses on the body. From infancy to old age, the body is systematically examined, tested, and probed for an endless variety of traits and skills that are believed to lie within. Intelligence, functional ability, locus of control, and memory are only a few of the characteristics that the objective body presents to us.

The *everyday* body is different (see Nettleton and Watson 1998). This is the body that is taken to be there in practice. It is a material entity suffused with meaning. It is the body that is there because people take it into account when organizing their thoughts, feelings, and actions. In this sense, it is a subjective body. Strictly speaking, this is the body-for-us, the body-for-me, or the body-for-them, depending on who takes it into consideration in responding to themselves and others. It is also the body-on-this-occasion and the-body-in-these-circumstances, the result of situational variability in its meaning. It is a hyphenated body because its presence in experience and its salient characteristics depend on what beholders construe them to be.

In contrast to the objective body, the "thereness" of the everyday body cannot be taken for granted. When individuals engage in face-to-face interaction, they cannot assume that their bodies are attended to in a particular way, if at all. Indeed, they might attend to each other as colleagues or competitors, clever or dim-witted, or pleasant or obnoxious, among a broad range of social and personal categories that frame the subjectivities of life separate from the body. In a given interaction, the body may have little or no relevance in its own right as an object of experience. It may be a virtually unnoticed surface of signs for other considerations.

On occasion, the body itself becomes an object of pointed attention. Its material presence is a central concern for those involved. There are times, for instance, when a person's intellectual, spiritual, or emotional qualities can distinctly influence others' perception of that person's physical body. One can be viscerally repulsed by the mere sight of a "despicable" acquaintance, even though he may be conventionally and "objectively" quite handsome. Conversely, the physical appearance of a "loved one" can be considerably "enhanced" as the attractiveness of the subject behind (or inside) the body is applied to the surface of signs the body presents to us. The practical consequence is that beauty—or its opposite—is in the eye of the beholder.

The physical body sometimes becomes a commanding presence in the beholders' interest in life. It is relatively common, for example, for a physical body to be so robust or beautiful (by cultural standards) that it becomes the focus of attention at every turn. Bodybuilders and super models are viewed almost exclusively in somatic terms, which are objectified to the extreme. Interaction commonly proceeds with an orientation to, if not a preoccupation with, bodily attributes. Beauty and physical appearance may overwhelm the presence of more personal, distinguishing traits because a surface of physical signs becomes significant in its own right. The same could be said of the physically deformed or disfigured. In casual encounters, a focus on the unsightliness of the body may profoundly shape (or preclude) interaction. Pretty (or repulsive) faces can be more important than the people and stories behind them.

It is in this sense that the everyday body is unfinished business. While it is a material entity, its presence in life cannot be assumed. Physical states or characteristics are continually subject to definition and evaluation. The body's material presence in the social world is not constant. Individuals are not just bodies to each other, although there are times and places where this may seem quintessentially so.

Yet not just anything goes. While the presence of the body is subject to the contingencies of interpretive practice, the body's materiality sits adjacent to what and who we are. Here Shilling's qualification "within certain limits" comes into play. The practice of everyday life finishes off the body, just as the body presents itself—at times precipitously—as a surface of signs for interpretation. Which one of these is underscored unfolds empirically in the practice of everyday life. Living in a nursing home, for example, is a circumstance that continuously features decrepit bodies. It puts the visibility of the body in a particular light—often the spotlight, so to speak—setting certain conditions for its defining practices. In other circumstances, the body may not come into awareness at all, being a marginal presence to participants' concerns.

Managing the Body's Visibility

The aging body is perhaps more likely than other bodies to be viewed as objectively visible; the physical ravages of the later years bring bodily concerns to the fore more than at any other time of life. But lived experience can temper its material intrusions. Both the aging body's objective presence and its meaningful visibility can be socially managed. Sarah Matthews' (1979) study of self-identity among older women shows how these women actively influence the everyday visibility of their bodies. Matthews argues that aging and being old are subjectively discerned. The visibility of the aging body is not simply a fact of the everyday landscape of the later years. It is a consequence, rather, of the presentation of self, both the social and the physical.

In introducing her research, Matthews turns directly to the priority of the social over the biological meaning of age for the women she interviewed:

> The research . . . stands as a challenge to the notion of the "naturalness" of old as a social category defined in biology. By putting aside taken-for-granted assumptions about old age, the social worlds of old widows in American society can be seen not as dictated by physical and mental decline but as shaped by social and historical forces. The informants for this research are social actors defined as old by the society in which they live and forced to deal with the social meaning of their chronological age. (P. 20–21)

Matthews goes on to describe an "everyday-life" perspective (p. 21), setting the stage for presenting her empirical material. She observed and did in-depth interviews with elderly respondents who attended a local senior center and others who lived in a housing project for older persons, extending this to interviewing and participant observation in the surrounding community. Many of Matthews' leading questions centered on the aging body: How do these older women experience others' reactions to their physical presence? How do they respond to the reactions? The answers to these questions tellingly show how unfinished the aging body is in practice.

One of Matthews' arguments is that others' reactions to older women are significantly related to how well acquainted they are with them. In interview after interview, the women refer to how old they feel in new surroundings, in interacting with strangers, or in public settings where "all everyone seems to see is an old women." In contrast, the women say that, among friends and in familiar surroundings, others see the person behind physical appearances. For these older women, the aging body is visible as a first set of clues that indicates who they are in situations where nothing else is known about them.

In meeting someone for the first time or when they are out in public, the women have a distinct sense of being viewed as old. The mere appearance of their bodies would seem to suggest to others they are, in fact, aged. Two respondents poignantly recount incidents that go to the significant part of the matter. Passing a group of children on the way to the grocery store, one woman recounts:

> I grinned at them because I like children, and one of them looked up and she said, "You're ugly, ugly, ugly." And I said, "Well, so are you." And one of them was going to hit me with a stick. . . . I was surprised to death. I must have had a long face because I didn't feel very good and it takes all of me to get there and all of me to get back. (P. 79)

Another woman reports the reactions she occasionally receives from other drivers, who figure that, as an old woman, she should not be on the road:

> There have been a few occasions with younger people. Well, when I say younger I don't mean in the middle twenties, I mean in the teens. I had the feeling they were saying, "The poor old soul," especially when I used

to drive a car. They had the attitude, the look on their face, "What the devil are you doing in a car? You belong home in a rocking chair." (P. 79)

Not just young strangers use the aging body as an initial set of identifiers. Older people themselves also use the body to assign identities to each other. The "newcomers" who had moved to the settings in which Matthews did her research, for example, were commonly viewed as old. In contrast, "residents" who had become familiar faces were known to others in more biographical-specific terms. Their bodies were less visible as a result. Residents were likely to be known as, say, "John the successful lawyer's mother," "the woman who has always been active in politics," or "the woman whose husband left her and for good reason" (p. 97). The aging body, in other words, is what initially is on display for newcomers in these settings. It is all that is available to categorize them, according to Matthews:

> The resident has a reputation; the newcomer is not so lucky. She arrives on the scene already old. Her move to the setting was probably precipitated by a negatively evaluated status passage. Recent retirement, either for herself or her husband, widowhood, or decreased physical capacity are the most likely explanations. . . . The most salient characteristic of newcomers, then, is their oldness and their imputed, and often accepted, devalued status as no longer independent, financially, emotionally, or physically. (P. 97–98)

At first blush, it would seem that the objective body is paramount in assigning identity in these circumstances. These old women, however, do not respond passively to others and their social situations. They actively manage their bodies' social visibility by reducing the number of situations in which they are likely to encounter individuals unfamiliar to them. They literally avoid situations where their aging bodies might be the only salient signs of identity. In support of this, these women suppress other evidence of being old, such as not telling their age and cosmetically trying to appear younger than they are. These efforts work to control their bodies' intrusions into everyday life. The aim is to reduce the salience and significance of their physical presence for designating who and what they are to others.

None of the women Matthews studied believed they were old, even while their bodies sometimes led others to view them that way. Indeed, as

Matthews (1979) explains, "Each old person considers herself to be just an ordinary person and forgets whenever possible that she has the trappings of oldness. But when she must attend to the trappings, she explains that she is not what she seems" (p. 76). Some actually express surprise when they view themselves in a mirror, seeing striking evidence of what they could be were it not for their self-management:

> I don't feel like I'm seventy-two. I'm surprised when I look in the mirror. I went down to get my hair cut the other day and I'm always surprised when I look down and see all that gray hair, because I don't feel gray-headed. (P. 76)

For these older women, unmitigated physical appearance can vividly present who they could be, were it not for the way they manage their bodies' visibility. For them, it is evident that the aging body is continuously unfinished business. While there are times and places when their objective bodies give them away, so to speak, there are other times and places when this is not so. For these women, the aging body's visibility is "occasioned." It is a complex, hyphenated reality, visible-sometimes but not at other times, visible-for-some, but not-visible-for-others. As Cooley ([1902] 1964) pointed out decades ago, the self is like a reflection in a social looking glass. An actual physical mirror can make this point abundantly obvious (see Furman 1997). But the women Matthews studied are not trapped in such mirrors. What is reflected are older people in the process of managing the visibility of their aging bodies, not simply aging bodies per se.

Rendering the Body Invisible

If Matthews teaches us how the body's sheer visibility can be managed, Sharon Kaufman (1986) shows us how the body can be rendered all but invisible in everyday life. Kaufman refuses to frame the life stories she hears in her research as the narratives of old people. Her goal, as she puts it, is "to study aging *through* the expression of individual humanity" (p. 6). Kaufman asks why preclude people's own sense of themselves by defining them from the start in terms of chronological age or the bodily ravages of late life? As Kaufman explains, "The old Americans I studied do not perceive meaning in aging itself; rather, they perceive meaning in being themselves in old age" (p. 6). This, in effect, brackets age and the body as orienting frameworks for guiding and responding to what is said in the interviews. Methodologically, Kaufman does not assume that age and the body are objective parameters of the lives she studies. Instead, the meaning of the aging body and its consequential visibility are treated as empirical questions. Kaufman thus works against gerontology's inclination to orient to the aging experience in terms of indisputable facts of embodiment.

The results are remarkable. While her respondents, who are seventy to ninety-seven years of age, do speak of their chronological ages, their appearances, and the travails of longevity, these seem unimportant to them in the narrative scheme of things. As the respondents tell their stories, it is evident that they resist both somatic and chronological framings of their lives. Conventional wisdom, for example, would suggest that these respondents might anchor their life narratives in significant generational experiences, such as having lived through the Great Depression and World War II. Kaufman, however, finds that these historical events and chronological signposts are consigned to the narrative background, just like the respondents' aging bodies. While most of them lived through the Great Depression and World War II and do refer to these events, they do not figure as major themes in their stories. Instead, the respondents construct who and what they are in terms of their own making.

Themes of the respondents' own making highlight these life narratives, superseding both the body and history. Many themes center on personal values. Three of the people Kaufman interviews provide graphic examples: Millie, who is eighty years old and had been living in a nursing home before Kaufman met her, constructs her life story around the significance of affective ties. Kaufman explains that most of the conversations she had with Millie over the course of the eight months she interviewed her focused on Millie's interpersonal likes and dislikes, especially who she was attracted to, cared for, or loved. Millie uses the word "attach" repeatedly in her narrative: "I grew attached to him and he to me," "I am so attached to her," "We developed an attachment to one another" (p. 33). "Love," too, is a significant part of Millie's vocabulary and, of course, her life story.

While affective ties provide the central meaning for Millie's narrative, it also features themes related to her marriages, her success at work, her social status, and her self-determination. But even as an eighty-year-old woman, Millie's body is virtually invisible in her commentary. Its absence is noteworthy, given the widespread presumption that the aging body is a central presence in old age. Even though she spent time in a nursing home, this did not lead her to thematize ailments. Her stint in the nursing facility is conveyed, instead, as a challenge to her self-determination. Challenges posed by her bodily condition are subsumed under the more general assault on her sense of who she was and wanted to be. Millie's narrative features someone who has successfully defended herself against the onslaughts posed by the aging body, hospitalization, and nursing care. Kaufman notes that Millie resolutely resists all efforts to impose a compromised aging body on her daily routine and sense of herself:

> Millie has also assumed control over the daily rounds in the facility, a difficult thing to do as many observers of large institutions have noticed. . . . One morning I arrived at the Home at 10:30 to discover that Millie was not in the lounge area, the place I usually found her at that time. She had changed rooms the day before and was now located on another floor. . . . She said to me: "I've been crying. The system is all changed. Upstairs they got me dressed so early. Here they come much later. I can't stand staying down here so long. It's like a morgue." . . . Within two days of this incident, she managed to get written orders from her doctor stating that she was to be dressed and upstairs by 9:30 so she could participate in the exercise class that took place then. (P. 46–47)

Two other respondents, Ben and Stella, assemble their life stories that highlight different themes. Ben, who is seventy-four years old, presents his life as a battle between his sober, responsible side and his carefree, romantic side. The theme crops up repeatedly as he talks of his past, his present, and the years ahead. At one point, he describes himself looking into the mirror and seeing his father, who, he explains, was "a very serious," "no-nonsense guy." Ben adds that this is also the kind of image of himself that he (Ben) conveys to the world, even though, he points out, "I don't feel that way. I feel carefree and happy . . . and I could easily slide or slip into a romantic adventure" (p. 48). Other themes of Ben's narrative center on his need for financial security and his religion.

Interestingly enough, when Ben looks into the mirror, he does not see his aging body, an aged face, or gray hair. Rather, he sees himself in relation to the two character types that thematize who he is as a person. He does not even contrast who he really is behind an aged body—a contrast that has been featured as the "mask of aging" (Featherstone and Hepworth 1991). The image of a corporeal mask covering the real self does not apply to him. Rather, the dichotomous self he has always felt he was, even into old age, is center stage. Ben's aging body simply is not visible in his story.

Stella was born in 1897 in the rural South. An important theme of her story centers on her need for achievement. According to Stella, "I don't look back at all. I only look forward to what I'm going to do next." Even her past is something she competes with, not something she looks back on or longs for. A second theme relates to the first—her aesthetic sense and desire for perfection. Stella links both themes with a need for relationships that, she explains, prompt her to create new roles for herself. The theme of striving for perfection connects with the two most important people in her life, her late mother and her deceased daughter. Stella describes everything they did as beautiful and perfect. Asked to portray her mother, Stella explains

> She was a creative person, and so pretty! And a perfectionist in everything. Things had to be done just right. And she would never get tired, just going all the time. [Now describing her daughter] She was so talented in art. I couldn't imagine where she got if from. I never had to criticize her for anything. (P. 66–67)

Stella's daughter died at the age of 14. As Kaufman explains, "[It was] a tragic event which had a profound effect on the development of Stella's identity. The child is frozen in Stella's memory on the brink of maturation and promise. There is only perfection to remember" (p. 67). Here again, while Stella is elderly and speaks of her daughter's death, she does not use the aesthetic and perfection themes as the bases of comparison with whom she has now become in old age. Old age is at most a background feature of whom she is now as a person. Once more, the aging body is transparent in the life story. Despite having what Matthews calls the physical "trappings" of oldness, Millie, Ben, and Stella virtually render their bodies invisible as they tell the stories of their past, their present lives, and what they hope for the future.

Denying the Aging Body

While some aging bodies are all but transparent, the "obvious" presence of such bodies for others is denied. This is a significant feature of perceptions of the aging body by some caregivers of the elderly. Jaber Gubrium's (1986, 1992) study of the everyday experience of caring for Alzheimer's disease (AD) sufferers illustrates this poignantly. The data Gubrium draws from interviews with caregivers and participant observation in caregiver support groups show that even for so-called vegetables, selfhood can be preserved when bodily evidence suggests that there is virtually nothing left of the person behind the disease. While the term "vegetable" is repugnant, it is nonetheless a common way of referring to those whose diseases have progressed to the point where existence is merely vegetative.

Because such individuals appear to just breathe, eat, and eliminate, and barely respond to external stimuli, they are sometimes said to be "empty shells," the barren result of a "disease that dims bright minds." Of course, not all AD sufferers become vegetative and, indeed, some may seem surprisingly physically fit despite their cognitive impairments. Still, for some sufferers who become vegetative—whose minds not only have failed, but whose postures in some cases have regressed to near-fetal positions—a "hidden" self or mind can be socially preserved through the interpretive efforts of their caregivers and significant others.

With remarkable resolve, some of the AD caregivers who Gubrium studied actively worked to sustain a semblance of self in an otherwise vegetative loved one. They accomplished this through a combination of existential doubt about the death of the self, belief in the sufferer's personhood, and selective attention to what they took to be bodily signs of continued presence in life. Such caregivers could be quite determined in their "self-preserving" efforts, which was evident in discussions about the persistent existence of minds under the circumstances.

An exchange between two support group participants, Jack, a sufferer's spouse, and Sara, another caregiver, is illustrative. Note how, in the following heart-wrenching exchange, Sara casts existential doubt on caregiver Jack's ruminations about his wife's "living death." When Jack wonders what to think about his wife's very demented condition, Sara raises the distinct possibility that a mind really exists behind what the body hides. Even AD's infamous neurological markers—amyloid plaques and neurofibrillary tangles—are challenged as evidence of the dementia and loss of personhood that lies behind them:

> Jack: That's why I'm looking for a nursing home for her. I loved her dearly but she's just not Mary anymore. No matter how hard I try, I can't get myself to believe that she's there anymore. I know how that can keep you going, but there comes a point where all the evidence points the other way. Even at those times (which is not very often) when she's momentarily lucid, I just know that's not her speaking to me but some knee-jerk reaction. You just can't let that sort of thing get your hopes up because then you won't be able to make the kind of decision that's best for everyone all around. You know what I mean?
>
> Sara: Well, I know what you've gone through, and I admire your courage, Jack. But you can't be too sure. How do you *really* know that what Mary says at times is not one of those few times she's been able to really reach out to you? You don't *really* know for sure, do you? You don't really know if those little plaques and tangles are in there, do you? I hate to make it hard on you, Jack, but I face the same thing day in and day out with Richard [her husband]. Can I ever finally close him out of my life and say, "Well, it's done. It's over. He's gone"? How do I really know that the poor man isn't hidden somewhere, behind all that confusion, trying to reach out and say, "I love you, Sara"? [She weeps]

Certain physiological evidence—words spoken in putatively "lucid" moments—is read as a positive marker of self. At the same time, neurological signs that all is lost are denied—"You don't even know if those little plaques and tangles are in there"—as Sara defies physical evidence to sustain what she "knows" still exists inside.

In another group meeting, Sara casts direct aspersions on the significance of the aging body for the existence of the self. Her response suggests that what is somatically evident or otherwise in place need not be existentially conclusive. In the process, she virtually tells Rita—a group participant whose husband is very demented—that the body is only a visible indicator of a mind if one treats it as such, placing the responsibility for being minded on those who have a choice in preserving it:

> Rita: I just don't know what to think or feel. It's like he's not even there anymore, and it distresses me something awful. He doesn't know me. He thinks I'm a strange woman in the house. He shouts and tries to slap me away from him. It's not like him at all. Most of the time he makes sounds but they sound more like an animal than a person. Do you think he has a mind left? I wish I could just get in there into his head and see what's going on. Sometimes I get so upset that I just pound on him and yell at him to come out to me. Am I being stupid? I feel that if I don't do something quick to get at him that he'll be taken away from me altogether.
>
> Sara: We all have gone through it. I know the feeling. Like you just know in your heart of hearts that he's in there and that if *you* let go, that's it. So you keep on trying and trying and trying. You've got to keep the faith, that it's him and just work at him, 'cause if you don't . . . well, I'm afraid we've lost them. That's Alzheimer's. It's up to the ones who care because they can't do for themselves.

For readers who are clinically oriented, these beliefs and actions might seem to be a form of psychological denial. But a clinical view is not the only way to interpret such exchanges. These conversations are also part of the mundane philosophical considerations of everyday life. At times, we all wonder about our selves and the selves of others. In the process, we make decisions and act on what we convince ourselves is "real" or relevant to our own and others' lives. We continually make judgments about existence and the operating status of our minds, thoughts, and feelings. As Mead (1934) instructed us long ago, selves and minds arise out of, and are part of, social interaction. They are social objects, in effect, and as such can be separated from what in this case is the aging body. As Sara would seem to argue, we are morally implicated in the continued existence of others' minds and selves: "If *you* let go, that's it."

This has two possible ramifications for the objectively visible body. First, bodily signs do not necessarily tell us what lies within. Second, if we abandon our social responsibility for constructing and preserving selves and minds, the presence of a physical body can be of little practical importance to us. Such practices of denying the aging body, paying attention instead to what the body cannot discern, renders visibility insignificant in its related everyday affairs.

Certain Limits

As variable and constructed as the body's visibility might seem to be, we do well to remember Shilling's words of caution: while the body is unfinished business and is transformed in society, its visibility unfolds within certain limits. Kaufman's respondents, Millie, Ben, and Stella, for example, were relatively healthy, even if they were aged into their eighties. Their lives were not enmeshed in incapacitating illnesses, physical breakdowns, or dementia. Likewise, the older women Matthews interviewed were in fair health and had relatively sound bodies and minds. They were not forced by frailty to be sedentary; they could control their whereabouts and encounters with others. The interpretive work these individuals undertook to manage the visibility of their aging bodies was made possible in part because their bodies cooperated in their interpretive ventures. Their bodies were serviceable—if unobtrusive—resources for constructing and managing the selves these older people worked to promote. Had their "obdurate" bodies been more recalcitrant—had they limited mobility, compromised communication skills, or required more than a modicum of special care—their visibility would have been far more difficult to manage. (See, for example, Pollner and McDonald-Wickler, 1985, for an instance where the objective conditions of the body seem to work harder against interpretation.)

Indeed, the aging body can intrude deeply into everyday life. It can try the interpretive fortitude and bodily transparency of the most insistent caregiver and most resistant old people. Still, such intrusions do not impose meaning on their own terms. Neither the subjective contours of embodiment nor the objective status of the body determines the other. There is a dynamic interplay between the two in practice. If the visibility of certain bodies is strictly limited for all practical purposes—such as among the friends and acquaintances of Matthews' respondents—this does not mean that these women fail to take their bodies into account on other occasions.

The sudden company of strangers or the aches and pains of getting about on foot during the day are occasional reminders that the objective body is a reality that more or less makes itself present in life. If the body seems starkly visible—as if it were insisting on being the center of attention—it does not mean that its presence will necessarily engross the lives of those concerned twenty-four hours a day. The visibility of the glaringly aging body is constructed in relation to, not separate from, the practice of everyday life. Certain limits may come in the form of trenchant intrusions, but these do not abrogate interpretive practice.

Kathy Charmaz's (1991) research on the experience of serious chronic illness nicely illustrates this point. Charmaz asks how those who suffer from illnesses such as cancer, lupus erythematosus, multiple sclerosis, arthritis, and cardiovascular disease construct their lives in relation to illness. Rather than assuming that such illnesses set objective limits on meaning-making, Charmaz takes her point of departure from the illnesses' everyday experience.

From in-depth interviews conducted over a number of years with 110 individuals, most of whom are older adults, Charmaz quickly learns that chronic illness affects the self in a way that acute illness does not. This is a difference in kind, not just degree. Assuming that one recovers from an acute illness, the illness runs its course fairly quickly and those affected return to their "normal" lives, once again taking their now relatively transparent bodies for granted. In contrast, those suffering from serious chronic illness live in relation to their illnesses for long periods. This results in life reconstructions that shift with the persistent—if fluctuating—pains and inconveniences posed by the illnesses. The visibility and meaning of the body alternate in the process.

Charmaz's interviews show that individuals can construct their illnesses in distinctly different fashions. Their definitions of their illness experience are affected by their place in the trajectory of the illness, as well as by the problems of daily living posed by specific symptoms. The visibility of a chronic illness sufferer's body moves into and out of view in the course of related experiences. Charmaz focuses on three types of response—chronic illness as life interruption, chronic illness as intrusive to life, and life as immersed in illness. As she takes us through her material and we hear respondents describe themselves, we learn that these are different *ways* of experiencing chronic illness; they are not each characteristic of particular individuals. The same individual may at times construct his or her illness as merely intrusive in his or her life and, at other times, construct life as immersed in the illness.

Respondents frame this in terms of "good days" and "bad days." On bad days, one may become immersed in one's illness, with the resulting pathological implications for one's identity. These are days when the aging body is felt to be most visible, the objective chronicity of which seems to predominate. On good days, one's illness may be experienced as having been a passing interruption in life. The individual is otherwise mostly engaged in the normal rhythms of daily living. On these days, the aging body recedes into the background of experience to become experientially invisible. The overall effect is that we are witness to subjects who not only construct the meaning of chronic illness, but who do so in relation to their bodies' fluctuating symptomatological presence in life. These subjects are not experiential robots, continuously caught in the objective pathologies of their bodies. Instead, they take account of the changing experiential contours of chronic illness in discerning who and what they are as sufferers.

Charmaz explains that "each way of experiencing and defining illness has different implications for self and for meanings of time" (p. ix). Repeatedly, the respondents couple statements about the ups and downs of their illness with thoughts about themselves, how their lives have changed, and what this means to them in the immediate scheme of things. Serious chronic illness and its daily vicissitudes are not just another series of embodied assaults on one's being, Charmaz explains, but make for complex and continuing changes in who one is as a person. Chronic illnesses, in other words, are more than sicknesses; their fluctuations provide the bases for repeatedly redesigning the selves their sufferers live by. To use Arthur Frank's (1995) telling language, these are identities that are "wounded" with little to hope for on bad days and, for the same individuals, identities that resiliently spring forth in fine health and promising futures on good days.

All this might easily have been missed had Charmaz oriented to her respondents' selves as having physical limits placed on them by their bodies. The underlying lesson here is that we shortchange our understanding of everyday life when we allow the objective body to interpretively overshadow a view to its subjective understanding. Equally instructive, especially for the discipline of gerontology, is the lesson that the experience of the aging body is occasioned and not fixed by a particular stage or condition of life (see Holstein and Gubrium 2000a, 2000b, 2002). At the same time, it is apparent that the objective body does intrude, materially challenging the interpretive acumen of its subjects. The everyday visibility of the body in chronic illness is limited in practice by both the body's fluctuating infirmity and the meanings constructed in relation to this fluctuation.

As important as they are, the aging body's objective fluctuations are not the only limits on its unfinished business. Limits also derive from the variety of institutions that influence the interpretation of bodies. Institutions of all kinds—from nursing homes to caregiver support groups and spiritual fellowships—provide established and localized ways of viewing the bodies presented within them (Gubrium and Holstein forthcoming). Nursing homes, for example, are settings in which the body comes into view as sick and close to death. While, of course, not all residents in such facilities are physically incapacitated, nor are they all terminally ill, it is nonetheless an environment where talk and action unfolds with these conditions discursively foregrounded (Gubrium and Holstein 2001b).

Again, this is not to suggest that such limits determine how the body is viewed or considered in these settings. Rather, these are conditions taken into account in the practice of making bodies meaningful. In listening to nursing home residents speak about their lives, it is evident that they construct who and what they are in relation to the "conditions of possibility" (Foucault 1979) for bodies typified in nursing facilities, not to mention the specific objective conditions of these bodies themselves. At the same time, residents supply biographical particulars of their own to specify the related interpretive interplay (Gubrium 1993, [1975] 1997). The visibility of the body is thus a confluence of personal, physical, situational, and institutional factors that are interpretively sorted in practice. While aging bodies in nursing facilities are typically made visible in terms of frailty, sickness, and death, there is not a standard interpretive template for highlighting the body. Indeed, there is considerable variation in the bodily images that emerge. And, interestingly enough, they are not always formal institutional images, nor are they necessarily somber and depressing.

In the following conversation, two wheelchair-bound African American nursing home residents discuss the vegetative identity of a fellow resident. The fellow resident, Miss Casey, is a known vegetable, partly because of the location of her bed in the nursing facility, where the "bags of bones" are placed. Note how Muriel and Ruby, the wheelchair-bound residents, humorously use Miss Casey's vegetative status to construct the visibility of their bodies in nursing home terms but incorporating biographical particulars of their own in the process:

> Muriel: Don't know how you stand it, girl. Why you go over there, down there by those rooms? I saw you lookin' in there.
> Ruby: What you mean? I was just passin'. That Miss Casey, the one just over yonder, couple doors over there? Oh my, she is a bag of bones. Oh, wee! She's just in there in bed and she's on her back. You be hardly knowin' she's alive. They got her hooked up to all kinds of stuff. Her mouth's hangin' open, like that. [Imitates Miss Casey] Oh, wee!
> Muriel: That one's a vegetable. Sweet Jesus, I don't know why they keep 'em alive. What good are they? The bags of bones they have in the place, it gives me the chills when I see 'em. I don't know how you can stand it, Ruby. Why do you look there, girl?
> Ruby: Who you talkin' to?
> Muriel: You, girl. [Chiding Ruby] You thinkin' of bein' one of them there vegetables? You look like you gettin' pretty skinny. I'll get me one of those pills that knock me dead before I get like that!
> Ruby: I'm no vegetable! Look at you, girl. That nappy hair look like ol' dried up corn silk. You better watch out, in a place like this here I can see you in one of those beds down there, like ol' Miss Casey. I be comin' down that hall and look in there and there you is, mouth open like this [imitates Miss Casey], like an ol' dried up melon, oozin' and bruisin'.
> Muriel: Now look at you, Ruby. You already a bag of bones. You *all* skin and bones! You no vegetable, you a skeleton!
> Ruby: Oh, wee! What you talkin' about, girl? You got no behind!
> Muriel: I'm leavin' this ol' place tomorrow. This here is bonetown. Ain't gonna be one of them vegetables like you Ruby. You gonna look at 'em so much, you gonna be one of 'em. [Laughing] You turnin' green already!

As the women banter and laugh about the bags of bones, Muriel describes how chilling it is to wheel past the vegetables, asserting that she would take a suicide pill before she would let herself come to that. Joking with each other, their own bodies come alive as a complex surface of related signs that take on meaning within their institutional context. The residents use and embellish what they know about their neighbor "Miss

Casey" to concretely describe what they themselves could become. With wit and sarcasm, the women present their bodies and selves, discursively constructing them and, in the process, bringing them into view out of both biographically relevant and institutionally significant linkages. Using recognizable terms, they indicate who and what they themselves could become "in a place like this here." If these woman humorously construct the visibility of their own bodies, they do so in relation to the nursing home's vernacular of embodiment. Shilling's certain limits are in place, of course, as they mediate the unfinished business of this segment of these residents' everyday lives.

Conclusion

Following Shilling's suggestion, we have approached the visibility of the aging body by drawing on contrasting objective and everyday perspectives. An everyday perspective brought the aging body into view as unfinished interpretive business. From this angle, we looked on the aging body as a project of interpretive practice. Rather than taking for granted that the aging body was an objective entity with a constant presence in experience, we explored the varied ways that the body is both highlighted and recedes from attention in everyday life. From the management of its visibility to its displacement by more significant concerns, the visibility of the aging body is articulated in relation to the competing circumstances and priorities at hand. This perspective ultimately suggests that the aging body, even in frailty, is not a constant presence in life, but, rather, is an object of experience that is continuously subject to meaning-making action.

The objective perspective emphasizes the aging body's independent "effects" on experience. But in the context of everyday life, a better word would be "intrusion." The latter suggests that while the objective body may shape experience, it does not determine it. The body is a presence that is taken into account when assigning meaning to the lives of aging persons. From daily fluctuations in the status of serious chronic illness to the body-conscious environments of nursing homes, the aging body intrudes and insists on its attendant visibility. This body has no essential meaning; its insistence is only a demand for meaning. It leaves open to interpretation the many ways that beholders can take it into account. Both certain limits and unfinished business are implicated in the process.

The visibility of the aging body, in practice, is a product of the constant interplay between obdurate, objective features of the body and the meaning-making activities and circumstances in which the body is encountered and interpreted. Documenting its resulting social organization gives us further insight into the body as a gerontological object. Emphasizing everyday interpretive practice permits us to treat the visibility of the aging body as an ongoing interactional project that is subject to the working intrusions of embodiment—two aspects of the body that are continuously intertwined. Aging, as a result, is disentangled from the body per se and inserted into the interpretive contingencies of being old.

This view has distinctive research implications. To start, it is important to resist the urge to assign independent priority to either the objective or the fully subjective body. Second, it is imperative that the ordinary, everyday contours of the aging body take center stage in orienting to questions of visibility. This means focusing on how the body presents itself to, and is understood by, all concerned—both those whose bodies are the topic of interest and those who attend to these bodies. Third, we do well to document the practical interplay between the aging body as an interpretive project and the aging body as an obdurate intrusion. The empirical outcome will be portraits and understandings of bodily visibility grounded in the broad everyday experiences of embodiment.

References

Blumer, H.
   1969 *Symbolic Interactionism.* Englewood Cliffs, N.J.: Prentice Hall.

Charmaz, K.
   1991 *Good Days, Bad Days: The Self in Chronic Illness and Time.* New Brunswick, N.J.: Rutgers University Press.

Cooley, C. H.
   [1902] 1964. *Human Nature and the Social Order.* New York: Scribner.

Featherstone, M., and M. Hepworth
   1991 The Mask of Aging and the Postmodern Life Course. In *The Body.* Edited by M. Featherstone, M. Hepworth, and B. Turner, 371–89. London: Sage.

Foucault, M.
1979 *Discipline and Punish.* New York: Vintage Books.
1988 *Technologies of the Self.* Edited by L. H. Martin, H. Gutman, and P. H. Hutton. Amherst: University of Massachusetts Press.

Frank, A. W.
1995 *The Wounded Storyteller: Body, Illness, and Ethics.* Chicago: University of Chicago Press.

Furman, F. K.
1997 *Facing the Mirror: Older Women and Beauty Shop Culture.* New York: Routledge.

Gubrium, J. F.
1986 *Oldtimers and Alzheimer's: The Descriptive Organization of Senility.* New York: JAI Press/Elsevier.
1992 The Social Preservation of Mind: The Alzheimer's Disease Experience. *Symbolic Interaction* 9: 13–28.
1993 *Speaking of Life: Horizons of Meaning for Nursing Home Residents.* New York: Aldine de Gruyter.
[1975] 1997 *Living and Dying at Murray Manor.* Charlottesville: University Press of Virginia.

Gubrium, J. F.
(eds.) 2001b Analyzing Interpretive Practice. In *Handbook of Qualitative Research.* 2nd ed. Edited by N. Denzin and Y. Lincoln, 487–508. Thousand Oaks, Calif.: Sage.

Gubrium, J. F.
Forthcoming. Going Concerns and Their Bodies. In *Cultural Gerontology.* Edited by L. Andersson. New York: Greenwood.

Hallam, E., J. Hockey, and G. Howarth
1999 *Beyond the Body: Death and Social Identity.* London: Routledge.

Holstein, J. A., and J. F. Gubrium
2000a *Constructing the Life Course.* Lanham, Md.: AltaMira Press.
2000b *The Self We Live By: Narrative Identity in a Postmodern World.* New York: Oxford University Press.
2002 The Life Course. In *Handbook of Symbolic Interactionism.* Edited by L. Reynolds and N. Herman. Lanham, Md.: AltaMira Press.

Kaufman, S. R.
1986 *The Ageless Self.* Madison: University of Wisconsin Press.

Kessler, S. I., and W. McKenna
  1978 *Gender: An Ethnomethodological Approach.* Chicago: University of Chicago Press.

Matthews, S.
  1979 *The Social World of Old Women.* Beverly Hills, Calif.: Sage.

Mead, G. H.
  1934 *Mind, Self and Society.* Chicago: University of Chicago Press.

Nettleton, S., and J. Watson, eds.
  1998 *The Body in Everyday Life.* London: Routledge.

Pollner, M., and L. McDonald-Wikler
  1985 The Social Construction of Unreality: A Case Study of a Family's Attribution of Competence to a Severely Retarded Child. *Family Process* 24: 241–54.

Rose, N.
  1998 *Inventing Our Selves.* Cambridge: Cambridge University Press.

Shilling, C.
  1993 *The Body and Social Theory.* London: Sage.

Turner, B. S.
  1984 *The Body and Society.* Oxford, U.K.: Blackwell.

Turner, B. S.
  (ed.) 1992 *Regulating Bodies.* London: Routledge.

CHAPTER EIGHT

THE BODIES OF VETERAN ELITE RUNNERS
Emmanuelle Tulle

This chapter will explore the ways in which Veteran or Masters elite long-distance runners and track athletes aged fifty to eight-six experience and talk about aging, especially how it affects their ability to train and compete in a physically demanding discipline. The focus of this chapter is on the deployment of the body and bodily signals in life history narratives of nine men and four women who have trained and competed regularly over a substantial period of time (most entered their discipline as young adults)—and in most cases continue to do so.

The argument presented here is as follows: In a bid to contribute to the development of a sociology of the body in the later years, I will examine the discursive context in which older bodies are understood and governed. This is important because traditionally older bodies, following an oft-quoted argument made by Öberg (1996), have largely been absent from the purview of empirical and theoretical investigations in social gerontology and in sociology. Yet older bodies are very real and play a vital and necessary role in the pursuit and achievement of agency and in the negotiation of identity (Hepworth 2000). By focusing on the "realization of age" among aging runners, I will show how the body is deployed in the athletes' biographical accounts of their achievements to date and how the body structures their plans for the future. This will provide an opportunity for laying some foundations for an understanding of the older body as one of the technologies through which the government of older people is operated, in addition to understanding the aging body as physical capital. In so doing, I will explore whether running, through the body, contributes to the accumulation of social capital.

For a Sociology of the Aging Body

The present discussion is located at the lived intersection of the sociology of the body and the sociology of later life. As Gilleard and Higgs (1998) note, the body has become a key aspect of understanding late life. Therefore, if we are to grasp this thing called late life, it is vital that we concentrate on its very moorings—the practical formation of the body and the varied ways in which self and identity are constructed in relation to its corporeal presence.

Along these lines, a growing literature has problematized the aging body in relation to the impact it might have on self and identity. Does old age, culturally understood as a period of bodily decline and deterioration, pose an obstacle to a positive sense of self? Mike Featherstone and Mike Hepworth (1989) and Simon Biggs (1997 and 1999) have discussed this issue in different ways. Featherstone and Hepworth have identified the strategies older people deploy to come to terms with bodily aging in an ageist cultural context in which value is placed on youthful, fit, and perfect bodies. From this, social worth is derived. In this context, the bodies of older people are clearly transgressive and people are encouraged to come to terms with their own aging by eliding the body from experience and locating the source of positive identity primarily in an ageless, unchanging self.

Biggs (1999), from a psychological perspective, critically explores the potential of masquerade and agelessness for maintaining a viable selfhood and concludes that such a strategy alienates people from their authentic identity. Polivka (2000), in a reflection on the opportunities presented by the postmodern life course and the destabilization of age-based boundaries for the fashioning of more socially, culturally, and personally satisfying experiences in later life, argues that the elision of the body is not conceivable or desirable. Indeed along with Biggs (1999), Katz (1997) and Andrews (1999), who reflect on ways in which we could envisage the rehabilitation of the aging body and its relationship to identity, advocate the celebration of old bodies, including very old ones, rather than their concealment through an ongoing pursuit of agelessness.

Nevertheless, the point is that older people interpret, give meaning to, and act on the sensations their bodies give off in context. Michel Foucault (1975, 1984) would argue that the body bears the marks of its own regulation. Whether in the prison or in the gym, social actors are encouraged to take up techniques to control bodily movement, shape intimate dispositions, and achieve particular bodily shapes. These give access to culturally appropriate forms of subjectivity. The potential for agency is discernible in the deployment of these "techniques of the self." Foucault's approach is reliant on an analysis of power predicated on its dispersion in the social body. All social actors are invested with a power that is prone to challenge and diversion.

Thus, we are all implicated in our own subjectification, yet we have the power to resist the application of power by others as much as those forms of control we apply onto ourselves. It is likely to influence the key decisions people make about the organization of their lives. For instance, it may be invoked in relation to decisions about the reliance on or rejection of welfare support to compensate for the actual or potential erosion of physical competence (Tulle-Winton 1999; Tulle and Mooney 2002) at key turning points but also in the mundane practices of everyday life. Through the engagement in forms of behavior that are corporeally and age appropriate, older people comply with their own government and thus position themselves as ethical subjects in their own right.

This type of analysis focuses our attention on the discursive conditions in which the body is brought into play. It does not, however, illuminate the ways in which social actors, in specific contexts, deploy their bodies as both the target of and support for social action and how, in the process, they situate themselves in the social structure. This important discussion is where I now turn.

Body as Capital

In order to understand this aspect of bodily self-maintenance, I turn to the work of Pierre Bourdieu (1979) and Loïc Wacquant (1993 and 1999), and their conceptualization of the body as "capital." Both have shown how the body is fully implicated in the project of situating itself socially. In other words, the shapes of our bodies, their dispositions, needs, and wants; and the way they move and are used are all references to our social location, our "habitus," as they term it. Thus, the way in which we work with and through our bodies in a range of contexts produces social capital commensurate with our position in the social structure. Bourdieu

(1979) shows that even the choice of sport available to social actors is consistent with their habitus—the system of dispositions that structures practices and gives rise to a specific set of aspirations.

In his ethnographic account of the lives and aspirations of young men living in a Chicago Black ghetto, Wacquant (2000) shows that boxing is more than the pursuit of a violent activity. First, one *becomes* a boxer, a fighter. Second, the urge to submit oneself to the appropriate training required for this process of change to take place is consistent with an ethic of hard work and discipline that Wacquant suggests only a fraction of the youngsters brought up in lower-income, inner-city areas will have and pursue.

In order for the transformation from street kid to boxer to be achieved, a disciplining of the whole life is required: of the self, of everyday life, and of the body. With respect to the body in particular, the work consists of learning and constant repetition of a new range of gestures and techniques until they are naturalized and internalized and have refashioned the bodily appearance. Only then can the possibility of using boxing as a source of livelihood be seriously contemplated. Wacquant (1993) concludes that the body is at once economic, cultural, and physical capital. Furthermore, the labor that is applied to the body in the pursuit of boxing prowess leads to what Hawee (2001) refers to as the transformation of the self.

Paradoxically, I would argue that the concept of capital presents opportunities for capturing the corporeality of later life and its impact on self and identity, despite the presumed association of aging with the erosion of the economic, cultural, and physical properties of the body. Is this decline wholesale? To what extent are aging bodies able to retain some of these properties? At the discursive level, what is the field of possibilities in which older bodies can be understood and used?

Biology and Aging

Recent work in the biology of aging reveals that there is no overarching biological theory of aging (Bengtson, Parrott, and Burgess 1996; Cristofalo, Gerhard, and Pignolo 1994)—theorizing in this area has been split between the location of aging processes at the cellular levels or at the organismic level. Research has shown that aging takes place in heterogeneous ways, not just across organisms but also within organisms. Cristofalo, Gerhard, and Pignolo (p. 1) argue that there is some justification for accepting a genetic theory of aging that affects organisms at the level of cells operating "in a hierarchical, dynamic and interacting network whose functional integrity progressively deteriorates with time." Thus, biological aging is not linear but "hits" the organism in different places in an increasingly synergistic fashion.

Another important area of development in the field of biology is the search for "biomarkers" of aging (Butler and Sprott 2000). That is, the series of thresholds signaling qualitative and quantitative changes in the organism, consistent with a significant increase in morbidity, deterioration of function, and risk of death. The biomarker concept appears to reflect a conception of human aging that is visible to observation and thus amenable to intervention. However, while the impression is gained that aging is a wholly internal, individual process, there is also recognition in the discipline that external (read social) processes can also influence aging. Thus, the speed and reach of aging may be altered by one's social position and exposure to risk factors for aging. The aim of intervention is not to extend the life span but to prevent illness and maximize individual life expectancy through an understanding of the interactions between internal aging and external factors.

Exercising Older Bodies

Older bodies are increasingly targeted as sites of health prevention measures that encompass healthy eating and the pursuit of physical exercise. For instance, Goggin and Morrow Jr. (2001, 58) note that physical activity is now widely accepted in the scientific community as beneficial for older adults, regardless of their health status, in "reducing or preventing functional declines linked to secondary aging." Thus, not exercising is constructed as a health risk. But how much activity should older people engage in? Given that successful agers should also "accept" the decrements of age and manage their aspirations and expectations accordingly (Baltes and Baltes 1993), this is quite a pertinent question.

Evidence exists to show that high levels of sports participation (say, among Veteran or Masters athletes) are beneficial for health but also that older bodies, including very old ones, can be challenged and have performance improved considerably with training. Benyo (1998) quotes the results of a study involving ten frail men and women whose average age was ninety and who took part in an "8-week programme of high intensity training of the leg muscles. . . . Strength increased by 174%, muscle area, measured by computed tomography (CT) scan, increased by 9%; and mobility substantially improved. Two participants who had previously relied on canes for walking were able to dispense with them after the training program" (p. vii–viii). Morley (2000) concludes that while aging leads to attrition in performance and that older athletes could never outperform younger athletes, older bodies are nevertheless capable of very strenuous physical exertion that can lead to improvement in performance.

With respect to the positive impact of exercise on health, in a longitudinal study of the impact of physical training on older male track athletes, Mengelkoch et al. (1997) conclude that risk factors for coronary heart disease (CHD) remained low and stable among those who had continued to train regularly for twenty years. DeSouza et al. (1997) found that regular physical activity (in this case long-distance running) among healthy postmenopausal women aged forty-nine to seventy reduced levels of plasma fibrinogen (which in high levels are linked to increased risks of CHD) and that this relationship persisted regardless of whether the women involved in the study were hormone replacement therapy (HRT) users or nonusers (HRT also lowers levels of plasma fibrinogen).

Washington, Shaw, and Snow (1998) show that postmenopausal women aged fifty to seventy-five subjected to a nine-month exercise regime showed improvement in lower-body strength consistent with a lowering of the risk of falling. However, the exercise regime to which the women had been subjected showed no change in hipbone density, partly because the jump exercises appropriate for this were not included until the fourth month of the study period, for "safety purposes." Furthermore, women had to get "physician clearance" before being accepted into the exercise program.

One study, carried out in Glasgow by Hood and Northcote (1999), appears to lend credence to the need for caution. They carried out a study of a small sample of male harriers drawn from the Scottish Veteran Harriers Club, among whom figure a high number of national and international champions, in which they found that "high intensity lifelong endurance exercise may be associated with altered [read deleterious] cardiac structure and functions" (p. 239). They also accepted that "moderate" physical exercise was beneficial, without specifying what that might refer to. However, it should be noted that some of the changes observed in the measurements that the athletes had undergone were similar to those affecting younger athletes. Thus, the risks posed to the heart by such activities were not simply age-related but a function of the intensity that engagement in high-level athletics demands.

What the preceding review suggests is that exercise, even at high levels of intensity, is beneficial and that the bodies of older men and women can be pushed quite hard in many cases. However, there is still reluctance to recommend anything more than modest levels of exercise due to expected health risks.

And yet there exist manuals for older athletes that reflect more ambitious aspirations. Benyo's (1998) book titled *Running past 50* is one such manual. Its aim is to help veteran runners continue running at high levels of performance for as long as possible. Thus, it contains advice not just on the prevention and management of injuries, but also on ways of improving performance through training and refueling, staving off boredom, and planning what he calls "adventure runs" or other endurance events. The book's message is underpinned by an acute awareness of the inevitability of nefarious bodily change. It appears to accept fifty as a "biomarker" of aging but also ventures the claim that running may, if not reverse, at least stave off physical and psychological deterioration.

How can this be translated into an in-depth understanding of the experience of aging? Most people, at any age, are not elite athletes. But older athletes reveal to us what effort their bodies can sustain and what performances they can generate in exercise. In other words, these are "pioneer" bodies because they push back the boundaries of what is expected. Given the context of regulation in which older bodies are allowed to operate, as well as the porousness of the boundaries that accompany these regulatory processes, how does this shape the experience of becoming older? What this chapter ultimately attempts to elucidate is how corporeality is deployed in the aging experience. Here, we attend to the language of age, the symbolic repertoire (Hepworth 2000) that is available to people when they experience and communicate age.

What is foregrounded in much of the theoretical work on bodies is the production of socially valued bodies. From this modal selves are deduced.

However, the sensate as a condition of possibility for agency also needs to be provided its own prominence, both empirically and theoretically. I suggest that a sociology of the body, particularly of the aging body, cannot address the issue of self and identity without exploring the ways in which social actors communicate with the intimate dimension of corporeality in order to engage in its regulation, either through the project of successful aging or through the negotiation of prescriptions of age-appropriate exercise behavior.

The work emanating from biology and physiology alludes to a complexity of structure and opportunity, which makes its presence felt in the intimate engagement of social actors with their bodies. Thus, the following questions beg to be addressed: What does it feel like to become older? What part does the body play in this experience, and how does that shape social action? How do people negotiate, interpret, and manage the various influences which frame the individual aging experience and which situate them as social actors in the world?

Methodological Implications

Berthelot (1983) argues that a sociology of the body should be underpinned by a methodological strategy that fulfills the need to find ways of capturing the three different levels described earlier at which the body is deployed and experienced and, in the process, shown how agency is made possible. We also need to be able to capture the sensate or at least to identify it in the mass of data produced in the course of empirical work. He advocates a combination of methods, such as interviews, life histories, and observation of a range of social actors to explore how they, themselves, "manage" these complex processes. How the body is brought to the surface in the production of these narratives is particularly relevant.

This is an area that is still, as yet, largely underdeveloped, although, as I have shown elsewhere (Tulle-Winton 2000), there are notable exceptions. Cunningham-Burley and Backett-Milburn (1998) tap into corporeality among middle-aged men and women through the experience of health and illness. Gubrium and Holstein (1999) explore how the residents of nursing homes used bodies (usually other people's) to make sense of the experience of institutionalization.

We also know that people have a sense of their own aging that does not follow a linear process and that is instead disjointed and hermeneutical in form and context. Öberg and Tornstam (2001) have carried out a survey investigating how people aged twenty to eighty-five made sense of their body image. They wanted to explore the importance of youthfulness and fitness in a context in which youthful bodies have high cultural currency. Respondents were asked to agree or disagree with a range of statements about age as a multidimensional concept encompassing look-age, ideal-age, and feel-age.

Both men and women reported feeling, looking, and wanting to be younger than their chronological age. This discrepancy between chronological age and subjective age increased with age. Thus at age eighty and over, respondents reported looking seventy, feeling sixty, and wanting to be fifty! Apart from the youngest males, there was dissatisfaction among both men and women with their own body shape, a process that remained constant for women, regardless of age, but which increased with age for men. Respondents also reported being youthful, although the proportion of those who did decreased with age. Respondents appeared to be sensitive to the obligation of maintaining youthfulness through fitness regimes and weight regulation. But what the survey could not investigate was what being youthful consisted of and what the *meaning* of age was in an aging society.

The Study

The study focuses analytic attention on veteran elite runners. I conducted life history interviews and periods of participant observation with twenty-one men and women aged forty-eight to eighty-six involved in athletics competitively or, if they have retired, whose active involvement has continued into their later years. I will concentrate on the accounts[1] of thirteen informants, whose characteristics are shown in figures 8.1–8.3.

Veteran athletes use their bodies more strenuously than people of similar ages not engaged in athletic pursuits. For example, among the ten endurance runners, eight (six men and two women) were still active and accumulated weekly mileages of between thirty and eighty miles. They ran between five and seven days per week and raced regularly in open and veteran races.[2] Of these, four (two men and two women) were

Age groups						Total
	50–54	55–59	60–64	65–69	70+	
Women	2	1	0	1	0	4
Men	3	3	2	0	1	9

Figure 8.1. Physical Activity by Age Group

Discipline		
	Endurance	Track & Field
Women	2	2
Men	8	1

Figure 8.2. Type of Physical Activity

Participation Level		
	Active	Retired
Women	4	0
Men	6	3

Figure 8.3. Participation Level in Physical Activity

hill or ultradistance runners. They pushed their bodies particularly hard, hill runners running up and down mountains, often over several days: and ultrarunners covering distances in individual races exceeding 50 km.

Even the three who had retired from intensive training and racing, while their levels of activity were considerably lower than the other ten, were still able to use their bodies at levels still deemed remarkable (not by themselves but by nonrunners) for their respective age groups. At the time of the interview these men were aged 58, 59, and 86. They ran from between three miles and twelve miles per week, spread over one to three runs a week. The reasons for the attrition in their ability to run were varied: the 86 year old underwent an operation three years before the interview that left him with a long scar across his abdomen. This caused the loss of core (that is, abdominal) strength and impaired his posture. He also reported loss of balance and being more sensitive to inclement weather conditions, both of which he attributed to the aging process.

The 58 and 59 year olds had heart conditions. In both cases it was extreme fatigue that brought the illness to their attention. The 58 year old had an uneven heartbeat that could not be controlled by surgical or drug intervention. Rest and a reduction in physical exertion were prescribed. The 59 year old suffered a heart attack and had been fitted with a pacemaker. The pacemaker had been set at 70 beats per minute (bpm), which did not enable him to run for an extended period of time. Because of this, he had to alternate running and walking. All three men hoped that, despite their considerable impairments, they would be able to improve on current performance and increase their weekly mileage and the number of times they went out running. Given this, it can be argued that these thirteen runners are part of what one of them described as an "elite group":

> A lot of the top class seniors they don't carry on as veterans. There aren't so many of us and as you go through the age group it becomes a more and more elite group. [DF, M, 56, LD]

Of the three T&F athletes, two were women aged 56 and 65. They trained and competed as often as the veteran athletics calendar (which is less full than the senior scene) allowed. The third one, who was male and aged 54, had retired from his sport (hurdling) and now jogged twelve miles per week. He cited loss of performance and aging as reasons for his retirement, and he did not consider veteran athletics as a desirable option for him.

One of the striking features of the data is the ubiquity of age in my informants' narratives. This is, of course, a function of the research itself that they knew was concerned with the experience of the aging body. However, specific questions about later life and the aging experience were not dealt with until later in the interview encounter, while unprompted, spontaneous, and varied references to aging were offered throughout the interviews, rather than in response to direct questioning.

Findings

The data generated a range of questions: How did the informants experience aging; how did it come to their notice; and how did they respond to it and communicate aging?

Aging as Loss

Loss of speed: In line with current literature on the subject (de Beauvoir 1970; Gullette 1997; Thompson 1998), all the informants recounted experiencing aging as loss or depletion. Loss of speed was mentioned most often. Whether suddenly or gradually, informants had become aware that they did not run as fast or jump as high as in the past. Regardless of age and the timing of entry into the sport, they reported that performance had peaked in their early forties, and that by their early- or mid-fifties, it had started to deteriorate in a way that required explication.

Usually, loss of speed was noticed in races, especially those that runners entered annually and that allowed for comparison of performances over time. Less often, but just as shocking to them, slowing down was experienced in training, especially if they trained with someone who was younger. They noticed it in both speed work or when running over a fixed distance:

> We set off on a Sunday, we used to set off together but now she [23 year old daughter] sets off down the road in front of me and I have gradually got to wind up the pace and I find that the first two or three miles I am

struggling a bit, running with her, and then I get into my pace. I suppose that is just getting the looseness, stiffness out of my joints. [DF, M, 56, LD]

When I go out on a Sunday, we run . . . , we used to run steady seven and a half minute miles for 12 miles and it was always 1.15, now it is maybe 1.31, 1.32 and I don't really feel I am deliberately going any slower but I think maybe we are jogging a bit slower than we used to, so there must be a decrease in performance somewhere I think. [JS, F, 51, MD]

Loss of strength: Informants also referred to loss of strength, of power, of drive in the legs, or even loss of spark, often simply wear and tear of the body. This suggests that they seemed to recognize the pervasiveness of the deterioration they were experiencing—a growing fragility that manifested itself either holistically or topically in the body:

ET: Do you take part in these races to win?

IL: In my age category. In the open races some of them only go as high as 50 and I know I will never win another open race, there is no two ways about it, I just . . . the physical power to win an open race is very, very . . . it has gone now. [M, 61, LD]

ET: Do you think your training . . . has become strenuous as you have got older?

JI: Oh yes. Most of my training. And I don't really keep to any kind of schedule, or anything like that, I just like to go for runs now. . . . I don't train as hard as I used to. I can't actually, to be quite honest with you.

ET: You can or you can't?

JI: I can't. . . . My biggest drawback has always been all the injuries I have had. I got a . . . back problem maybe three and a half, four years ago and I felt . . . not lost the power in my legs, but I think I lost a lot of drive from my legs. [M, 65, LD]

Loss of control: Third, loss was an outcome over which the runner had no control. Aging deprived the athlete of performance. In this case, aging seemed to often be passively experienced:

ET: Did you feel that slowing down yourself?

HS: Yes, well the speed really wasn't there I think. The speed was missing. It had deserted me I think. [M, 54, T7F/r]

There is always something going. I think it is just wear and tear and age is catching up on me. [M, 65, LD]

The runners linked this to the notion of inevitable and natural decline, encapsulated in comments such as:

It has got to happen. [KT, F, 50, UD]
I think my peak was when I was 27 or 28 so then you are on a downward spiral. [IL, M, 61, LD]

Realization of Age

Outside the body: The notion of loss, in its association with aging, gains in saliency if we explore how informants became aware of reduced performance. Informants initially claimed that the loss of performance was not sensed. In other words there was nothing in the practice of running and the physical sensations experienced that signaled a drop in speed. In fact, most said that it was when checking their times during (split time) or after a race, or even when reviewing entries in their diaries, that they noticed they had lost speed:

DF: This year I did the Glasgow Marathon in 2.48. I have slowed by 24 minutes in 17 years.
ET: Does that seem like quite a lot to you?
DF: Well it has taken me by surprise the way my times have slowed down. I feel I am running just as fast as I was but I know I am not. [M, 56, LD]

ET: Is it something that tells you inside?
JBF: No I just know I am not going as fast. I mean, I just think . . . I was running Zeerzinale this year and I did 3.16 or something and my best time is 2.55 and I was aware that I wasn't running as fast. . . . well I mean I was taking split times anyway but the body can't . . . felt it was not running as fast here but there isn't much I can do about it.
ET: Right. It is interesting that you said the body felt it wasn't going as fast.
JBF: In some races I know I am not quite as fast. I mean, the body doesn't notice I am going slower but yes I am slower. [M, 50, HR]

242

Sensing the loss: However, as the quote by JBF [M, 50, HR] and a closer look at the data reveals, there was some ambiguity in the ways in which runners became aware of the loss of speed. On the one hand, they claimed that these changes were not felt in the body and were brought to their attention by external agents, like split and finish times. On the other hand, they also reported sensing these losses and experiencing other sensations that were associated with loss of performance. For instance, the loss of power, drive, and spark alluded to earlier meant that they were less able to generate what JI [M, 65, LD] referred to as "a good turn of speed" in quite the same way as they had done in the past. Furthermore, they often referred to needing longer recovery time, experiencing muscle soreness and fatigue following hard races.

Aging as involution: DF's [M, 54, LD] gradual speed loss was also brought to his attention when training with his daughter. He had trained with her since she had shown promise as a junior athlete. Her training was focused on winning the selection for the Scottish team. DF, who in the early years of his daughter's running career led the pace during training sessions, had been overtaken in speed by her and was now forced to train harder—not to keep up, which he could no longer do—but to minimize the gap which had opened between them and which was not recoverable. When asked to explain this widening gap, he simply said that "she's improving and I'm declining."

However, he could only increase the intensity of training up to a point due to bodily concerns. While her coach allowed her to bring her heart rate up to 140 bpm, his had to stay at 120 bpm. For him this meant running at a pace of less than seven minutes per mile, a pace that was considerably slower than he desired or had ever expected. However, of obvious pertinence here, he experienced serious fatigue, a sensation echoed by JS in the following comments:

> JS: As I said, I feel when I am running I feel I am running just as fast as I have always run. . . . I know I find I don't recover the same as I used to. I used to quite often be able to do races on consecutive days and now it is very rarely that I will do that and then it will take two or three days to recover from a hard training session. . . . I feel tired. It is not so much aches and pains. I just go out and feel I can't run hard. [DF, M, 56, LD]

ET: And are you finding that apart from perhaps an increase in injury that you are having to work harder now to achieve the same?

JS: I have to work harder to achieve the same time, aye. The fact that I haven't . . . you know the best of the 10k was the 35.15, that was when I was 46, and since I was injured I have not gone beyond 36.30, I have not beaten 36 yet. Because I haven't been . . . I used to do 8x1000 on the track but I find I cannot do that now because it is too much. I get too tired and I have less energy. I used to do it between Tuesday and Thursday no bother, but I find if I do too much on a Tuesday, I don't recover enough for Thursday. [F, 51, MD]

Responding to Loss

As these accounts alert us, loss of performance called for a direct and immediate response. Responses to changes in performance varied, from forced, and in one case voluntary retirement from competition, through the development of complex strategies to mask, or at any rate stave off, further decline.

Accepting loss: Acceptance varied by the degree of reluctance with which it was accompanied. IL [M, 61, LD], who at the start of our interview had stated that aging was "not a happy situation," went on to say that he had nonetheless achieved a "cheerful" acceptance of his aging, which he claimed was made possible by the greater wisdom that comes with aging. Thus, for him accepting the inevitability of aging was part of a greater project that he termed "self-realization," apparently consisting of a trade-off between physical loss and psychological gain:

ET: Does that make you feel sad or disappointed that your times . . . that you are having to change your expectations of what you can achieve?

IL: No, not at all. As I say, it is a bit of self-realisation and you have got to accept that you won't be there . . . you still like to think you could but it is not feasible, let's put it like that. So you have got to be realistic about the whole situation.

One might wonder whether the acceptance of old age was tinged with, or even more profoundly underpinned by, a moral stance. I will return to this theme later in the chapter.

Resisting loss: The claims to acceptance were in many cases made concurrently with efforts to resist, on the one hand, aging, and, on the other, social and cultural expectations about appropriate behavior in the later years. Training harder to compensate for speed loss was targeted at the aging body. Continuing to run against the expectations of nonrunners or against the advice of medical professionals was overtly designed to resist what was perceived to be insensitive, even insulting advice, as shown by JI's experience quoted in the proceeding:

> I went with that cartilage I told you. I went there, I went to the National Health and the doctor told me to go and play bowls. I was 55 and he told me to go and play bowls. I said "I don't want to play bowls, I want to be a runner, I have been a runner all my life and I am still running well apart from this knee that is hurting me." He said "Well just don't run." I said "That's not the point. If it is hurting me when I run there is something the matter with it, don't you agree?" I tried every argument with him but he wouldn't do anything for me, he just told me to come back in three months. So I went private and the guy told me "I think it's your cartilage." So I had to pay about £1,700 to get my knee operated on and get my cartilage sorted out and I was back running in three weeks, so. [JI, M, 65, LD]

This statement raises at least two key issues: the issue of a running identity and the moral dimension that appears to underpin the relationship of runners to those outside the sport. To echo Vertinsky (1998), while physical activity may be encouraged in the later years, unspoken but nonetheless strict boundaries exist around the extent and intensity of this involvement. Whether from lay people or medical professionals, prescriptions to try moderate, or even to give up, physical activity appear consistent with the construction of middle-aged people at risk for ill health and needing to rest, whose energies should be diverted to other, perhaps more appropriate foci, such as grandparenthood, coaching youngsters, or administering the sport. In this way, room is made for young athletes and also avoids the ridicule that HS—himself aged fifty-four—had associated with veteran athletics. In this process, the running identity becomes contested and efforts must be made to regain it (in this instance by going for private treatment). The battle lines shift from those that the injured body imposes on the runner to those imposed by external agents, such as doctors.

Regulating behavior: What is also worthy of note is that these prescriptions are focused in several directions: first, as we have just explored, by others onto the runner; but also—second—by runners onto other runners; and, third, by the individual runner onto him- or herself. Because of this, the subjects would question the appropriateness of running or competing in T&F events among people perceived to have inadequate abilities. This presumption was made because these runners' bodies were incorrectly shaped (poor posture), they were too slow, too weak, or simply "too old."

In the following quote, BS [F, 65, T&F] was asked whether she was attracting attention from others when she went out running. She had indeed become well recognized in the neighborhood by her white hair, and people were used to seeing her running in the neighborhood. In the course of our interview, she talked of an older woman who was also often seen running in the neighborhood. This is how she commented on her activities:

> There is an older . . . well I don't know, I am presuming she is older than me, I think she looks older than me and she runs a bit and she looks as through she is a Scandinavian and I think . . . I don't know whether she might have been a fell runner or something and I look at her and wonder why she runs. She is so kind of stooped and sometimes I think that doesn't [benefit] her, even if an athlete can't think that it is doing them any good when you are shuffling and I keep thinking she would be much better having a walk and concentrating on her posture. But that's just me.

Despite others claiming elsewhere that old age was an imposition in very intimate ways, BS [F, 65, T&F] engages in the same process in relation to others. What is described here, beyond the mere association of age with decline and disability, is the association between *looking* old and the legitimacy of engaging in particular forms of physical activity.

Extending this line of argument, BS [M, 58, LD/r] goes even further when he describes the impact of aging on performance and training intensity:

> ET: Do you think it is inevitable that as one gets older that things begin to change?
> BS: Yes, certainly. I . . . both . . . two different points probably to that. One, OK obviously your body is getting older and you can't expect to run so fast but I think that the quality of training that you can cope with when you are younger, which is something I don't think you can cope

with when you're older. OK you can go out and do your long easy runs and all that sort of stuff, OK, but the quality training that is required to run fast I don't think the older person is suited to doing that and certainly not if they have had a full career of being, for instance, an early athlete.

In these two examples we see that the achievements of very old runners were not universally applauded. They were in fact often devalued by not being classified as running, but instead described at best as jogging, and at worst as shuffling. And these older runners' participation in the sport was frowned on, to the extent of advising that, as both informants just quoted in the preceding did, the runners give up and concentrate their efforts on alternative forms of physical activity or on more gentle forms of training, such as walking.

Thus, the look of age was a trigger for regulation, through reflexivity and the obligation by the self to become conscious of the body's failings and to take appropriate remedial action. Looking old was the external manifestation of more intimate forms of agedness, which BS (M, 58, LD/r) expressed as fragility borne out not just of the aging process but also of overtraining earlier in the life course.

Here again we find a strong moral content, as well as the refusal to confront the possibility of performing at levels well below those attained in the past. In effect, these informants regulated their own behavior, and that of others, on the basis of age, but also on a more emotional basis, fueled by the need to preserve a sense of competence, of which their achievements to date were evidence. They engaged in age-appropriate behavior, and this appeared to result from an interplay of accepting public constructions of age and of emotional responses to an unwanted scenario. It could be argued that the process of adapting to physical deterioration that informants advocated for others and for themselves is part of the moral struggle contained in the felt obligation to submit to agedness—to lower one's expectations of achievements.

Furthermore, these informants were caught in an ambiguous position: on the one hand they were prone to engaging in the regulation of their own behavior and that of others, using age relevant criteria; on the other, by the mere fact of continuing to run or train (at whichever level), they also resisted those very same age-based expectations of appropriate behavior. It appears that it is where these two contradictory stances met that key decisions were made, about whether to run, how hard to train, and how to reach the correct balance between maintaining the body in the right condition and risking serious injury. Thus, the experience of the later years is characterized by ambiguity. This is further reflected in the way people discuss themselves and their bodies at later stages in their lives.

Language of Age

In the course of the interviews, informants made a number of claims about their age. They navigated between fixed and relative notions of age. They talked of their experience of age as an embodied process, accessible through bodily sensations or through appearance. But they also invoked other markers, such as cultural and social markers of age, to make sense of their temporal location in the life course.

Being old: On a few notable occasions, informants located themselves firmly in old age by describing themselves as geriatric, "on the slide," or a "has been."[3] The quotes below exemplify this quite well:

I think as well when you get injuries when you are older and things start ... you think "I am getting older, I can't go on forever!" [JI, M, 65, MD]

I had slight niggling injuries, like wee tears here and there and everywhere but I didn't have any problems until I got older with those. ... But once I got older I found certainly it was very frustrating in some respects as well. [IL, M, 61, LD]

This is elucidated further when BS (F, 65, T&F) discusses postponing dinner preparations for her family in order to go for a run. She tells us that "you can't say 'sorry I am going to the gym.' That would be silly at our age."

Do these comments signal an acceptance of agedness? There were indeed variations in the statements made about age. SW [F, 56, T&F] was the most articulate in her rejection of agedness, while being aware that physically she was beginning to exhibit its attributes. She talked at length about her growing dissatisfaction with her body. For instance, her neck now displayed deep wrinkles not present in her earlier years. She had noticed a hardening in the contours of her jaw line, which she attributed to aging. She also was dissatisfied with her hands and fingers. This woman was in fact physically elegant—she was graced with height and a very erect carriage and her bone structure was the underpinning for a remarkably smooth face, free of deep wrinkles and enjoying a glowing complexion. She was aware that she was fortunate in her appearance, but her aging caused her some anxiety. Thus, she preferred to claim she was middle aged, although this was not a positive conclusion. Rather, it was borne out of an awareness of the ambiguity of her situation, as neither young nor old.

Other informants had fewer hesitations to call themselves old. These comments were rarely made in response to a direct question about age. Rather, they were volunteered as part of a commentary on the changes in their running that they had experienced to date (see for instance BS [M, 58, LD/r] who accounted for his loss of form by calling himself geriatric). Most notably, however, no one used the word *elderly*. In contrast, only one informant made no mention of age in fixed terms.

Correspondingly, there appeared to be no reluctance to talk about the age of other older people—sometimes their contemporaries—in fixed terms. JS [F, 51, MD] and BS [F, 68, T&F] made reference to other women using phrases like "an old biddy," "an old bat," or more benignly—because she was talking about herself—"an old lady with white hair."

Feeling youthful: There was a constant to-ing and fro-ing between relative and fixed notions of age and, in the case in the preceding, youthfulness. The claim to youthfulness was not only possible because of the involvement in strenuous physical activity but also because of the informants' appearance. Thus, the appearance of age seems to be a useful asset to bridge the gap between being and feeling age. Physical features like wrinkles, graying hair, or hair loss betray age. However, informants could legitimately claim they were and felt youthful by using other bodily attributes which they possessed and which they associated with *not* being old.

The features of age that their own bodies displayed (wrinkles, gray hair, balding) were perceived as unavoidable because running could do little to prevent them. However, other features denoting old age were identified in those of their contemporaries who did not exercise. Unflattering references were made to fat people, saggy abdomens, people getting breathless crossing the road, or struggling to walk at a brisk pace. Being old means letting oneself go, both physically and socially. Expressed differently, people became old through the performance of age.

Markers of Age

Some informants played with the idea of a specific chronological point that marked entry into old age. Entry into the fifty-five to sixty age group was perceived by a few as a significant marker of old age. Informants seemed to find that declining speed and the disappearing possibility of beating younger runners in races were more obviously observable in this age group. Old age was defined at several levels: as an embodied process and as a process linked to attitude and lifestyle, as well as chronologically, socially, and culturally.

This was not always present, however. As DM [M, 86, MD] remarked, old age was more than its chronological, institutional, or attitudinal characteristics or declining performance. It was also about finitude, the decreasing number of years ahead and the shift in aspirations that uncertainty about life expectancy imposed on people as they got older, whether runners or not:

> DM: There is a saying about age is just a number, but I think it is more than just a number.
> ET: So tell me what are the . . . bits that make it more than a number?
> DM: Well (pause) . . . your age . . . obviously you get older every year, there is no doubt, there is no getting away with that and certainly none of us is going to live until we are 150, at least I don't think so, as far as I know. I think there has got to be a stage where you say, well I have had my chips, it is time you departed from this world. . . . I am certainly not looking forward to that part.

Conclusion

What I have attempted to do is to explore the ways in which corporeality was deployed by aging runners in their life narratives, particularly through the realization of age. In order to achieve this goal and to understand the very discourses through which aged bodies are understood and made sense of, my focus has been on the mundane aspects of aging.

The Sensate Body

The body is emerging not simply as a tool that allows people to continue engaging in their regular activities but is itself acting as a field of possibilities. The constraints and opportunities presented by the body are perceptible to social actors through a close intermeshing of intimate bodily sensations and of age-based prescriptions of appropriate behaviors disseminated in the wider cultural and social context in which people are becoming older.

The body was salient in the runners whose accounts I have just presented. By pushing their physical capacities well beyond those of nonathletes, runners mapped out a field that was indeed replete with possibilities. The investment of time, the discipline to which they subjected their bodies and also their lives, the exhaustiveness and thoroughness of the training they underwent, and the results it yielded in terms of performance are all testimony to the incredible reserves of strength and ability older bodies can deploy.

None of the informants claimed they subjected themselves to these regimes in order to reverse aging or to alter the appearance of age. Nevertheless, it is quite clear that the labor in which they were engaged was more than the pursuit of a beloved hobby. Or to put it another way, although there may have been no conscious desire to use running as a way of resisting bodily and social aging, unwittingly it fulfilled a range of aims, some of which were socially valuable.

The body was deployed in several ways: (1) As an instrument that, for some, allowed the pursuit of a sport at high levels of competitiveness and performance; (2) as a tangible entity on which the sport itself was inscribed and in the process reflected the achievement of socially valuable bodily attributes; (3) as a structure on which were inscribed the modes of regulation associated with intensive participation in athletics; and (4) as the carrier of signs and messages about the quality of its internal functioning.

Running as a Technique of the Self

Running is also a field in which runners confront aging corporeally. Despite claiming that they had not *sensed* the loss of speed manifested in performance attrition in races in training, runners nevertheless also reported being aware of attrition in physiological efficiency and needing more time to recover from races and hard training sessions. This, as their narratives displayed, was quite obviously important to them.

Thus, by training harder, by resting more, or by abandoning competition, runners engaged in forms of regulation in order to remain active in the sport but also to retain the physical hallmarks of the athlete that had social and cultural value: fitness, slimness, and a youthful "silhouette." Are these responses consonant with Foucauldian "techniques of the self?" Yes, because they invite runners to fulfill particular social aims, for instance the achievement of successful aging, the "sensible" navigation of age-based prescriptions of appropriate behavior and aspirations, and the application of regimes of discipline to regulate life and the achievement of a graceful old age.

Veteran elite runners are in an ambiguous position, however. By their very participation in the sport, they transgress boundaries of what is physiologically acceptable. The dominant impression gained from the available literature on exercise in later life is that exercise has health benefits, but it is also cautious about specifying the upper limits of strenuousness to which exercise should be taken. The exception is the literature aimed at older runners that places no such limits beyond those placed by the aging body itself. Some informants reflected the mainstream position by, in effect, engaging in the regulation of other runners, through the articulation of prescriptions aimed at preventing them from overdoing it or from having inappropriate expectations of achievements—the runners articulated the obligation to come to terms with old age and adapt to appropriate levels of training.

However, in other ways these runners engaged in socially valuable projects. Through their training, they projected onto their lives and onto their bodies the discipline that elite athletics requires. As they got older, there was a sense in which such disciplining or single-mindedness was also inappropriate and, thus, transgressive. So through running, informants were able to resist social and biological aging while being confronted with it.

The Older Body as Physical Capital

Elsewhere in the data, some informants observed that running was a lifestyle, so pervasive was it in the organization of their everyday lives. But

I would argue that it plays a more fundamental role than that. Just as it did for the relationship Wacquant's (1993) boxers developed with the practice of their sport, my informants' running can be understood as the art of living or the art of existence; the involvement of time in its practice; the opportunities it gave for the fashioning of a moral framework around socially valued modalities of age; and, finally, the labor carried out on the transformation into a runner's body and its maintenance as such. Thus, while the veteran runner's body may not have economic capital, nevertheless it continues to have physical capital. What is emerging from the data is the need to consider physical capital in at least three ways:

1. As instrumental capital—that is, as a tool with particular biomechanical characteristics that made it suitable for running into the later years. Here we find that aging places the instrumental body at risk through involution and loss and alters the ability of the body to recover from injury.

2. As health capital—running keeps the older body healthy (or postpones the onset of a serious illness like CHD) and is even believed by some informants to slow down biological aging.

3. As aesthetic capital—the older runner's body has aesthetic characteristics that are associated with self-control, health, and youthfulness.

Running in later life contributes to what Bourdieu (1979) refers to as the accumulation of social capital. In this context, social capital would be the ability to maintain a runner's identity despite aging and the many constraints placed on the body engaged in the activity.

The Dialectic of Age

Social capital does not, however, remove the precariousness of the self as one ages. This is reflected in the observed dialectic between being and feeling age and between agedness and youthfulness, which mapped out a space within which informants were able to navigate fairly flexibly to account for the instability, not only of available concepts of age but also of their own location in the life course relative to their contemporaries. Thus, rejecting old age and claiming to feel younger cannot be understood outside the bodily changes that although not pathological nevertheless act as reminders of the phenomenological passage of time. In other words, the corporeal cannot be elided, even when there is no underlying pathology, from the experience of aging.

As IL appeared to suggest, the process of self-realization that is involved in "coming to terms" with the attrition in performance is primarily corporeal. In their confrontation with their own aging, older runners are constantly striving for a resolution of the dialectic between being old and feeling young(er) and ultimately between the fleshiness of the body and the work on the self resulting from the realization of age.

Notes

1. Unfortunately, the participant observation sessions had to be curtailed because of a persistent long-term injury to my left knee, which prevented me from running for twelve months. By mid-summer 2001, I anticipated being able to resume training with some of my informants because recovery from my injury was progressing well. Thus, I returned to training and took part in two 10-km races in the early autumn. Unfortunately, my return to form was beset by another injury—this time to my lower back—which is affecting neural pathways down my left leg and proving difficult to treat. So, once again, I am unable to run. Therefore, the data are drawn mostly from the life history interviews carried out in autumn 2000.

2. Participation in athletics is structured by age, starting with junior categories through to seniors. Older athletes also have their own age-based structure, which is gendered. The age threshold for becoming a veteran (U.K.) or Masters (U.S.) athlete is thirty-five for women and forty for men. Subsequently, athletes' performances are organized into five-year age groups. Most important, age structures access to competitions, and this affects long-distance runners and track and field (T&F) athletes differently. Veteran long-distance runners can enter either "open" races, that is, senior races, with no upper age limit; or veteran races, that is, races reserved for veteran athletes. In contrast, veteran T&F athletes are not able to compete in the senior events and have to rely on what some of my informants referred to as the "Veteran Movement" for the organization of competitions.

3. This was in fact made as a positive statement by BC (M, 59, LD/r) who could no longer emulate past achievements following his heart attack and the fitting of his pacemaker. Though he bemoaned his current situation, he comforted himself by stating that he preferred being a "has been to a never been."

References

Andrews, M.
1999 The Seductiveness of Agelessness. *Ageing and Society* 19: 301–18.

Baltes, P. B., and M. M. Baltes
1993 *Successful Aging: Perspectives from the Behavioral Sciences.* Cambridge: Cambridge University Press.

Bengtson, V. L., T. M. Parrott, and E. O. Burgess
1996 Progress and Pitfalls in Gerontological Theorizing. *The Gerontologist* 36: 768–72.

Benyo, R.
1998 *Running Past 50: For Fitness and Performance through the Years.* Champaign, Ill.: Human Kinetics.

Berthelot, J. M.
1983 Corps et Société: Problèmes Méthodologiques Posés par Une Approche Sociologique du Corps. *Cahiers Internationaux de Sociologie* LXXIV: 119–31.

Biggs, S.
1997 Choosing Not to Be Old? Masks, Bodies and Identity Management. *Ageing and Society* 17: 553–70.
1999 *The Mature Imagination: Dynamics of Identity in Midlife and Beyond.* Buckingham, U.K.: Open University Press.

Bourdieu, P.
1979 *La Distinction: Critique Sociale du Jugement.* Paris: Les Editions de Minuit.

Butler, R. N., and R. L. Sprott
2000 *Biomarkers of Aging: From Primitive Organisms to Man.* Tucson, Ariz.: International Longevity Center-USA.

Cristofalo V. J., G. S. Gerhard, and R. J. Pignolo
1994 Molecular Biology of Aging. (UI: 94151716) *Surgical Clinics of North America* 74(1): 1–21.

Cunningham-Burley, S., and K. Backett-Milburn
1998 The Body, Health and Self in the Middle Years. In *The Body in Everyday Life.* Edited by S. Nettleton and J. Watson, 142–59. London: Routledge.

De Beauvoir, S.
1970 *La Vieillesse*. Paris: Gallimard.

De Souza, C. A. et al.
1997 Plasma Fibrinogen Levels in Healthy Postmenopausal Women: Physical Activity and Hormone Replacement Status. *Journal of Gerontology: Biological Sciences and Medical Sciences* 52A: M294–M298.

Featherstone, M., and M. Hepworth
1989 Ageing and Old Age: Reflections on the Postmodern Life Course. In *Becoming and Being Old: Sociological Approaches to Later Life*. Edited by B. Bytheway et al., 143–57. London: Sage.

Foucault, M.
1975 *Surveiller et Punir: Naissance de la Prison*. Paris: Gallimard.
1984 *Histoire de la Sexualité, Vol III, le Souci de Soi*. Paris: Gallimard.

Gilleard, C., and P. Higgs
1998 Ageing and the Limiting Conditions of the Body. *Sociological Research Online* 3(4). www.socresonline.org.uk/3/4/contents.html [accessed December 14, 2002].

Goggin, N. L and J. R. Morrow, Jr.
2001 Physical Activity Behaviors of Older Adults. *Journal of Aging and Physical Activity* 9: 58–66.

Gubrium, J. F., and J. A. Holstein
1999 The Nursing Home as a Discursive Anchor for the Ageing Body. *Ageing and Society* 19: 519–38.

Gullette, M. M.
1997 *Declining to Decline: Cultural Combat and the Politics of Midlife*. Charlottesville: University of Virginia Press.

Hawee, D.
2001 Emergent Flesh: Physiopoiesis and Ancient Arts of Training. *Journal of Sport & Social Issues* 25: 141–57.

Hepworth, M.
2000 *Stories of Ageing*. Buckingham, U.K.: Open University Press.

Hood, S., and R. J. Northcote
1999 Cardiac Assessment of Veteran Endurance Athletes: A 12 Year Follow-Up Study. *British Journal of Sports Medicine* 33: 239–43.

Katz, S.
1997 Foucault and Gerontological Knowledge: The Making of the Aged Body. In *Foucault: The Legacy*. Edited by C. O'Farrell, 728–35. Kelvin Grove, Australia: Queensland University of Technology.

Mengelkoch, L. J. et al.
1997 Effects of Age, Physical Training and Physical Fitness on Coronary Heart Disease Risk Factors in Older Track Athletes at Twenty-Year Follow-Up. *Journal of the American Geriatrics Society* 45: 1446–53.

Morley, J. E.
2000 The Aging Athlete. Journal of Gerontology: *Biological Sciences and Medical Sciences* 55A: M627.

Öberg, P.
1996 The Absent Body: A Social Gerontological Paradox. *Ageing and Society* 16: 701–19.

Öberg, P., and L. Tornstam
1999 Body Images of Men and Women of Different Ages. *Ageing and Society* 19: 629–44.

Polivka, L.
2000 Postmodern Aging and the Loss of Meaning. *Journal of Aging and Identity* 5: 225–35.

Thompson, N.
1998 The Ontology of Ageing. *British Journal of Social Work* 28: 695–707.

Tulle, E., and E. Mooney
2002 Moving to "Age-Appropriate" Housing: Government and Self in Later Life. *Sociology* 36(3).

Tulle-Winton, E.
1999 Growing Old and Resistance: Towards a New Cultural Economy of Old Age? *Ageing and Society* 19: 281–99.
2000 Old Bodies. In *The Body, Culture and Society: An Introduction*. Edited by P. Hancock et al., 64–83. Buckingham, U.K.: Open University Press.

Vertinsky, P.
1998 Run, Jane, Run: Tensions in the Current Debate about Enhancing Women's Health through Exercise. *Women and Health* 27: 81–111.

Wacquant, L.
1993 Pugs at Work: Bodily Capital and Bodily Labour among Professional Boxers. *Body and Society* 1(1): 65–93.
2000 *Corps et âme: Carnets ethnographiques d'un apprenti boxeur.* Marseille, France: Agone.

Washington, J., J. M. Shaw, and C. M. Snow
1998 Weighted Vest Exercise Improves Indices of Fall Risk in Older Women. *Journal of Gerontology: Biological Sciences and Medical Sciences* 53A: M53–M58.

Wiswell, R. A. et al.
2001 Relationship between Physiological Loss, Performance Decrement, and Age in Master Athletes. *Journal of Gerontology: Biological Sciences and Medical Sciences* 56A: M618.

CHAPTER NINE

AGING AND THE DANCING BODY
Steven P. Wainwright and Bryan S. Turner

ocial gerontology has been dominated historically by a set of practical and applied research issues. In recent years, the development
of both Foucauldian perspectives (Katz 1996) and discursive
analysis of age and aging (Green 1993) have introduced new paradigms
that draw attention to how "senility" as a discourse of social management
was, and is, historically produced. These new paradigms are important
because they drive research toward an understanding of the administrative system by which an aging population is constructed. Through these
innovative developments, the concept of aging has been incorporated
into Michel Foucault's concept of governmentality: namely, the administrative arrangements by which the problems of an aging population
can be productively managed.

In this chapter, we recognize the value of Foucault's concepts of discourse, regulation, and resistance in research on the process of aging, but
we contend that Foucauldian approaches can easily slide into the "radical
social constructionist" claim that aging is simply, or merely, a discourse. It
is important therefore to distinguish between "age" as a category of governmentality and aging as a process that must be understood through the
study of *embodiment*. If age is a classificatory system for the management
of resources, then aging is a performance or ensemble of embodied practices. Foucault's paradigm of bio-politics takes "population" as the product
of an administrative order, but this conceptual framework thereby ignores
or suppresses the process of embodied aging. We maintain that this conceptual strategy ignores the bodily experience of aging and argue for a re-
vised social constructionism that focuses on the embodiment of aging.

Our critical response to Foucault is located within a study of aging, injury, and the body with special reference to ballet dancers. We illustrate our argument by drawing on our ongoing research with professional ballet dancers and comment on the decline of the charismatic dancing body through aging in the specific field of classical ballet. In particular, we suggest that aging is contingent on the dancer's occupational community and, more generally, that aging is specific to the social context in which it occurs.

Because the majority of professional ballet dancers will be retired before they are thirty years of age, we need to recognize that the meaning of an aging body is context dependent, or in this case, occupationally dependent. Our research examines the intersection between individual aging, narratives of aging, and the structural constraints of ballet as an occupation, an occupational community, and a sector in the "art industry." In other words, our research provides a useful reflection on two classical sociological issues (body/culture and individual/society) through the study of a social process: namely, the aging ballet dancer.

This chapter describes dancers' and ex-dancers' perceptions of their bodies, of aging, and of their careers. Our argument works on three levels: first, as an account of dancers' and ex-dancers' "lived experience" of embodiment; second, as an example of the fruitfulness of the contrasted theoretical paradigms for empirical research of the writings of both Michel Foucault and Pierre Bourdieu; and third, as a philosophically grounded critique of radical social constructionist views of the body. In this chapter, the empirical data that are used to illustrate our argument are taken from interviews with ex-dancers. This group presents us with a cohort where the aging body is highly pertinent. We begin with a critical reading of a Foucauldian approach to the aging body and then present a brief overview of some of the key literature on the dancing body. These two sections set the scene for our discussion of our own empirical work on aging, embodiment, and career in ballet. Finally, in our discussion section, we draw out the implications of our chapter for future research on the aging body in gerontology.

Foucault and the Aging Body

Foucault's seminal work (1979a) on surveillance and discipline, *Discipline and Punish*, provides us with a useful way of conceptualizing the discipline of professional dance. Echoing Foucault, Clarke and Crisp (1984, 84) note how

> the dancer is the only adult who subjects himself daily to classroom discipline. . . . Although athletes must always maintain a rigorous training schedule, dancers alone can never relax and escape the watchful gaze of a teacher who corrects the greatest performers as strictly as the newest apprentice. Humility in the face of the physical aspects of the art is an essential part of a dancer's career.

Moreover, such physical discipline must be matched by a dancer's mental discipline. For "ballet pushes us to the edge of who we think we are. . . . Basically, from the moment we begin serious training, nothing is ever good enough" (Bussell 1998, 4). However, as his theoretical career unfolded, Foucault (1979b, 1987, 1988a) turns away from a focus on the inscription of powerful discourses on the "docile body" and toward a concern with the ways that individuals can resist power through the transformation of the self. "Technologies of the self," as he termed them, are practices that "permit individuals to effect by their own means or with the help of others a certain number of operations on their own bodies and souls, thought, conduct and way of being so as to transform themselves in order to attain a certain state of happiness" (Foucault 1988b, 18). The danger, of course, is that such an individual project can lead to a stultifying "politics of introversion" (McNay 1992).

However, Foucault also offers a fruitful way to understand what it is like to be old. A Foucauldian perspective encourages researchers to focus on the conduct, regulation, and government of old people (Biggs and Powell 2000). To be more specific, the decline and infirmity that is often allied with old age is managerial property (Katz 1996; Gullette 1997). Social research from the 1940s to the early 1980s offered what Turner (1996) describes as merely versions of the functionalist theory of Talcott Parsons. Old age was almost exclusively seen as a biological event. However, later sociological theories suggest that the experience of old age amounts to more than physical and biological change. A more recent body of work, therefore, argues that aging is influenced and produced by a host of economic, social, and cultural processes (see, for example Featherstone and Hepworth 1989; Arber and Ginn 1995; Victor 1991; Featherstone and Wernick 1995).

Old age cannot be reduced to the visible impact of biological processes on the surface of bodies, because what is required in addition to this is an account of the factors that induce people into being constructed as old. Over the last decade there have been a number of theoretical innovations that together establish this turn to social constructionism. In particular, the life course perspective (Silverman 1987), Third Age theory (Laslett 1989), the mask of aging approach (Featherstone and Hepworth 1989), and discourse analysis (Green 1993) have transformed social gerontology into a sociology of power and classification as it looks toward the construction and management of old age in late modernity.

These contemporary theoretical concerns form a part of what Phillipson (1998) refers to as "the reconstruction of later life": in other words, a refocusing away from accounts that emphasize the homogeneity of later life toward those that "document new lifestyles, institutions and identities among elderly people" (Phillipson 1998, 140). The ways in which old age is represented and given meaning, and especially the methods used by old people to make sense of visible bodily changes and physical impairments, act as inevitable reminders that old age is real and has real consequences in people's everyday practices (Chaney 1995; Featherstone and Wernick 1995). Senescence then becomes a mask that covers the "ageless self" (Kaufman 1986) that lies beneath the body, and thus most old people report not feeling old in themselves—unless they are physically unwell (Thompson 1992).

However, "old people" do feel betrayed by their aging bodies because bodies act as reminders of the inevitability of their aging in themselves and for others (Bytheway 1993). This shifts the source of identity to the self that on this view does not age but remains fixed sometime in "early adulthood." Harper (1997), therefore, argues that this process of self-recognition in later life can be understood as the tension between the experience of what she calls interiority and exteriority. To capture this tension between the sense of the self as unchanged and ageless and of the physical body in decline, she suggests we should see the old body as both a lived body and as a social body. The intimate experience of becoming and being older shapes and is shaped by daily living. The lived body is phenomenological: it is a body of bodily sensations. By contrast, the signs the aging body gives off to others mark the presence of the social body. This conceptualization of the aging body allows for the corporeality of old age to be taken into account while also attending to the social and cultural context of old age.

Focusing on the connections between bodies, identity, and management of old age involves describing the processes that generate these relationships. One such process is the practice that Foucault designates as government: namely, the "techniques and procedures for directing human behavior. To be more precise, this is a specific technique to reach social and political ends by acting in a calculated manner on individuals of a particular group (Rose 1989). Indeed, the modern liberal state produces the conditions that allow for the regulation of populations but also for the creation of self-regulating subjects" (Barry, Osborne, and Rose 1996). The latter can be achieved through the adoption by social actors of self-practices that control behavior and intention in line with what is socially desirable while at the same time paradoxically fashioning a sense of a true, individualized self.

Thus, government in the Foucauldian sense is the interaction between techniques of regulation and interiority, which produces the individual as the subject of government. This self is shaped by specific projects of governmentality. The subject is the intersection between that which is proposed by outside agencies that we should do and our own intentions for the fashioning of the self. This process has also been referred to as the "conduct of conduct" (Foucault 1988b) and amounts to a form of population and individual control. Its aim, as paradoxical as it might seem, is to achieve a better existence for individuals and the well-being of populations.

There is an extensive debate about the usefulness of Foucault's philosophical works for sociological research. Uncertainty about and dissatisfaction with Foucault's approach has developed around the apparent overemphasis of the mechanisms that are constitutive of social life, regardless of the social actors operating within these frameworks. Because Foucault does not discuss the tension between structure and human intentionality, it cannot be, according to some social theorists, applied to sociological investigation (Fox 1998; Mouzelis 1995). The focus of a Foucauldian analysis is on the wider discursive level; that is, the sets of meanings, practices, and knowledge that underpin and inform what it is possible to accomplish and to know and through which human agents are constituted. In Foucault's conception, discourses are independent of human agency and set the conditions within which truth claims can be made and human action shaped and interpreted.

This is not, however, the only area of his thoughts to be critiqued. Another vitally important area has been Foucault's conception of the body and the self that has been readily critiqued and criticized. Fox (1998) argues that Foucault gives primacy to the conditions for particular modalities of embodiment and ignores the body as a lived entity. The Foucauldian body is realized or created by discursive networks and via the interplay of power relations to which the application of discourse gives rise. It is, therefore, a passive body, a body shaped by discourse, rather than an active corporeal body perceived through social and cultural lenses. It must be noted, however, that Holstein and Gubrium (2000) present us with a somewhat different view, arguing that we can indeed apply Foucault's concept of "conditions of interpretation" to local cultures such as human processing agencies while articulating the subjective nature of the self as an embodied construct. This is an important step in that it bridges Foucault with more microlevel, interactionist concerns. Extending this, Foucault has provided sociologists with the potential to make visible processes that were otherwise invisible, however difficult this theoretical leap might be.

Diet, Weight, and Anorexia

Nutritional regimes provide us with a useful example of a research area that has been illuminated by a Foucauldian approach to government of the self. More specifically, "consumerism points to a discipline of the surfaces of the body in which the self is enhanced and displayed by the absence of flesh" (Turner 1995, 25). Having a body that meets the stringent demands of classical ballet that displays such "an absence of flesh" is an essential prerequisite to a balletic career. The waiflike appearance of female, and even male, ballet dancers can be disturbing even for those that themselves were once professional dancers, as Jessie, a professional dancer, notes in the quotation below:

> Jessie: I'll always remember going back to the company. I hadn't been around the company at all for about two years, and I walked back into Barons Court [rehearsal studios] one day. I was absolutely shocked be-

cause I saw all these sort of waiflike, very tired-looking people walking around, and I thought, "Gosh I used to be one of those" that's what they look like. And of course you don't realise it, and now I think maybe they're not. There's more an athleticism about dancers these days I think, but I was shocked at that point, because they are all incredibly thin. They're much thinner, except for one or two, than the ordinary person is, and it really conditions your mind I think.

Jessie's wonderfully illustrative statement is also an example of, drawing on Bourdieu (1984), what might be described as a dancer's habitus (interpretive schemes that alert the person to how the world functions and provide specific guidelines for mundane action, or better, for routine embodied practices). Thinness is not, necessarily, something that you especially notice when your social world is that of the ballet rehearsal studio and stage—simply because thinness in this social world is the norm. However, after her two-year break from the company, and the consequent shifting of Jessie's habitus to the nondance world, then these "waiflike tired bodies" came as a jolt to her recently acquired set of aesthetic dispositions. A biographical reconstruction now sees thin bodies as deviant bodies, a radical shift in focus. Once dancers had retired from "classical ballet," then a combination of a less strict dietary and exercise regime invariably led to weight gain. Georgina alerts us to this:

> Georgina: As regards changing, body changing, well I haven't changed that much at all. I've been, most of my dancing career I've been eight stone, eight and a half maximum, and now I'm nine. I've put on half a stone since I left, since I stopped dancing.

While there exists a copious amount of literature on the problems of anorexia nervosa in ballet, it was not an important concern of the interviewees. Our research, as noted, was about the balletic body in general terms and not about the specific issue of anorexia. Here is the one example in which the concern did surface. The topic emerged as a spontaneous response to a broad question:

> Interviewer: How do you feel that growing older has affected the way that you see your own body?

Jessie: Well . . . struggled a little bit, at points when I was dancing, with my weight. You know, I think, there's no doubt about it that I was really verging on the anorexic for some of the time. There was a period when I was like the classical anorexic. You can't see it when you're there, absolutely can't see it. Got very very thin. . . . Was sort of eating a piece of cucumber and a lettuce leaf, you know, getting quite silly for a while. And for whatever reason, I couldn't begin to say why, I sort of came out of it. . . . I just couldn't switch my brain off from thinking about what I was eating. And it was really until after I'd had the kids and I was working again full time. I think at that point I was so busy, and not busy thinking about myself, but busy thinking . . . about family and work. I just didn't have time to think about food anymore. But it was a very long and gradual process, so now I just don't have a problem with food at all. I just eat when I'm hungry, and I don't eat when I'm not hungry.

Fear of fatness and the pursuit of thinness are the most significant properties of anorexia (Bruch 1978). As Turner (1995) notes, "[i]n religious terms [anorexia is] . . . a form of asceticism in which there is a struggle to achieve a spirituality through the management of the flesh" (p. 107). His comment on the ethereal dimension of anorexia is particularly apposite for female ballet dancers who, in *Giselle* for example, portray "ghostly virgins" on stage. As Tamara Rojo, one of the world's leading ballerinas, recently remarked: "*Giselle* is my favourite ballet. You have to go further than your own body. You have to become a soul, so that the public sees that soul and not the balletic body" (Lawson 2002).

Returning to and summarizing our basic argument, the Foucauldian notion of government is an attempt to make connections between the wider structural context in which old age is experienced and the lived experience of older people. It is a reminder that old age is the product of particular types of relations of power, binding those that define old age and talk about it with those that reproduce and resist it. We argue that the fundamental problem with the Foucauldian notion of government is that it does not entail an account of the phenomenological body; in short, as a perspective, it does not lend itself to the study of processes, practices, and performance, as the research illustrates. So how do we reconcile this? In the next section, we turn to Bourdieu and his anthropologically inspired emphasis on the embodiment of social practices.

Bourdieu and the Balletic Body

Bodies matter because our experience of them is the justification for much social research and, more fundamentally, for a social life. Partly as a consequence of this fact about our corporeality, there has been, in the last twenty years or so, an impressive growth in academic research on the body. While there were exploratory contributions to the anthropology and sociology of the body in earlier decades (Blacking 1977; Turner 1984), there has been a outpouring of books subsequently that have been concerned with "putting the body back into sociology" (see, for example, Leder 1990; Featherstone, Hepworth, and Turner 1991; Turner 1992; Nettleton and Watson 1998; Williams and Bendelow 1998; McKie and Watson 2000).

A sociology of the body is characterized by an abundance of theorizing, but despite the voluminous literature, a systematic empirical research tradition is still lacking (Turner 1996). Research on the body has been castigated, in brief, for privileging theorizing, for bracketing out the individual, and for neglecting the practical experiences of embodiment (Watson 2000). More specifically, seldom has attention been focused on the ways that "specific social worlds invest, shape, and deploy human bodies" (Wacquant 1995, 65). Indeed, "one of the paradoxical features of recent social studies of the body is how rarely one encounters in them actual living bodies of flesh and blood" (Wacquant 1995, 65). Such a disembodied view is both strange and distressing.

The growing academic dance literature mirrors this same propensity toward theoretical work. There is a similar scarcity of empirical research on the sociology of Western theater dance (Thomas 1995) and especially on ballet. Research on the "body and dance" is, broadly speaking, dominated by work that emphasizes history (Adshead-Lansdale and Layson 1994; Franko 1993; McCarren 1998), textuality (Cranny-Francis 1995; Fraleigh 1995; Goellner and Murphy 1995), ethnicity (Tomko 1999), and gender (Hanna 1988; Grover-Haskin 1998). In addition, work on the "dancing body" does, sometimes, combine several of these themes (see Desmond 1997; Carter 1998). However, little of this dance research draws on firsthand observation of, and interviews with, dancers. Instead, most of this scholarship relies on secondary or indirect sources (written historical records, videos, and so on) or involves a meta-theoretical debate on the mélange of deconstructive approaches to the textuality of dance (Adshead-Lansdale 1999).

The academic work at this end of the spectrum has more in common with literary criticism than with social research. The point about dance is, from a sociological perspective, we must appreciate its significance as a performance, not simply as a text (Shusterman 1992). It requires us to pay attention to embodiment, practice, and execution and to the movement of bodies in time and space in a fashion that is unlike reading Shakespeare's sonnets. We emphasize we are not arguing that research on textuality is without worth. It most certainly is worthy. But we are claiming that such research represents a very limited approach to both dance in particular and to the social world more generally. We assert our primary empirical research on dancers' bodies will, therefore, make a useful contribution to understanding the differences between age as a system of classification and aging as an embodied process. In addition, our research is obviously relevant to the field of "dance studies" and to the field of the sociology of the body.

As we have asserted, contemporary writings in dance studies are dominated by postmodern readings of "dance as text" (Adshead-Lansdale 1999; Fraleigh and Hanstein 1999). Although there is a long tradition of anthropological work on dance (see Kaeppler 1978; Buckland 1999), empirical work on the sociology of dance is meager. A notable exception here is Helena Wulff's (1998) international ethnographic study of the culture of some of the world's great ballet companies—the Royal Swedish Ballet, The Royal Ballet (U.K.), American Ballet Theatre, and the Ballett Frankfurt. In addition, her book covers the transnational nature of "ballet worlds," the career trajectory of dancers (from school to retirement), and the process of producing performances (the contrast between a view from the dancers and a view from the critics).

Unfortunately, Wulff's emphasis on breadth inevitably means her study lacks the qualitative depth often associated with ethnographic research reports (Hammersley and Atkinson 1995). As noted anthropologist Clifford Geertz (1973) might argue, it isn't "thick" enough. Buckland (1999, 11) points out that, "Wulff's pursuit of her ethnographic communities over four countries is relatively unusual in that it dispenses with anthropology's classical notion of bounded cultures." Moreover, the body in the ballet career receives little attention in her study. Our research, therefore, seeks to elaborate some of the insights from Wulff's pioneering research via a more focused study of the salience of Bourdieu's theoretical framework through qualitative research on the embodiment of dance within one ballet company, namely, The Royal Ballet in London. For ballet is surely a (perhaps the) paradigm case of embodiment. Bourdieu is widely acknowledged to have made a seminal contribution to the sociological study of the relationship between habitus, practice, and culture (Fowler 1997). Moreover, Bourdieu's concepts are grounded in the body (Shilling 1993) and are, therefore, especially salient for research on the body as a lived entity, not simply as a constructed one.

Aging, Biography, and Career in Ballet

Aging forces the dancer to face her body and her declining career as biographical constructions (Hamilton 1998). This possible epiphany, or biographical rupture, invites dancers to reflect on their bodily habitus. The actual decline in a dancer's physical capital—what we describe as "the ontology of ageing"—undermines radical social constructionist views that collapse biology into a branch of discursive sociology. The decline of the body in ballet performance cannot be easily or readily neglected. This exchange between Caspar and the interviewer illustrates this in great detail. In short, to see and feel the body experience its relative decline is both demoralizing and frustrating:

> Caspar: I did daily class for a few years afterwards because it's ingrained in you. It's not a thing that is easily given up. It's a discipline that's there. You feel rather like your playing truant if you don't do it! You feel guilty, even if you don't have to do it. I mean there's one guy who's the same age as me (64) who religiously does class every day! I got out of the habit! I don't expose myself the way the dancers look now!
>
> Interviewer: Is that partly because you see these young beautiful things doing class effortlessly, and that was something that you could no longer do?
>
> Caspar: Yes. It's demoralising. Well you thought you could do it, but you can't. The ability has gone. Of course you can go on doing class forever, but it doesn't mean to say that the audience is going to appreciate it! There are certain standards that must be kept up. And the standards are continually getting better and better.

Here, we can note how the physical decline of the dancer's body, the ontology of aging, is a threat to both a dancer's career and to her or his very identity. Ballet is such an all-consuming career that it is inevitable that self-identity becomes, essentially, decided by it. Ballet is more than a vocation, it is a calling. Dance is certainly something that the ballet dancer's body can do, but being a ballet dancer is also the embodiment of a particular type of self or personality. It is, in essence, a "master identity" (Armato and Marsiglio 2002; Charmaz 1994). Classical ballet dancers do not divide their world into offstage and onstage, because personality, career, and performance are integrated by the discipline of their art.

A popular biography of Margot Fonteyn noted that "her sense of order is as apparent off-stage as on—in the organisation of her day, her punctuality, the arrangements of her dressing room, the darning and patching of the practice tights that in war-time even a ballerina must preserve with care" (Anthony 1945, 16). In other words, being a ballet dancer is not just something that you *do*, it is something that you *are*. This customarily means that there is a disposition toward delaying the inevitable end of a dancing career. Jessie's and Casper's narratives illuminate this point wonderfully:

> Jessie: You can see that a dancer's powers are declining, and you can see that it's going to be downhill from here on in—and not uphill. Some people are going to have to hear things that they don't want to hear, and cannot see for themselves. So for some people it is very painful and very difficult.

> Caspar: Dancing is not easy. You have to go through a certain amount of pain, through the pain barrier, and if you can't do that, you don't have the ambition and the drive to rise above all that, there's no point. I just wish one's body didn't deteriorate! It would be great to be able to do it all still. In fact you feel in here [points to his head] that you can. You have to believe what people tell you, and normally people in this company are very truthful—they try to let you down gently. But one always feels one can still do it. It's like the run to catch the bus, and then you realise that you are not going to catch it!

Both of these examples can be certainly be analyzed as philosophical constructs. The notion that "they think they can do it" chimes with a radical social constructionist view of epistemology where, essentially, "the world" is little more than a social construction. For some concerned with aging and the body, aging is wholly socially constructed (see Featherstone and Wernick 1995; Phillipson 1998). We, like many others, argue that such a radical epistemology of constructionism is indefensible given the everyday, common practices the body finds itself located in (Turner 1992; Wainwright 1997). Likewise, from our notion of the ontology of aging, we suggest that there is an inevitable physical decline as an organism ages and that this occurs within specific cultural framings. For ballet dancers this means that their careers as performing classical ballet dancers are invariably over by early middle age (Greskovic 2000). Rudolf exemplifies this constraint on the career in this commentary, as he tells us of his experiences soon after retiring from the ballet:

> I retired at 38. I would say the last 3 years [I was] increasingly aware of aches that hadn't been there in the past, and also the fact that you take a little bit longer to recover from a particular exertion. When I first did that (points to a photo on his wall of himself as Tybalt in *Romeo and Juliet*) I was fine. But as I got a little older my wife would always notice when I got out of bed and creaked! When you talk about ageing, the danger that happens to people in their late thirties is that their brain thinks they can do it and the body doesn't, and that's when you run the risk of hurting yourself. There are suddenly things that you could do last year and you threw yourself into but, gravity takes over and you hit the floor a little earlier than you thought! It's a young person's job, it always has been.

From the perspective of a lay audience, it is obvious that with aging, aches and pains gradually become more common. For the professional dancer, there is also an increased chance of injury. The extreme physical demands of ballet can, literally, wear your body out. In one interview, Megan echoed these sentiments as she discussed bodily decline within the context of ballet:

> Well Kenneth [MacMillan, then Director of the Royal Ballet], I've absolutely got to stop soon. I just hurt everywhere and I'm 39!

Moreover, as the body ages, it begins to take appreciably longer for a person to recover from injuries. The increased vulnerability of the dancer's body requires a vigilance that can turn into an obsession with "the fragile body." Dancers can become chronically and eccentrically addicted to special diets, exercises, and medications that they hope will manage their increased frailty and vulnerability effectively. Note how dancers Lisa and Megan discuss this:

> Lisa: It takes longer to warm up properly. You also have standards, and you can't go below a certain standard and it takes a longer time to get there. So more energy is going into reaching the same level. It's a bit like an alcoholic, isn't it? You have to drink a little more to get the same effect!
>
> Interviewer: I wouldn't know!
>
> Lisa: Well, nor would I, but that's what they say. You just have to spend longer getting to the same point!

> Megan: I danced less and less, yes. I remember giving up Swan Lake with a huge sense of relief. Because as time went on the only way to cope with something so demanding was to wrap myself in cotton wool and to be so precious that it was horrible! You took care of every little toenail and every little blister on your foot. Every pair of Pointe shoes was worked in miraculously. You planned your rehearsal, and you planned what you ate and when you ate it and how many hours sleep you had. It was unbelievable. The dedication. There was no other way I could do it. I remember saying to my husband, "Oh you haven't agreed to go to a cocktail party and reception for your company on Tuesday! I've got Swan Lake on Thursday." He'd say, "But this is Tuesday!" I'd say, "But darling, I'm 35! Ten years ago I could have done that. Don't ask me to come to a cocktail party and stand in high heels on Tuesday." All that sort of rubbish. So, a huge sense of relief when you actually think, "God, I was so obsessed with my body and myself and now I can actually live." I never walked from Covent Garden to Leicester Square [5 minutes] because it was too far! So I think there is a huge sense of relief when you let go of that preciousness.

In fact, our interviews with nine injured dancers (between the ages of twenty-three and twenty-nine) all confirmed that these changes in the physical hardiness of the dancer's body appear well before middle age. For example, the youngest person we spoke to in our sample of "older dancers" was thirty-three years of age. Percy was still doing some classical dancing, but even he acknowledged that this discipline was becoming much harder. At the time of the interview, he was also a part-time administrator. He was retiring from dancing and becoming a full-time administrator at the end of the season. What is striking here is the way that much greater care had to be taken to avoid injury even with a relatively young "thirty year old dancing body."

Interviewer: Do you find class is physically harder now that you are getting older?

Percy: Oh God, yes! Going into arabesque is a struggle now. [When I was younger, in class] I was right at the front! I'm not now; you'll find me at the back! I hide in the corner now!

Interviewer: Is the pain just part of your everyday life as it were?

Percy: Yeah, like I said, as you get older it gets worse. There's more niggles, things hurt a lot more. I'll come off stage, or I'll wake up the next morning and my Achilles tendons feel like the first few steps they are going to snap and I never had that before. My body tightens up a lot quicker than it used to do.

Interviewer: Does the warm up take longer?

Percy: I never warmed up when I was younger! I used to just go and do a quick warm up five minutes before and then go on. I can't do that now. I have to do a full 25 minutes' warm up. Ten years ago there is no way I would have done that. Two pliés and I was on! And my body could get away with it. You think, "Oh God, if I don't do this now I could be injured" whereas I never thought that as a young dancer.

Interviewer: So how do you feel about this decline in your physical ability? If I dare ask!

Percy: It is hard. I'm glad in a way, because I'm glad of not having to do class. Because for so many years now of doing it every day. Just to suddenly pack up and go, but I'm not just suddenly stopping. I'm still in the same profession in a way. It is hard. Part of me wants to just completely stop. I was thinking of doing that. I think I will probably go to the gym and do an all round body thing, then do company class here.

In this example Percy had, effectively, offset his declining physical capital by drawing on and by "cashing in" his acquired cultural capital as a discursive resource so that he remained a part of the Royal Ballet's social world. In contrast with Percy, one teacher, who is sixty-three, was very positive about his physical abilities. Speaking confidently, Dexter tells a completely different story:

> Interviewer: How do you think growing older has affected the way that you see your body?
> Dexter: Not at all. I'm still fit. I don't [do] ballet exercise. I mean I obviously demonstrate, and I can still lift. I can lift Darcey Bussell up there (points above his head). I can do it all.

However, another dance teacher, also sixty-three, disagrees with Dexter. Dudley speaks of a phenomenological concern with how people actually perceive what they can and cannot do. In essence, he points to the dancer refusing to leave the master identity, the defining point of their lives, even as the body declines:

> Interviewer: Do you think that when you come to teach classes that dancers accept that their physical prowess is on the decline? Because the impression I get from talking to some people is that they almost feel that, even though they're now in their 60's, they could go out on the stage and still perform as they did when they were 19.
> Dudley: That's in their mind! The mind is a funny thing because the mind thinks it's doing it, and it's not. Ballet is definitely for the young. [Natalia] Makarova, who I worked with a lot, she said to me one day "Just when you are beginning to realise how it all should be done, your body packs up." One day, when she was going to retire, she had a little party. She sat there and she said, "I'm going to retire" and we all cried. And she said, "Why are you crying? Why aren't you happy for me that I can move on. You have to move on in life. And anyway, everything I've done, most of the good things, are on film. And if I do it now the doing it is in your imagination, it's not actually happening." She was like 44. Gels [Gelsey Kirkland] walked away from it at 35. Cynthia Harvey at 39. Maya Plisetskaya is still dancing, unfortunately, at 72 and in a way it's sad. It's a sickness. It's a mental sickness. They cannot get off the stage. You have to take a hook and pull 'em out!

As we have already argued, drawing on Bourdieu's conceptual schema, ballet dancers effectively offset their declining physical capital by drawing on and developing their stock of cultural capital—their incorporated knowledge of ballet. This was certainly a common theme throughout our interviews. Jessie speaks specifically of this in the following narrative:

> Of course I knew all the people here because I'd been at school. I came back and it's been wonderful. It is a marvellous way of being able to, sort of, capitalise and use all of the things.

In fact, Jessie had been asked by the director of the Royal Ballet to "rejoin" the company as an administrator. In Bourdieu's terms, we see how an amalgam of social, symbolic, and cultural capital is enacted. The heritage of ballet becomes sedimented into the dance teacher's body. For some, educating and developing the artistry of younger dancers offsets, to some extent, the loss of "the performing self." However, the embodiment of being a dancer, of "dancing in a world of pain and magic" (Villella 1992), is inevitably lost once the artists cease to dance on stage. Dominic, who had been a principal dancer with the Royal Ballet, became one of the company's principal character artists almost twenty years ago. However, he still passed "technical tips" on to the next generation of dancers, not losing touch with a defining part of who he considers himself to be:

> Interviewer: Some people have said that when they were young class was a chance for them to show off and it was a chance for them to get promoted within the company.
> Dominic: Oh yes. Yes it is very competitive. Round about 50 I began to learn a few things. So I try and help the young people now by telling them what I never learned. Because I couldn't do things I went to the best teachers, and I listened to what people said. I couldn't apply it very well. But I understand now, and I try to pass that on. I was always very tense, and one of my biggest problems with Ed is that he is very tense (demonstrates a difference in tension in the arms). I'm trying to get Ed to have a little bit more relaxation, because I was the same. I say "You don't want to be like me! For God's sake, learn from my mistakes!"

In this next example, Dominic is molding the physical capital—of how relaxed your arms are—of a rising young male dancer. Just calling this physical capital is, we think, misleading. Through watching over sixty studio and stage rehearsals of the ballet *Onegin*, one of the authors became acutely aware of how something as commonplace as the heaviness of a dancer's arm movements provided a window into the emotions of the character they were portraying (or better, the dancer literally became the character). For example, in Lenski's solo in Act 2 of John Cranko's ballet of [Alexander Pushkin's novel *Eugene*] *Onegin* (Brinson and Crisp 1980), every movement should show the audience that this is a man who "is a tortured soul." Every second of this four-minute solo is filled with yearning, despair, and utter despondency. For Lenski and his best friend, Onegin, are about to duel with pistols (as Onegin has insulted Lenski by flirting with Lenski's fiancée). Dancing narrative ballets is, therefore, not simply about dancing the right steps. What matters is convincing the audience that the characters on stage are real, so that the audience identifies and connects with the emotions and the fate of "real people." *Their* feelings become *our* feelings. As the next narrative illustrates, this level of artistry—the very embodiment of ballet—is only achieved by passing the culture of ballet on from one generation to the next:

> Interviewer: One of the things that we are particularly interested in is how the culture of ballet is handed down from one person to another. For example, *Firebird* is passed on from [Tamara] Karsavina through [Margot] Fonteyn and [Monica] Mason—and then onto the current generation.
>
> Dominic: I thought Monica did that very well, that [BBC] Masterclass [on *Firebird*]. You mustn't be overly referential. Generally the things that deserve to survive do. If we have a really efficient method of safe keeping history—you can come back to scripts and paintings that have fallen out of favour and then someone will discover them and say "Oh my, these are very good." So if you've got good notation and video, which is what you have now, then if it passes out of fashion then maybe in 20 years time it may be all the rage. It happens in every art form. In the past there were too many good pieces that were lost.

One of the joys of dancing springs from the ballet dancer's ability to become someone else for a short period of time, no matter how brief, and to express the sort of searing emotions—from love to despair—that are rarely a part of our day-to-day lives. Not surprisingly, giving this up is usually extremely difficult:

> Interviewer: You said that you danced for the sheer joy of dancing, and you no longer have that joy of dancing.

Lisa: No you don't. There's no real replacement for being a performer. But there's a wonderful transition of helping others to do it. I remember coaching Belinda Hatley, on *Giselle*. When I watched her I was just so thrilled because she was really exactly how I would have liked to have looked. There was something very rewarding about that.

There is some evidence that great dancers continue to develop their major roles through coaching the next generation of dancers, even though they themselves no longer dance their former roles (see Newman 1992). That said, retirement was, generally, not something to which our interviewees were looking forward. The expected loss of self was often quite obvious in comments by the dancers:

Dexter: I've got to retire in a year's time, which I'm not very happy about. I've been here for 46 years and I've done all the roles and I've coached for a long time. Peter Wright [former director of the Royal Ballet's sister company] said to me: "People like you shouldn't retire. You've got too much to offer. Lavatory attendants should be forced to retire at 65, not people like you!"

Unfortunately for Dexter, and many other dancers, Jeremy Isaacs, former head of the Royal Opera House (ROH), where the Royal Ballet staff are employed, brought in compulsory retirement for all ROH employees (Isaacs 1999). But the dancers were not going to give up this "piece of themselves" so easily and developed inventive means of achieving this important goal. Three of the ex-dancers we interviewed now have websites as "legendary ballet stars" and another, Dudley, is revered as a legend in the States:

By the time I was 28 I decided, that having been at it since I was 10, that I was burned out. I was having certain problems with my back and I went to see an orthopaedic surgeon and they said "If you don't stop you're going to have trouble." So I stopped. I had some back problems and then a knee problem and then a foot problem. Those injuries caused me to re-think and I had to, and I use the word very strongly, I had to re-invent myself. I had to come back and re-invent myself. And fortunately in our business the older you get, if you survive, you become legendary. In the States now they call me "This legendary star maker."

This is an example of the evolution, perhaps revolution, in a dancer's habitus that we discussed earlier in this chapter. As we have seen, coaching dancers is one way to utilize an accumulation of cultural capital. Another is to become a principal character dancer. However, such a move can be too onerous or humiliating or both, for dancers who have enjoyed "stellar careers":

> Dominic: It's very difficult, very difficult. Irek Mukamedov [Royal Ballet principal, and widely regarded as the world's greatest male dancer in the 1980s and early 1990s] would be fantastic in the sort of roles that I'm doing. He'd be absolutely wonderful. But the ego gets in the way. "I'm Mukamedov" [does a swaggering Russian accent]. Once one's been at that height, then it's very difficult to graciously go into the cameos and subsidiary roles. I asked to do Dr. Coppelius [Coppelia], as I'm the right age, but I was told I couldn't [by the Director]. Perhaps the new Director will see things slightly differently. You don't run out of ambition, you see!

For many performers, whether they are musicians, actors, or dancers, performance itself has an almost therapeutic dimension. For example, "theater" allows the private introvert to become a public extrovert. An embodied performance allows the dancer to make bodily improvements, if you will. In other words, performance reworks the self.

> Interviewer: What do you think you've gained from it in terms of, say, your personal growth as it were?
> Casper: I was a very shy child and I've certainly gained a lot of confidence and got over that. It's taken a long time. But I think also performing on the stage, is not a get out. I don't know how to put this but you find that a lot of performers are actually very shy people and it's a way of overcoming all that. When you get out on the stage you find you can get beyond that shyness and you can communicate with people, and I've found that over the years I've been able to bring that back into my life and be much more confident about myself.
> Interviewer: I suppose I find your matter-of-fact view of your retirement surprising, in a way, because obviously dancing has been your life, as it were.
> Casper: Yeah. I think it's because I've been here such a long time, and that it has taken up an awful lot of my life, that I'm looking forward to

drawing back from it. I don't want to become, totally cut off from it, alienated from it. I'm planning on making quite a nuisance of myself here, even when they're not paying me! I'm not going to bring the shutters down, and go and retire to the country because I've got a flat just across the road so I only have to cross the road! I don't intend that, I'd be lost. I think I'd be totally lost.

Ironically, not being a "star dancer" could prolong your career as a dancer of "classical roles." For older soloists, and even "secondary" principal dancers, did not have to bear the public's expectation of physically exhilarating performances and exemplary, even "perfect," classical technique that are expected of the stellar principal dancer. The expression of bodily capital was perhaps not as excruciatingly deconstructed, part by bodily part:

Interviewer: So how did you notice your physical decline as a dancer?

Dominic: Well I was still doing genuine dancing in classical roles, I was always a sort of, in classical terms what you might call a group soloist, for instance, in *Cinderella* I would be one of the four cavaliers. If you needed four or six blokes to get up and do classical steps together I would be one of those—like the cavaliers in the prologue to *Sleeping Beauty*. I was a cavalier in *Cinderella* when I was 45. Ironically, I was still doing serious classical steps on the stage long after many people who had been far better than I, who had become Princes and all the rest of it, leading male dancers, had left! Because the level that I was doing it was just about acceptable at my level, but it would never have been acceptable at the Prince level. That was ironic.

The aesthetic of classical ballet, its demand for perfect bodies coupled with an amazing ballet technique, means that there are no "classical dancing roles" for dancers once they reach an age of around forty. Sadly, institutional ageism is as rife in ballet as in other areas of contemporary Western society. Previously discussed in light of compulsory retirement, Dominic exemplifies this in another context:

Dominic: There is still an ageist thing in dance. Some people do use older people and there are some outstanding examples of that. I mean dancing, using their bodies, not just wandering around acting which is what I do nowadays, dancing in their 70's and 80's. You get these companies specialising in old people like White Oak.

Interviewer: But that is modern dance rather than ballet isn't it?

Dominic: Yes, modern dance. You can't do classical dance. With modern dance then Merce Cunningham can brood impressively in a corner at 80. Tragically, if you're trying to do classical stuff—and Rudolf [Nureyev] destroyed his own legend—then you mustn't go on. It is difficult, but it is something I should be tackling. If you've got a company of 80 people and you've got 10%, eight who are "of an age," lets say, and you create for them then that is important. The influence in the company tends to be quite good because it [the dancer's heritage] gets passed on.

Ballet is an art that is literally inscribed on the body. Both ballet technique and, as we have seen, especially, ballet artistry is handed from one generation to the next (Bland 1981; Guest 1988). Certainly, the "balletic body" is a biographical one embedded in dancers and companies rife with romantic pasts. Loyalty to the company is thus an important component of the role of the classical ballet dancer. Retirement from one of the grandest companies of all, the Royal Ballet, was usually seen as a dreadful, perhaps destructive prospect:

Interviewer: How are you thinking about retirement?

Oscar: I'm absolutely petrified. I've got to retire next year. I'm absolutely petrified.

Interviewer: Will they allow you to come back and dance your ugly sister (in *Cinderella*)?

Oscar: I wish they would darling! They might say, "He's too old." I would love to!

As noted earlier, ballet permeates every aspect of a dancer's life. One's life is judged by its relevance to dancing. When one can no longer dance, one's self is radically challenged and so a strong restructuring must occur. This restructuring is often undertaken with a strong sense of loss as one must look to a future biography that has been "disrupted":

Interviewer: Did you feel any sense of loss when you gave up dancing?

Dexter: Oh I did, because that was all I ever wanted to do. I've had a wonderful life really. If I lived my life again I would be an actor, not a dancer, because I could still be doing it now. Be doing big stuff now. I didn't come into it to teach. I came in to perform, and that's all I ever wanted to do. I had a good innings. 23 or 24 years is quite a good innings for a dancer. But for an actor, it's no time at all really. You are half way through it then. I think I was lucky that I've turned out to be a good coach. I wouldn't be here if I wasn't, would I? So I must be quite good. But it's not the same. I mean, I've been going to Barons Court since 1951, till I came here a year ago. I didn't know anything else. It's been my whole life. That's why I'm not all that keen on retiring.

Continuing this line of thought, ballet is such an all-consuming occupation that it is difficult for professional dancers to have the time to reflect on what they might do once they retire. One famous dance teacher we interviewed recalled a conversation with Sylvie Guillem, who has been (and still is) perhaps the world's leading ballerina:

Dudley (about Sylvie Guillem): She's making millions all over the world. I said to her "At a certain point what are you going to do?" She said "I want a Winery." Maybe she'll just walk away from it. But you don't know. What happens between now and then, and how she really feels about it.

Interviewer: That's one of the things that we're interested in. Particularly if you get to the top, then your whole self-identity is tied up with being a dancer, and it has been from the age of 10 and now you're getting to 40 and you have to re-invent yourself. You seem very happy to do that, but one of the things we thought was that a lot of people might not be at all.

Dudley: Yes, yes. They panic. Their whole identity has been around the toe shoes. Sometimes something comes along, or there's a jolt in their life, and they can pull into another direction, and others can't. And you never really know which one of those people . . . are capable of doing something else. The panic sets in when your whole identity has been around your physicality. You've never explored anything else, you know.

Ballet is such an all-consuming career that it is inevitable that your self-identity is, essentially, determined by it, present, past, and future. Retirement, in general, is not just a source of stress for the psyche and a loss of a familiar social world; but it is also often the cause of financial worries as well. Like Margot Fonteyn before her, who famously retired from dancing classical roles at sixty so that she could pay the high costs of her paraplegic husband's medical care (Fonteyn 1975), Lisa spoke of her need to continue her dancing career "just to pay the bills":

Interviewer: I am still not quite sure why you gave up, as it were, because you still seemed to have lots of energy and to be dancing very well.

Lisa: I gave up because I was in a financial situation with the company that made it unbearable. It put a lot of stress on being fit to dance because I went onto a guest contract, which wasn't a monthly salary. You got paid for what you did, and it put a tremendous amount of stress on us. I needed a salary, I had two children and I just needed a salary.

Interviewer: You don't have to answer this if you don't want to. But was that your idea to go onto the guest contract?

Lisa: Oh no! No, no, it wasn't. It certainly wasn't, and I tried not to have it too. I don't think its right that ageing dancers should go onto guest contracts because you need to be a guest artist when you are young and available and you can do it and want to do it. A reduced salary would have been preferable, so that it's constant. It seemed like I was going to have to wait for so much work, and would I be fit to do it, probably not. It's happening to another dancer at the moment. I know what they are going through.

Interviewer: So are you saying that although a lot of the time you were still quite fit to dance, in a sense, you were more likely to get injured towards the end of your career—the stress and strain was showing?

Lisa: Yes. I had always danced for joy before, and then suddenly I was aware that I was dancing for money and it put the focus completely differently on it, and it became stressful. I think any injury after that was because of stress. Not because I danced any differently, and not necessarily because I was getting older. Although one is told that the body ages, and I'm not too bad! It's got a little heavier, so it's under a bit more strain now! But it still gets me here and home again!

Interviewer: So how did you feel at the end then when there was some decline in your physical abilities as it were? You seem to have been almost pushed, if that's the right word, into giving up dancing.

Lisa: Well that *is* the right word. And lets face it if I hadn't been then I'd still be here now, because some people just don't know when the right time is to give up.

Our next quotation from our interviews provides a synthesis of the principal themes in this chapter of embodiment, habitus, physical capital, cultural capital, aging, and career in ballet:

> Megan: I still feel some days as if I'd love to be able to jump up and move. There's suddenly a piece of music playing in the studio or there's a particular role. I mean, in the ballet I am doing at the moment. God, I loved it so much and just have such vivid memories of the joy of that ballet and those performances. I think all of us do that did leading roles in that ballet. But in a sense you just think what would it be like to wind the clock (back), and do it now with all the knowledge one has now. And there is something so sad that dancers' careers really are relatively short. Because just at that point when you are in your mid-thirties, I think, you just begin to understand so much more about the world, and yourself and life and other people and emotions. But you can no longer dance like you could when you are 25. So it's a cruel business. It has wonderful rewards for probably very few people to go on in the business in the way they'd like to.

The empirical data and theoretical constructs presented here push us in an interesting direction. The embodiment of dance is captured in the term "muscle memory" that is often used by dancers in everyday conversation among themselves. Essentially, this is the ability of their bodies to remember particular sequences of dance steps perhaps years after they last danced them. Similar everyday examples of such embodied practices include riding a bike, swimming, and playing the piano—everyday bodily practices. Bourdieu's concept of habitus is a shorthand way of describing a wide range of embodied social practices.

Dancers' narratives exemplified the inevitable decline of the "aging dancers'" physical capital, but the mechanisms through which this is offset are by a lifetime of practical knowledge, or cultural capital, of the ballets they danced in. In short, biographically gained cultural capital compensates for physical capital. There comes a point, however, when artistic capital can no longer supplement the deterioration in the dancer's physical prowess. With aging, the male dancers in particular cannot achieve the elevation and flight that are required by classical ballet. Retirement from dancing the classical roles of the ballet repertory is then inevitable. Yet this occurs at a time when most professional careers are still developing. As one might put it, "it's a cruel business" indeed.

Discussion

The evolution of self-identity is a common theme in contemporary sociological literature. Variations on this theme include the notions of turning-point experiences (Strauss 1959), biographical disruption (Bury 1982), epiphanies (Denzin 1989), fateful moments (Giddens 1991), transformational experiences (Wainwright 1995), and disrupted lives (Becker 1997). The main point we wish to make is that these sources have a resonance with our account of aging, injury, and career change in ballet. A recent piece by Brian Gearing (1999) on narratives of identity in ex-professional footballers provides an interesting comparison with our narratives of the embodiment of ballet. Gearing draws on Giddens' (1991, 53) claim that *"self-identity is not a distinctive trait, or even a collection of traits, possessed by the individual.* It is the self as reflexively understood in terms of her or his biography" (italics in original). Gearing found that the past experience of ex-footballers continues to give meaning to their lives as they move through middle and old age. More generally, our life story is our self-identity (McAdams 1993). Or as Holstein and Gubrium (2000) argue, our selves are embedded within our biography, past, present, and future.

A specific aim of this chapter has been to embed a critique of radical social constructionism (and discourse analysis) in empirical research on the aging dancer. This agrees with the position taken by Bourdieu (2000, 108), who has recently argued that

> it is not sufficient to change language or theory to change reality. . . .
> While it never does harm to point out that gender, nation, or ethnicity or race [or aging] are social constructs, it is naive, even dangerous, to suppose that one only has to "deconstruct" these social artefacts, in a purely performative performance of resistance, in order to destroy them. . . . One may . . . doubt the reality of a resistance which ignores the resistance of reality.

We suggest that "aging ballet dancers" trying to dance the classical roles of their "youth" is an example of the futility of ignoring the resistance of reality—the reality that the body is aging physiologically as well as culturally in a context that bounds its decline tightly. The aging body of the ballet dancer, simply put, cannot do what it used to be able to do.

Thus, the dancer must use the resources he or she has, the lens through which they see the world, and continue to draw on a "master self" in order to maintain their place in the social world, or at least, their place as they see it.

In his ethnography of the Welsh National Opera, Atkinson (2000) criticizes existing "cultural studies" research on opera for being "sociology at a distance." Much work in dance studies and, more broadly, in cultural sociology is open to a similar charge. Our current research on the body in dance uses interviews to glean firsthand accounts of the embodiment of ballet. In this chapter, our focus has been on aging and career, empirically examined through narratives of dancers. We intend to extend this work through interviews with dancers who forge a second career away from dance (as solicitors, physiotherapists, musicians, and so forth) and intend to build the research project longitudinally by, for example, reinterviewing informants after they have retired from their current teaching and administrative posts. Classical ballet provides us with unique and unexplored areas of the aging body. We have looked at veteran runners (Tulle, chapter 8 in this volume), personal care (Twigg, chapter 5 in this volume), and even organ transplantation (Freidin, chapter 2 in this volume). The ballet presents us with another venue to see the body as a practical achievement. It is a significant topic for producing more comprehensive social research on the reciprocal relationships between the lived body and society.

References

Adshead-Lansdale, J., ed.
   1999 *Dancing Texts: Intertextuality in Interpretation*. London: Dance Books.

Adshead-Lansdale, J., and J. Layson
   1994 *Dance History: An Introduction*. London: Routledge.

Anthony, G.
   1945 *Ballerina: Further Studies of Margot Fonteyn*. London: Home & van Thal.

Arber, S., and J. Ginn
   1995 Choice and Constraint in the Retirement of Older Married Women. In *Connecting Gender and Ageing: A Sociological Approach*. Edited by S. Arber and J. Ginn. Buckingham, U.K.: Open University Press.

Armato, M., and B. Marsiglio
2002 Self-Structure, Identity, and Commitment: Promise Keepers' Godly Man Project. *Symbolic Interaction* 25: 41–65.

Atkinson, P.
2000 *Days at the Opera: The Ethnographer and the Repetiteur.* European Sociological Conference, University of Exeter, September 1–2.

Barry, A., T. Osborne, and N. Rose
1996 *Foucault and Political Reason: Liberalism, Neo-Liberalism and Rationalities of Government.* London: UCL Press.

Becker, G.
1997 *Disrupted Lives: How People Create Meaning in a Chaotic World.* Berkeley: University of California Press.

Biggs, S., and J. L. Powell
2000 Surveillance and Elder Abuse: The Rationalities and Technologies of Community Care. *Journal of Contemporary Health* 8: 43–48.

Blacking, J., ed.
1977 *The Anthropology of the Body.* London: Academic Press.

Bland, A.
1981 *The Royal Ballet: The First Fifty Years.* New York: Doubleday.

Bourdieu, P.
1984 *Distinction: A Social Critique of the Judgement of Taste.* London: Routledge.
2000 *Pascalian Meditations.* Cambridge, U.K.: Polity.

Brinson, P., and C. Crisp
1980 *The Pan Book of Ballet and Dance: A Guide to the Repertory.* London: Pan Books.

Bruch, H.
1978 *The Golden Cage.* Cambridge: Harvard University Press.

Buckland, T.
1999 All Dances Are Ethnic—But Some Are More Ethnic Than Others: Some Observations on Recent Scholarship in Dance and Anthropology. *Dance Research* 17: 59–68.

Bury, M.
1982 Chronic Illness as Biographical Disruption. *Sociology of Health and Illness* 4: 167–82.

Bussell, D.
1998 *Life in Dance.* London: Century.

Bytheway, B.
1993 Ageing and Biography: The Letters of Bernard and Mary Berenson. *Sociology* 27: 153–65.

Carter, A.
1998 *The Routledge Dance Studies Reader.* Routledge: London.

Chaney, D.
1995 Creating Memories: Some Images of Aging in Mass Tourism. In *Images of Aging: Cultural Representations of Later Life.* Edited by M. Featherstone and A. Warnick. London: Routledge.

Charmaz, K.
1994 Identity Dilemmas of Chronically Ill Men. *Sociological Quarterly* 36: 657–80.

Clarke, M., and C. Crisp
1984 *Dancer: Men in Dance.* London: British Broadcasting Corporation.

Cranny-Francis, A.
1995 *The Body in the Text.* Victoria, Australia: Melbourne University Press.

Denzin, N.
1989 *Interpretive Interactionism.* Newbury Park, U.K.: Sage.

Desmond, J. C., ed.
1997 *Meaning in Motion: New Cultural Studies of Dance.* Durham, N.C.: Duke University Press.

Featherstone, M., and M. Hepworth
1989 Ageing and Old Age: Reflections on the Postmodern Life Course. In *Becoming and Being Old: Sociological Approaches to Later Life.* Edited by B. Bytheway et al. London: Sage.

Featherstone, M., M. Hepworth, and B. S. Turner, eds.
1991 *The Body: Social Processes and Cultural Theory.* London: Sage.

Featherstone, M., and A. Wernick, eds.
1995 *Images of Aging: Cultural Representations of Later Life.* London: Routledge.

Fonteyn, M.
1975 *Autobiography*. London: W. H. Allen.

Foucault, M.
1979a *Discipline and Punish*. Harmondsworth, U.K.: Penguin.
1979b *The History of Sexuality: An Introduction*. Vol. 1. Harmondsworth, U.K.: Penguin.
1987 *The History of Sexuality: The Use of Pleasure*. Vol. 2. Harmondsworth, U.K.: Penguin.
1988a *The History of Sexuality: The Care of the Self*. Vol. 3. Harmondsworth, U.K.: Penguin.
1988b *Technologies of the Self*. Edited by M. Luther et al., 16–49. Amherst: University of Massachusetts Press.

Fowler, B.
1997 *Pierre Bourdieu and Cultural Theory: Critical Investigations*. London: Sage.

Fox, N. J.
1998 Foucault, Foucauldians and Sociology. *British Journal of Sociology* 49: 415–33.

Fraleigh, S. H.
1995 *Dance and the Lived Body*. 2nd ed. Pittsburgh, Pa.: University of Pittsburgh Press.

Fraleigh, S. H., and P. Hanstein, eds.
1999 *Researching Dance: Evolving Modes of Inquiry*. London: Dance Books.

Franko, M.
1993 *Dance as Text: Ideologies of the Baroque Body*. Cambridge: Cambridge University Press.

Gearing, B.
1999 Narratives of Identity among Former Professional Footballers in the United Kingdom. *Journal of Aging Studies* 13: 43–58.

Geertz, C.
1973 *The Interpretation of Cultures*. New York: Basic.

Giddens, A.
1991 *Modernity and Self Identity: Self and Society in the Late Modern Age*. Cambridge, U.K.: Polity.

Goellner, E. W., and J. S. Murphy, eds.
1995 *Bodies of the Text: Dance as Theory, Literature as Dance.* New Brunswick, N.J.: Rutgers University Press.

Green, B. S.
1993 *Gerontology and the Construction of Old Age.* New York: Aldine de Gruyter.

Greskovic, R.
2000 *Ballet: A Complete Guide.* London: Robert Hale.

Grover-Haskin, K.
1998 *Dance and Gender.* Brighton, U.K.: Harwood Academic Press.

Guest, I.
1988 *The Dancer's Heritage.* 6th ed. London: Dancing Times.

Gullette, M. M.
1997 *Declining to Decline: Cultural Combat and the Politics of the Midlife.* Charlottesville: University Press of Virginia.

Hamilton, L. H.
1998 *Advice for Dancers: Emotional Counsel and Practical Strategies.* San Francisco: Jossey-Bass.

Hammersley, M., and P. Atkinson
1995 *Ethnography: Principles in Practice.* London: Routledge.

Hanna, J. L.
1988 *Dance, Sex and Gender.* Chicago: University of Chicago Press.

Harper, S.
1997 Constructing Later Life/Constructing the Body: Some Thoughts from Feminist Theory. In *Critical Approaches to Ageing and Later Life.* Edited by A. Jamieson, S. Harper, and C. Victor. Buckingham, U.K.: Open University Press.

Holstein, J., and J. Gubrium
2000 *The Self We Live By: Narrative Identity in a Postmodern World.* New York: Oxford University Press.

Isaacs, J.
1999 *Never Mind the Moon: My Life at the Royal Opera House.* London: Bantam Press.

Kaeppler, A.
1978 Dance: An Anthropological Perspective. *Annual Review of Anthropology* 7: 31–49.

Katz, S.
1996 *Disciplining Old Age: The Formation of Gerontological Knowledge.* Charlottesville: University of Virginia Press.

Kaufman, S.
1986 *The Ageless Self: Sources of Meaning in Late Life.* Madison: University of Wisconsin Press.

Laslett, P.
1989 *A Fresh Map of Life: The Emergence of the Third Age.* London: Weidenfeld and Nicolson.

Lawson, V.
2002 An Elegance of Energy: An Interview with Alina Cojocaru and Tamara Rojo. *Sydney Morning Herald.* April 29.

Leder, D.
1990 *The Absent Body.* Chicago: University of Chicago Press.

McAdams, D. P.
1993 *The Stories I Live By: Personal Myths and the Making of the Self.* New York: Morrow.

McCarren, F.
1998 *Dance Pathologies: Performance, Poetics, Medicine.* Stanford, Calif.: Stanford University Press.

McKie, L., and N. Watson
2000 *Organising Bodies: Policy, Institutions and Work.* London: Macmillan.

McNay, L.
1992 *Foucault and Feminism.* Cambridge, U.K.: Polity.

Mouzelis, N.
1995 *Sociological Theory: What Went Wrong?* London: Routledge.

Nettleton. S., and J. Watson
1998 *The Body in Everyday Life.* London: Routledge.

Newman, B.
1992 *Striking a Balance: Dancers Talk about Dancing.* New York: Limelight Editions.

Phillipson, C.
1998 *Reconstructing Old Age: New Agendas in Social Theory.* London: Sage.

Shilling, C.
1993 *The Body and Social Theory.* London: Sage.

Shusterman, R.
1992 *Pragmatist Aesthetics: Living Beauty, Rethinking Art.* Cambridge, Mass.: Blackwell.

Silverman, P.
1987 *The Elderly as Modern Pioneers.* Bloomington: Indiana University Press.

Strauss, A. L.
1959 *Mirrors and Masks: The Search for Identity.* Glencoe, Ill.: Free Press.

Thomas, H.
1995 *Dance, Modernity and Culture: Explorations in the Sociology of Dance.* London: Routledge.

Thompson, P.
1992 "I Don't Feel Old": Subjective Ageing and the Search for Meaning in Later Life. *Ageing and Society* 12: 23–47.

Tomko, L. J.
1999 *Dancing Class: Gender, Ethnicity and Social Divides in American Dance, 1890–1920.* Bloomington: Indiana University Press.

Turner, B. S.
1984 *The Body and Society: Explorations in Social Theory.* Oxford, U.K.: Blackwell.
1992 *Regulating Bodies: Essays in Medical Sociology.* London: Routledge.
1995 *Medical Power and Social Knowledge.* 2nd ed. Thousand Oaks, Calif.: Sage.
1996 *The Body and Society.* 2nd ed. London: Sage.

Victor, C.
1991 Continuity or Change: Inequalities in Health in Later Life. *Ageing and Society* 11: 23–39.

Villella, E.
1992 *Prodigal Son: Dancing for Balanchine in a World of Pain and Magic.* Pittsburgh, Pa.: University of Pittsburgh Press.

Wacquant, L. J. D.
1995 Pugs at Work: Bodily Capital and Bodily Labour among Professional Boxers. *Body & Society* 1: 65–93.

Wainwright, S. P.
1995 The Transformational Experience of Liver Transplantation. *Journal of Advanced Nursing* 22: 1068–76.
1997 A New Paradigm for Nursing: The Potential of Realism. *Journal of Advanced Nursing* 26: 1262–71.

Watson, J.
2000 *Male Bodies: Health, Culture and Identity.* Buckingham, U.K.: Open University Press.

Williams, S. J., and G. Bendelow
1998 *The Lived Body: Sociological Themes, Embodied Issues.* London: Routledge.

Wulff, H.
1998 *Ballet Across Borders: Career and Culture in the World of Dancers.* Oxford, U.K.: Berg.

INDEX

ABOUT THE CONTRIBUTORS

Christopher A. Faircloth is a research health scientist at the Rehabilitation Outcomes Research Center (RORC) at the North Florida–South Georgia V.A. Medical Center in Gainesville, Florida. He was previously a National Institute on Aging post-doctoral fellow with the Boston University Gerontology Center and received his Ph.D. in sociology from the University of Florida. He has published in a wide variety of areas including the everyday experience of chronic illness, community construction in senior public housing, qualitative methods, and family. His current research focuses on bodily construction in therapeutic environments for stroke victims.

Bill Bytheway is a senior research fellow in the School of Health and Social Welfare at the Open University. He has a degree in statistics and has been engaged in sociological and health service research for over thirty years. He has been an active member of the British Society of Gerontology since it was founded in 1971. He is the author of *Ageism* (1995) and was editor of *Ageing and Society* between 1997 and 2001.

Betina Freidin obtained her masters degree in social sciences at the University of Buenos Aires. She published the book *Los limites de la Solidaridad* (2000) based on a qualitative study on organ donation in Argentina. At this time, she is doing her doctoral work in sociology at Brandeis University in Waltham, Massachusetts.

Jaber F. Gubrium is professor and chair of sociology at the University of Missouri, Columbia. His research focuses on the description organization of personal identity, family, life course, aging, the body, and adaptations to illness. He is the editor of the *Journal of Aging Studies* and author or editor of over twenty books, including *Living and Dying at Murray Manor; Caretakers; Describing Care; Oldtimers and Alzheimer's; Out of Control; Speaking of Life;* and *The Self We Live By.*

James A. Holstein is professor of sociology at Marquette University. He has studied diverse people processing and social control settings, including courts, schools, and mental health agencies. He is the author or editor of over thirty books, including *Court-Ordered Insanity; Reconsidering Social Constructionism;* and, with Jaber F. Gubrium, *The New Language of Qualitative Method; The Self We Live By; Inner Lives and Social Worlds; Constructing the Life Course, Aging and Everyday Life;* and *Ways of Aging.* In addition, he is the editor of the journal *Social Problems.*

Elizabeth W. Markson is the author of numerous articles and books on aging, including *Social Gerontology Today: An Introduction,* and coeditor (with Lisa A. Hollis-Sawyer) of *Intersections of Aging.* Currently she is academic director of the Boston University Gerontology Center, and she is professor of socio-medical sciences and community medicine; research professor of medicine at the Boston University School of Medicine; and adjunct professor of sociology at Boston University.

Peter Öberg has been researching social gerontology from 1985 at Kuntokallio Gerontological Centre for Training and Research in Finland and the Academy of Finland in research topics such as loneliness and ways of life among the elderly. In 1997, he defended his thesis, *Life as Narrative: On Biography and Aging* at the department of sociology, Uppsala University, where he now works as a researcher. His latest projects have been on aging, body image, and identity.

Dana Rosenfeld is assistant professor of sociology at Colorado College. She received her doctorate in sociology from the University of California, Los Angeles, and was a National Institute of Mental Health postdoctoral research fellow at the University of Kentucky College of Medicine for two years. Her research focuses on aging and the life course, identity and identity politics, gender and sexuality, and the body. She is the author of several articles and book chapters on the identity work of lesbian and gay elders, and her book on the same subject is in publication. Currently she is considering the impact of biomedicine and sexual technologies on male bodies.

Emmanuelle Tulle teaches sociology at Glasgow Caledonian University, Scotland. She has a long-standing interest in later life, both empirically and theoretically, and publishes regularly in academic journals and edited collections. Her empirical work has spanned a broad spectrum, covering various aspects of social work, retirement housing, and now sport. She has contributed to new theoretical developments combining perspectives drawn from critical gerontology, social and sociological theory, the sociology of the body and, more recently, the biomedical sciences.

Bryan S. Turner is professor of sociology at the University of Cambridge, U.K. He has published extensively in medical sociology, sociological theory, and the body. With Mike Featherstone, he is the editor of the journal *Body & Society*.

Julia Twigg is professor of social policy and sociology at the University of Kent at Canterbury, U.K. She has written widely on issues of old age. She recently undertook a study of help with personal care entitled *Bathing: The Body and Community Care*, which explored the issue from the perspectives of both older people and the workers who provided such help. Previously, she has written on the subjects of food and of informal caregiving. She is currently working on a book on the body and policy.

Steven P. Wainwright is a research fellow at King's College University of London. He has published in the fields of medical sociology and aging.